A World beyond Politics?

NEW FRENCH THOUGHT

SERIES EDITORS
Thomas Pavel and Mark Lilla

Pierre Manent

A World beyond Politics?

A DEFENSE OF THE NATION-STATE

Translated by Marc LePain

 NEW FRENCH THOUGHT

PRINCETON UNIVERSITY PRESS · PRINCETON AND OXFORD

French edition © Librairie Arthème Fayard, 2001 *Cours familier de philosophie politique*, by Monsier Pierre Manent

English translation © 2006 by Princeton University Press
Published by Princeton University Press, 41 William Street, Princeton, New Jersey 08540
In the United Kingdom: Princeton University Press, 3 Market Place,
Woodstock, Oxfordshire OX20 1SY

Library of Congress Cataloging-in-Publication Data

Manent, Pierre.
[Cours familier de philosophie politique. English]
A world beyond politics? : a defense of the nation-state / Pierre Manent;
translated by Marc LePain.
 p. cm.—(New French thought)
Translation of: Cours familier de philosophie politique.
Includes bibliographical reference and index.
ISBN-13: 978-0-691-12512-1 (hardcover : alk. paper)
ISBN-10: 0-691-12512-0 (hardcover : alk. paper)
1. Political science—Philosophy. I. Title. II. Series.
JA71.M26413 2006
320′.01—dc22   2005025068

British Library Cataloging-in-Publication Data is available

Publication of this book has been aided by the French Ministry of Culture

This book has been composed in Adobe Bauer Bodoni

Printed on acid-free paper. ∞

pup.princeton.edu

Printed in the United States of America

10 9 8 7 6 5 4 3 2

Contents

Preface to the American Edition

THE PURPOSE of this book was to offer, first to students at Paris's *Institut d'Etudes politiques*, then to the general French readership, a hopefully impartial overview of the political order—or disorder—of today's world. By impartial, I mean that I tried to lay out the objective frame of political things in which we are fated to choose our partisan allegiances. It is true that the partisan spirit inherent in political life has taken on a new intensity among us with the recent and sharp parting of ways between Europe and America. Some will doubt that such an impartial assessment is anywhere available. And not a few Americans will wonder aloud whether anything even remotely useful can come from a French pen. These considerations notwithstanding, let me introduce my case to the American public.

Americans and Europeans are currently being driven apart by the very thing which is supposed to hold them together—their *common commitment to democracy*. On both sides of the Atlantic we more and more identify ourselves with democracy, but we understand it in two different, even opposite ways.

Permit me to begin with the far side of the Ocean. For more than half a century now, Europeans have been "building Europe." They have been trying to transform a loose grouping of democratic nations into a coherent whole, into a new, unified body politic. Now the most important and most problematic point is that this proposed new political body is *defined* by the fact that it is purported to be a *pure democracy*. By this expression I mean that what the Europeans are trying to do is to *separate* the democratic regime completely, or rather the machinery of democratic politics (composed of "institutions" and animated by "values") from any underlying conception of what it means to be a *people*. However democratic its regime, a people is never simply defined by its democratic character: its members are attached to a circumscribed territory, accustomed to particular mores, molded by a more or less ancient religion. But Europeans have embarked on the bold adventure of building a democracy without a people. The ravages and dishonor of a century of wars, the less than convincing adventures in empire-building, have persuaded most Europeans, or at least their governing classes, that their future lay with a clean break with their whole past, and that henceforth belonging to this or that people should be devoid of any specific political meaning or import.

Across the Atlantic, it seems to me that an opposite development is gathering strength. While Europeans, as I have just said, are trying to separate their democratic virtue from all their other characteristics, and accordingly to disentangle themselves from their culpable past, Americans seem more than ever willing—and this disposition extends well beyond the partisans of the current administration—to *identify* everything they do and everything they are with democracy, as such. A political decision is more or less justified as soon as it has been taken in accordance with the rules of American democracy, or as it responds to American public opinion. The way of life of the American people, whatever its effects on the lives of other peoples who are not participants in the American contract, is beyond criticism because it is the way of life of the American democracy. Americans increasingly identify American democracy with the universal as such.

Thus, while Europeans are busy separating their democratic "governance" from everything they were and have done in the past, Americans seem more willing than ever to identify everything they are and do with the democratic goodness of their government. It is true that, as Tocqueville famously said, "Americans were born equal instead of becoming so," they were so to speak born as a democracy. It is true too that their conscience is not burdened by anything resembling the Holocaust. In the eyes of many Americans however, the fate of the Native Americans and slavery in the South, just to mention the most obvious, justify a distinction between some aspects of the American past and "what America is all about." But that is precisely the point: the historical evil that occupies but a corner, however significant, of the American conscience—and it troubles the latter because it is profoundly *un-American*—has come to overwhelm European life and conscience to such an extent that European nations, in the name of "constructing Europe," have embarked on a methodical process of self-erasement. In brief, Americans identify democracy with the people it forms, while Europeans radically separate democracy from the peoples among which it is distributed.

These opposing perspectives paradoxically bring about the same—or at least equally grievous—underestimations of the intractable character of the political world. They equally belittle the political and human meaning of a mankind naturally divided among different peoples. Both Europeans and Americans are prone to understand the right political ordering of the world as the extension of their respective brands of democracy. Americans, through the extension to the whole world of the United States's writ, Europeans, through the extension beyond Europe's geographical borders of Brussels's "mechanisms and values," wildly exaggerate the docility or plasticity of the peoples of the world, including Western peoples. I am afraid that after discussing the respective merits of "hard power" and "soft power," we are bound to discover the limits of Western power generally.

This apprehension has accompanied me throughout the writing of this book. Whether it honed or dimmed my sight is a question for the reader to decide.

Pierre Manent
Paris, France
November, 2004

A World beyond Politics?

A T THE BEGINNING of his *Poetics*, Paul Claudel writes: "I am not considering the future, for it is the present the gods urge us to understand. Now and then, a man raises his brow, sniffs, listens, considers, and finds his position: he thinks, sighs, and taking his watch out his pocket, reads the time. *Where am I? What time is it?* These are the inexhaustible questions we ceaselessly ask the world."[1] As we begin our political inquiry, these same questions motivate us; this same inexhaustible question urges us. To begin means to find one's bearings.

How shall we orient ourselves in the social and political world? In what way can we best begin our inquiry? I believe that, in relation to politics, the first question to ask is: *What is it that holds authority for us?* "For us" does not mean here for Peter or Paul, or for political science students, or for this or that social class or age group, but for all of us as citizens of a contemporary democracy.

Now, I believe that if we make the effort to answer in the simplest and at the same time broadest way, we will say roughly that *we*, the citizens of a democracy in a new millennium, recognize the authority of *science* in the theoretical domain and of *liberty* in the practical domain. These are the two most widely recognized authorities in our societies. Of course, some among us also recognize other authorities, such as, for example, the authority of a Church or a religious Law, and this recognition can lead to conflicts of authority. But the most compelling authority, the one that inspires our laws and, beyond the laws, sets the tone of our society, is indeed the twofold authority of science and liberty.

When I say that science and liberty are our two great authorities, I obviously set aside the question of their truth or goodness. One can well think, as some ecologists do, that science is leading us to a catastrophe or, as do religious Fundamentalists, that liberty is drawing us further and further away from the divine law. It remains that these two authorities, these two "values" if you wish, effectively dominate our life. *Our societies are organized for and by science and liberty.* This is a *fact* and is, I believe, the main tenet of our present world.

But what do these great words "science" and "liberty" mean here? Are these notions not both hackneyed and vague? As for science, can we speak of science, when there are several sciences, very different from one another, and distinctions, and even oppositions, for example, between the natural sciences for which mathematics is an indispensable and essential tool, and the human sciences that seem to resist mathematization? Do quantum physics and sociology, for example, equally partake of science? The ambiguities surrounding the notion of liberty appear even greater. Which liberty are we speaking of? Did some of the greatest conflicts of the past century not arise from the fact that men conceived different ideas of liberty? What common ground is there, for instance, between the liberty of the liberals and that of the Marxists, except for the fact that each party declares that what the other party offers is nothing but slavery topped by imposture?

These difficulties are quite real and we must keep them in mind if we wish to remain alert to the complexity of the phenomena. I believe nonetheless that it is legitimate to speak of science and liberty, at least inasmuch as they orient decisively the life and movement of our society. Beyond the complexity and ambiguity of these two notions, there is in each a very simple *active principle* that needs to be brought out in all its force.

Let us start with science. The modern meaning of the term is not only exact knowledge; it is not simply exact knowledge methodologically, that is to say, one whose exactitude is obtained and guaranteed by the application of the scientific method. These aspects are very important; they belong to the very definition of science. But beyond these aspects there is something more fundamental, a truly unprecedented *project*. Its aim is to see the world as it is, not as it ought to be, that is, to make the world entirely *visible* to the mind's eye. Thus this project has a twofold aspect, moral and epistemological.

From the moral point of view, the scientific project brings forth the *will* to banish from our perspective on the world all that has to do with our desires and our wishes—to banish all "illusions." The first and most striking expression of this will is to be found in Machiavelli's *The Prince*, thus in a political context that goes back to the early sixteenth century. In chapter 15 of *The Prince* we read:

> But since my intent is to write something useful to whomever understands it, it has appeared to me more fitting to go to the effectual truth of the thing than to the imagination of it. And many have dreamt of republics and principalities that have never been seen or known to exist in truth; for it is so far from how one lives to how one should live that he who lets go of what is done for what should be done learns his ruin rather than his preservation.[2]

Such is, formulated for the first time by Machiavelli, the *realistic* project of modern science. And such is the moral character of this science.

From the epistemological point of view, the scientific project is defined by the methodical effort to bring the world before the mind's eye in such a way that the world, inasmuch as it is to be known, is henceforth *entirely* before the mind's eye, in other words, is henceforth *without mystery*. The great German sociologist Max Weber, in a lecture given in the immediate aftermath of World War I and to which I shall return shortly, formulated this idea in a particularly forceful way. Speaking of the growing intellectualization and rationalization of life due to modern science, he states that they mean "the knowledge or belief that if one but wishes one *could* learn anything at any time. Hence it means that principally there are no mysterious incalculable forces that come into play, but rather that one can, in principle, master all things by calculation."[3]

These two aspects of the modern project of knowledge converge in the mathematization that characterizes modern science, by contrast with Greek science, for example. Regarding the first aspect—the rejection of "illusions" and "imaginations"—, it is clear that mathematical theorems do not reflect our desires and are indifferent to our wishes. And whereas men are divided by the different ideas they entertain about the Good, they are all necessarily in agreement on the validity of mathematical demonstrations. In this sense, modern science reconciles people. As for the second aspect, it is no less clear that mathematics is entirely intelligible, since it is precisely mathematical demonstration that provides the model of perfectly conclusive reasoning. Here we have, if not modern science in all its aspects, at least the project of modern science as it was defined at its inception and has worked to this day.

I now come to the second great authority, liberty. It seems more difficult to give a synthetic definition of liberty than of science. Are we speaking of religious, or political, or again economic liberty? Are we speaking of the "external" liberty to "do what I want" without anyone stopping me, as Hobbes and Spinoza conceived of it in the seventeenth century, or are we speaking of my "interior" liberty, by which I determine myself, give myself the law, as Rousseau and Kant conceived of it in the eighteenth century? However interesting and important these differences within the modern notion of liberty may be, they do not impinge on the effectual and dynamic truth of modern liberty, namely, that *man is the sovereign author, in fact and by right, of the human world.* He is and ought to be its author. The world, in any case the human world, "society," does not have as its author God, or the gods, nor nature, but humans themselves. This fundamental truth of our condition, which in earlier societies was hidden and repressed, becomes visible in democratic societies. Democracy *enacts and develops* this human sovereignty. Every great election by universal suffrage, for example, gives life to the idea that the members of society, the citizens, are the authors of their own conditions of existence since they freely choose as their representatives those who will determine these conditions through legislation. Therein also lies the strongest and at the same time the noblest motive of the adversaries of modern democracy, of those who were once called "reactionaries." They hold that there is something supremely dan-

gerous for man, in truth something impious, in the democratic ambition
to organize the world "as we wish" instead of obeying the divine law or
following the proven customs handed down from past generations.

The sketch I have just drawn is a summary for sure, but I believe that it
gives a largely accurate idea of the two great "spiritual masses," to use
Hegel's expression, that make up the world in which we are attempting to
find our bearings. And all would be for the best in the best of worlds if
strange phenomena did not arise as soon as we place these two masses side
by side, science and liberty *together*.

Let us take a question that is much debated today, the question of genetic manipulation. Society, "democracy," is thought by many entitled to
if not prohibit these manipulations purely and simply, at least to regulate
them. In this way we would be affirming our collective liberty. At the same
time, there is the no less widespread feeling, possibly among the same
people, that this legislation would be pointless, that "science cannot be
stopped," and that moreover one has no right to stop science! In fact, if
the juridical situation, in different countries, is rather confused, it seems
indeed that in practice genetic research is just about completely free. In
short, our science seems to be stronger than our liberty, irresistibly
stronger. But then what becomes of our liberty? Can one still speak of our
liberty, our sovereignty, when science is our true and lawful sovereign?
Besides, for a fairly long time now certain philosophers, such as Heidegger,
have maintained that we live under the rule of science, that science is our
fate, and that our much-vaunted liberty is illusory.

On the other hand, it seems that the contrary is also true, that liberty is
stronger than science. No democratic government would dream of founding its legitimacy on science, for example, on the knowledge that science
gives us of human nature or of human history. This was what totalitarian
regimes claimed to do. Communism claimed to put into practice the scientific knowledge, elaborated by Marx, of the laws of history, under the name
of "historical materialism." Nazism for its part claimed to put into practice
the scientific knowledge of the laws of human nature, in particular those
governing the "inequality of the races." The crimes committed in the twentieth century in the name of the laws of history or nature would without
doubt be enough to turn any democratic government away from the temptation to found its action on science. But there is a further, more fundamental motive in addition to this one. For us, citizens of the democracies—and
those who govern us are on this score citizens like us—*there is no science
of what is good for us*, of what is good for man. What is good for us,
individually or collectively, we discover or invent by ourselves and for ourselves, at every instant and in full liberty. What is good for us does not
belong in the domain of science but of "values," and these values we

choose, some even say we "create," freely. In this sense, for us, liberty is stronger than science.

On the basis of these two examples, we see that, now science intimidates liberty, reduces it to silence, now liberty in return bids science to be silent. Thus, we are tempted to say, just as the men of the Middle Ages had to orient themselves in a world that was at once organized and disorganized by the confrontation of the two great authorities of the pope and the emperor, so we, citizens of the modern democracies, have to orient ourselves in a world that is at once organized and disorganized by the confrontation of the two great authorities of science and liberty.

A moment ago I alluded to the distinction and even the separation that is familiar to us between the world of science and the world of values. We take this separation as if it were a given. At the same time, as we have just seen, this separation is not really a separation, since now science rules liberty and now liberty rules science. This separation is thus less a given than a wish. We would like to resolve real or potential conflicts between the two authorities by separating the combatants. This wish was first formed when the two authorities asserted themselves in their fullest force, that is, near the end of the nineteenth century. Philosophers and sociologists at the time elaborated a doctrine aimed at resolving, or rather preventing these conflicts. This doctrine is still ours. It is the doctrine that wants to distinguish rigorously facts from values. The scientist is concerned with facts; the man chooses or creates freely the values by which he wants to live. There is no science of values, no objective knowledge of the good. You are familiar with this doctrine: it is the one that holds sway today.

It is not for us to study this doctrine in a thorough way. But we ought to take stock of it and make at least a broad evaluation, for several reasons of unequal urgency. The most urgent is the following: Does this book have to do with science or with values, which in this case could not be any other than *my* values? If it has to do with science, you ought not to miss a single statement, and indeed you ought to give your consent to all that is said. If it has to do with values, that is to say my values, why would you pay attention, why would my choice of values interest you? This alternative is not satisfactory, of course, but it seems to be implied in the current understanding of the separation between facts and values. This calls for closer examination.

It is remarkable that the most famous and most influential text on this question should consist of two lectures given by a university professor. The first, which I have already quoted, is devoted precisely to the vocation of a university professor as a scholar. I refer of course to the lectures of Max Weber, "Science as a Vocation" and "Politics as a Vocation," delivered at the University of Munich in December of 1918, at a time of great political, social, and moral confusion. As I have already indicated, these brief texts are among the most impressive and influential writings of the twentieth century. I will offer a brief analysis of the first lecture, by far the more important for our purposes, the one that concerns the work and vocation of the scholar.

Speaking before students and colleagues, Weber asks himself what his duty is as a professor, what his audience can demand of him. He replies:

> One can only demand of the teacher that he have the intellectual integrity to see that it is one thing to state facts, to determine mathematical or logical relations or the internal structure of cultural values, while it is another thing to answer questions of the value of culture and its individual contents and the question of how one should act in the cultural community and in political associations. These are quite heterogeneous problems.[4]

Weber makes a rigorous distinction between science, which establishes facts and relations among facts, and life, political or otherwise, which necessarily involves evaluation and action. I have already underscored that not only is this idea familiar to us and so to speak a given, but it constitutes in some way our official doctrine. Yet, it is not easy to grasp because it seems that we cannot adequately understand human phenomena if we are incapable of evaluating them or if we refuse to do so. To cite an example, How can one begin to describe what goes on in a concentration camp without disclosing its inhumanity, that is, without evaluating it, without making a "value judgment"? Besides, as some commentators have observed, Weber himself, in his historical and sociological writings, does not tire of evaluating even as he establishes facts, or rather, *in order to* establish facts. Otherwise, how could he make a distinction, a very important distinction in his religious sociology, between a "prophet" and a "charlatan"?

But before criticizing Weber, it is incumbent on us to listen to him. How does he prove this thesis that seems quite difficult to accept provided we give it some thought? He refers approvingly to John Stuart Mill, who affirmed that if one proceeds from pure experience, one arrives at polytheism. In other words, the diverse aspects of the experience of life are so disparate—they draw us in such different directions—that it is impossible to reduce them to any unity (if such unity were possible, one would arrive at "monotheism"). In Weber's terms, this means that human life is characterized by an irreconcilable conflict among "values." Thus Weber discovers, or asserts, two kinds of heterogeneities that commentators often confuse: a heterogeneity between science and life on the one hand and a heterogeneity or even a struggle among values in life on the other hand.

In any case it is clear that for Weber intellectual honesty forbids us to teach, and before that to believe, that science could teach us how to live or how to institute the political order; and this same intellectual honesty forbids us to believe for example that a thing is good because it is beautiful or vice versa. But why is Weber so preoccupied with intellectual honesty? Might this virtue, which is both intellectual and moral, be especially endangered today? Or, on the contrary, has it made decisive advances in modern times that would warrant safeguarding? Perhaps one could say that in his eyes both are true: in a world dominated by modern science, intellectual honesty is singularly valued and sharpened, and at the same time it runs particular risks.

There is something particularly problematic in modern science, and that is its incomplete character. It is definitely and essentially incomplete—it cannot be completed. Weber asks why one engages in doing something that in reality never comes, and can never come, to an end. Why are human beings forever striving to know what they know they will never know? The meaning of science is to have no meaning. Intellectual honesty consists in not arbitrarily giving it a meaning—by saying for example that science makes it possible to construct a more just world—in continuing the work of science despite this absence of meaning. But this honesty is almost superhuman or inhuman, since men desire nothing more than to find meaning in what they do. Accordingly the temptation to give meaning to scientific activity is almost irresistible. Thus, innumerable scholars and teachers arbitrarily ascribe meaning to their scientific activity or its tentative results and in doing so they transform themselves into little prophets, little demagogues.

These scholars and teachers let us know their personal convictions—as they have a right to do—but they present them as the result of pure science, and therein they lack honesty. This behavior is lamentable, but it flows almost necessarily from a major trait of our situation. In modern society only science can be the object of public affirmation or approval. It is the only publicly acceptable thought content. Other "values," for example esthetic or religious values, no longer have any right to be accepted in the public forum, or no longer have sufficient strength to be accepted in the public forum. Near the end of his lecture, Weber states:

> The fate of our times is characterized by rationalization and intellectualization and, above all, by the "disenchantment of the world." Precisely the ultimate and most sublime values have retreated from public life either into the transcendental realm of mystic life or into the brotherliness of direct and personal human relations. It is not accidental that our greatest art is intimate and not monumental, nor is it accidental that today only within the smallest and intimate circles, in personal human stations, in *pianissimo*, that something is pulsating that corresponds to the prophetic *pneuma*, which in former times swept through the great communities like a firebrand, welding them together. If we attempt to force and to "invent" a monumental style in art, the result is

the many miserable monstrosities that are produced as monuments in the last
twenty years. If one tries intellectually to construe new religions without a new
and genuine prophecy, then, in an inner sense, something similar will result,
but with still worse effects. And academic prophecy, finally, will create only
fanatical sects but never a genuine community.[5]

One can only be impressed by this eloquent description of a social world
that is still our own, that is even, so to speak, more and more our own.
The public forum more and more stripped of religious signs, the flight into
the "private" sphere, the poverty of public architecture, and the multiplication of odd "new religions"—all these phenomena have only developed
further, coupled with the increasing power of science to shape all aspects,
including the most intimate, of our life. The loss of substance of public life
is such that at times it seems that it is constituted now only by the publi-
cization of private life, or private lives.

In the passage I have just cited, Max Weber deplores the practical consequences of the separation that he recommends as a matter of principle
and requires that we respect out of intellectual honesty. In fact, why is
life more and more private if not because the public domain is more and
more dominated by a science that has nothing to say about our life? And
this is the same science whose integrity Weber wants to respect. In any
case, one of the great merits of Weber is precisely to have underscored
with incomparable vigor a fundamental aspect of our society that I will
address shortly, namely, that it is founded on separations, that it is a
definite organization of separations. The major separation in his view is
the separation of science and life: between science that has no meaning
for man and does not tell him how to live, and life that has no unity, that
is shot through with and so to speak defined by the conflicts of values,
by the "war of the gods," in which each man must *choose*, without any
rational warrant, his god or his demon.

This separation between science and life is solidly linked to the constitutive separation of the political order between the public and the private:
science rules the public domain, it is the only value effectively accepted in
the public realm; life, authentic life, is to be sought in the private realm,
authentic life is private life. Thus we are strangely divided: we have faith
in science, we make it sovereign in the public forum, that is to say, we join
together the two strongest ideas in the mind of man, the idea of truth and
the idea of the Republic, and at the same time we decide to live so to speak
apart and elsewhere: outside the public sphere, in the private; outside science, in values.

At the very moment when we bring to light the strange and almost absurd character of our undertaking, we suddenly understand its meaning.
In the first moment, when we join together science and the public realm,

science and the State if you wish, we create the framework and the conditions of our life; in the second moment, we aim at exercising our liberty. The separations that Weber underscores, like those we will consider next, are rooted in this duality of moments. Modern man, democratic man, wants first to create the framework of his life, the most neutral and even the emptiest framework, in order then to live all the more freely. He affirms science in order to better affirm liberty. Of course, he can only affirm each by affirming their separation.

I have just said that democratic people want first to create the framework of their life in order then to live all the more freely. This is a proposition that appears rather inoffensive and that, in its very platitude, does not probably correspond to the idea you have of political philosophy! In reality, it sums up an extraordinary change in humanity's perspectives. To understand the enormity of this historic innovation that defines modern democracy, it is enough to think for a moment of the perspective on life that our premodern ancestors had. They had no idea at all of this division, this separation into two moments. For them to live was to obey the law. Of course, there were several kinds of law—religious law, political law, family law—and these different laws could come into conflict. But people knew that life consisted chiefly in obedience to law. We do not want to obey the law; we want to be free. To be free, we must create the conditions of liberty. Science and the state allow us to create these conditions. And the public forum is more and emptier so that we can be more and freer.

CHAPTER 1

The Organization of Separations

ALL OF US have a certain prior or prescientific knowledge of the political regime in which we live. As members of society, as citizens, we know from observation, from experience, so to speak from immersion, a whole lot of things about our democracy. But among all these things that we know or believe we know about democracy, which ones are true and important and which are illusory or insignificant impressions? How can we organize our perception and transform it into analysis? How can we verify our analysis?

We are tempted to proceed in the following way. We ask ourselves first what democracy *wants* to be, or *claims* to be, and we answer that democracy is the power of the people or, in a more developed way, democracy is a political regime wherein all the powers draw their legitimacy from the people, wherein all the powers are exercised by the people or its representatives. All other aspects, first of all what jurists in France call "public liberties," flow from this principle. The choice by the people of their representatives holds meaning only if the citizens are informed and thus can communicate freely and in security, in short, if the people enjoy public liberties. But hardly have we stated that our regime is representative than doubts assail us. They have to do precisely with the reality or the validity of representation. In what measure are the representatives of the people representative of the people? As soon as we study the mechanism of representation more closely, as soon as we consider, for example, the electoral system—electoral law, party organization, and financing—and more generally the actual political system—financial powers, media, "ideological" powers—we begin to have doubts about the reality of democracy. These doubts are confirmed by experts in political sociology who explain that an oligarchy thrives beneath the surface appearance of democracy. The minority of those who hold material and cultural capital, they say, manipulate the political institutions to their benefit. Thus, at the end of this path that seemed so natural to us, we no longer know where we are.

On the one hand, the specialists in constitutional law and in public law help us to describe the intents and the mechanisms of democracy as a representative regime. But on the other hand, political sociology draws our attention to phenomena that are alien and even contrary to the constitutional principles of democracy and tends to suggest that these principles are illusions and perhaps even impostures. If we have the least concern for intellectual coherence we find ourselves in an uncomfortable perplexity. We are caught, between the principle and formal mechanisms of democracy on the one hand and, on the other hand, the reality of democracy, or at least certain real aspects of democracy that seem to contradict its principles by hampering its mechanisms or rendering them hollow.

We no longer have the means to progress toward truth since a kind of self-paralyzing mechanism occupies our mind. Every time we advance a consideration regarding the principles or formal mechanisms of democracy, we confront its reality, those so to speak inadmissible aspects that contradict them; and every time we consider the oligarchic, more generally nondemocratic aspects of democracy, we remember that in spite of everything the principles and formal mechanisms are present, they are at work, and they must indeed have some real effects. Such is, I believe, the malaise of our democracy today, a malaise that is at once civic and intellectual, political and scientific. How can we get out of it? Is it not inherent to the very structure of our regime? I think it is possible to resolve the scientific difficulty I have just underscored, or in any case to formulate the problem of democracy in another way.

The opposition we have brought out and that has so perplexed us—between the official constitution of democracy and its inadmissible oligarchic reality—is so sharp and so disturbing only because the two opposing or contrasting aspects are the concern of two altogether different disciplines that whet and maximize the opposition, in this case constitutional law or the formal theory of democracy on which it is founded on the one hand, and political sociology on the other. I do not say that the opposition is artificial, only that it receives exaggerated prominence from the fact that the two aspects are taken over by two distinct disciplines, each of which, wishing to preserve its specific character and legitimacy, accentuates precisely that which makes its results incompatible with the results obtained by the other discipline. More generally, if it is in any event difficult to describe adequately our democracy because it is an extremely complex human phenomenon, this difficulty is artificially aggravated indeed by the fact that the different aspects of the phenomena are taken over by disciplines that are different and most often incapable of communication. That said, we make the following observation: the partition of the social world into rigorously separated disciplines, aspects, and powers is a general and characteristic trait of the democratic regime. It is a characteristic trait of democracy that makes democracy particularly difficult to characterize. We can make this our starting point.

Democracy is an *organization of separations*. I do not know whether it
is its most fundamental trait, but I believe that it is its most distinctive
trait. It puts distinctions and even separations where other regimes do not
put or did not put any. This fact drew a great deal of attention when the
modern regime first appeared. Speaking of what he calls "nations devoted
to industry," Adam Ferguson wrote in 1767:

> Every individual is distinguished by his calling, and has a place to which he
> is fitted. The savage, who knows no distinction but that of his merit, of his
> sex, or of his species, and to whom his community is the sovereign object of
> his affection, is astonished to find, that in a scene of this nature, his being a
> man does not qualify him for any station whatever: he flies to the woods with
> amazement, distaste, and aversion.[1]

Of course, Ferguson is dealing here with developed nations in general,
which are not necessarily democratic. In fact, at the time he is writing, even
the English regime was not truly democratic, but it was representative, and
the only regime in Europe and in the world to be so.

Democracy confirms and multiplies the separations produced by the development of civilization. The more a regime and a society are democratic,
the more they produce professions, distinctions, and separations that present clear advantages over nondemocratic and less democratic regimes.
The superiority, or at least the superior vitality, of American democracy
derives in good part from its inexhaustible inventiveness in the matter of
new distinctions. Introducing a new service is often nothing more than
introducing a distinction, a division where until then there had been but
one undivided position, service, or task. The phenomenon I am evoking
has been known for a long time and described under the name of "division
of labor." I have deliberately held back from introducing this expression
because I believe that the phenomenon is much broader than the one designated by the expression "division of labor," an expression that tends to
direct attention in an exclusive way to the economic sphere. In fact, the
division of labor is only one aspect, albeit a very important one, of the
multiplication of distinctions and separations that characterize our regime.
Indeed, Sieyès, who played such an important role at the start of the
French Revolution, describes political representation as a development, an
application of the principle of the division of labor. That is tantamount to
saying that the principle goes well beyond the field of economics. This
movement, as can easily be seen, feeds on itself. New distinctions, that
is, new professions or positions, are aimed at acknowledging differences
perceived within positions that were hitherto indivisible, but also at con-
necting the elements that were separated by the previous distinctions. Professionalization multiplies professions, distinguishing them, of course, and
separating them from one another; and the development of public relations

positions is intended precisely to connect professions separated by professionalization itself. One separates in order to connect and connects in order to separate. Characterizing his time that was the start of our own, Ferguson speaks of "this age of separations."[2]

If the movement of distinction or separation is a fundamental aspect of modern democracy, one can distinguish several broad categories of separations. I see at least six:

- separation of professions, or, division of labor;
- separation of powers;
- separation of church and state;
- separation of civil society and the state;
- separation between represented and representative;
- separation of facts and values, or science and life.

Of course, these six headings are not watertight; they overlap in part. The separation of church and state can be considered as a particular case of the separation between civil society and the state. At the same time, it is a particular case that has taken on such importance that it is necessary to give it a special heading. Civil society took its form when the church left the government or cogovernment of the body politic, or was forced out of it, to take its new place as an essential element of civil society. One could find numerous other overlaps. In any case, it seems to me that we have here the great separations that define our democracy, the six great themes of the democratic symphony.

The common point of these six separations is that they are all of them imperatives; our description is prescriptive. These separations *must* be put into effect, and thereafter they *must* be preserved. Why? Because these separations are necessary for liberty. Better yet, they define liberty as the moderns understand it. Modern liberty is founded on an organization of separations. The modern regime institutes its separations for the sake of liberty. Modern liberty is inseparably linked to these separations.

I have just spoken of the "modern" regime, of liberty "as the moderns understand it." Indeed, this concern for separation is specific to the modern era; inversely, it is alien to earlier societies. In predemocratic societies, the accent is explicitly, emphatically, at times obsessively placed on social unity, on concord. These societies are forever representing their unity, displaying the spectacle of their unity. Anything that separates or threatens to separate, anything that divides or threatens to divide is fought, repelled, and concealed. There is indeed a division, a separation that is recognized and even proclaimed in predemocratic societies, the division between the governors and the governed. But the affirmation of this division is precisely the means of assuring unity and concord since, inversely, when this distinction is blurred, when one no longer knows who commands and who obeys, discord sets in and unity gives way to disorder, to anarchy. In predemocratic societies, this structure characterizes not only the political order but is duplicated or replicated everywhere: in the family, in corporations, in the church, the university, etcetera. The old order is founded on command; it turns on the command-obedience relation.

This can be seen in a particularly obvious way in what we call the ancien régime. But this was no less true, albeit in another manner, in ancient republics and democracies. One may well see the origin and first model of our liberty in the liberty of democratic Athens or republican Rome. At the same time, there are as many differences as there are similarities between these two liberties. The liberty of the Greek citizen is defined by the fact that the roles of the one who commands and of the one who obeys are not determined by birth, as they will be under the ancien régime, but that everyone, once a citizen, is now commander and now commanded. Ancient liberty is defined by this alternation. Thus it too rests on the command-obedience relation. As for its exercise, this liberty is put into practice by the citizens' participation in the deliberations and decisions of the body politic. Greek citizens converged on the agora as their gathering place. The very movement of ancient public-spiritedness is the opposite of separation. Modern citizens on the contrary withdraw to the voting booth. How did modern liberty come to rest on a system of separations?

It could be said, in a very general way, that modern politics was set up precisely to abolish or at least to get around the command-relation that was the pivot of ancient politics, whether it was free as in Athens or not free as under the ancien régime. Once again, ancient liberty was a certain modality of this relation, namely alternation. Modern liberty is a very methodic effort to escape the grip of this relation. This methodic effort has for its instrument the separations of which we speak.

An example, which is more than an example, will make it easy to understand how this is so. As we have recalled, modern democracy is a representative regime. Since the government represents the people (its "interest," its "will," etc.) the actions of the government are in the strong sense of the term *authorized* by the people. Consequently, when the government commands me to do something, it is that I have authorized it in principle to give me this command. One might say that I command myself through the intermediary of the government. In the end, I obey only myself. The represented-representative separation allows one to get around the apparently inescapable necessity of the command-obedience relation. Whereas ancient liberty was organized around alternation, modern liberty is organized around representation.

It will be said that what I have just described is but the illusion, the ideology of political representation, that in reality I obey well and truly the government and not myself and that moreover the idea of representation has justified some of the worst political oppressions in human history. It was precisely because they were convinced they represented the people that the Jacobins, for example, wrought on the French—the real people—a terror that has remained in people's memories as *the* Terror. Political representation does hold terrible possibilities. It remains that, once the idea of representation was elaborated, the command-obedience link was circumvented or became secondary. So that representation may not turn into oppression, it is necessary and it is enough to complete the separation between the represented and the representative with the separation between powers, the "separation of powers." According to a logic I had sketched above in broad terms, a new separation succeeds in solving the problem raised by the first separation. To describe modern democracy is first to describe the dynamic linkage of these two separations.

This linkage first appeared in England and was described, one might say definitively, in the first half of the eighteenth century by Montesquieu. The first description is the best because it is wholly enlivened and enlightened by the surprise of the New. It is found in chapter 6 of Book XI and chapter 27 of Book XIX of *The Spirit of the Laws*. The mechanism Montesquieu describes is wondrously simple and its effects wondrously wholesome. If there is anything like political science, surely it is to be found in this analysis of Montesquieu, which I shall summarize in very broad strokes.

There are thus two separations, one between the represented and the representative—in other words, between civil society and governmental institutions—and one between powers. Two powers are involved in this context: the executive and the legislative (the judicial, residing in the jury, in men drawn from the body of the people and returning there once their task is accomplished, is "so to speak invisible and null," says Montesquieu). The legislative, composed of representatives of the people, is in principle the sole representative power. But Montesquieu observes that, in reality, the executive also has a representative function. It has its supporters, above all those who feel badly represented by the legislative. Thus we have a political game with four protagonists: on the level of government, two powers, the executive and legislative; on the level of society, two parties, the party of the executive and the party of the legislative. What gets the game or the mechanism going are the wishes, wills, desires, and fears of the members of society. The latter will seek to attain their ends through the intermediary of the power they favor and whose favors they hope to obtain. But their will can hardly have an immediate or direct effect, since the power whose favorable action they hope for is limited, circumscribed, and held in check by the other power. Because society is *represented* by a *divided* power, the citizens will be *powerless* to do much harm to one another.

But, it will be said, if one of the two powers is supported by such a large majority that it crushes the other power and the minority of the citizens, who supports the latter? Montesquieu answers that such oppression is hardly to be feared, thanks to what he calls "the effect of liberty." If one of the two powers, he tells us, threatens to take over too much and to achieve complete domination, the citizens will lend assistance to the other; they will change party. In other words, in keeping with the "effect of liberty," the two parties corresponding to the two powers will always be nearly equally strong. This is confirmed by the historic experience of the democracies. But why, when this experience was barely beginning, was Montesquieu already so certain of this "effect of liberty"? His reasoning, which is inseparably political and psychological, I will summarize in the following way.

The citizens are indeed the partisans of one or other power that they favor and from which they hope for advantages, but they are always in the first place members of society inasmuch as society is distinct from the two powers, the one they like no less than the one they dislike. Accordingly, if one of the powers gains too much advantage, a certain number of its partisans, the more lukewarm at first, will themselves feel threatened, not as partisans of this power but as members of civil society. In such a system, in fact, the citizens generally have a twofold preoccupation: that the power serve their interests, of course, but *also* that it not weigh too heavily on society; and they generally have a twofold feeling that the power they support "represents" them, that it is "their" power, but *also* that it is different from them, that it represents them badly, that it will betray them. It is the necessary play of this twofold preoccupation and twofold feeling that guarantees that the citizens will necessarily come to the aid of the power that will become too weak, the power that is threatened.

There is a sort of "double game" of the citizens with the power that is inherent to the logic of representation: once a power, any power, is thought to represent the citizen, the latter's desire for identification is inseparable from a feeling of alienation. As can be seen, this organization of powers organizes in fact a sort of general impotence, the impotence of citizens to have much effect on one another and the impotence of the divided power to oppress the citizens. This mechanism of power producing the impotence of power is what Montesquieu calls *liberty*. In fact, since men in such a system cannot act by commanding one another, they have no other perspective for their activity and ambition than to "assert their independence as they please," that is to say, to turn their desires and their efforts to domains that are foreign to power or to politics strictly speaking, to domains where properly speaking one does not exercise power over other members of society. The citizens have only to exercise their talents and to become rich or famous by exercising their talents. In a political regime ordered in this way, life consists mainly of *economics* and *culture*.

It is extraordinary that this analysis by Montesquieu, elaborated in a context apparently so different from our own, remains completely valid today. One could have thought it would lose all pertinence when an element so fundamental to the analysis as the separation of the executive and the legislative had disappeared from reality. We know that this separation disappeared in England around the mid nineteenth century when "government by cabinet" was established. Such a government, in which the prime minister is at the same time the leader of the majority in the House of Commons, concentrates the executive *and* the legislative in its hands.[3] Yet this joining of executive and legislative powers in the same hands in no way meant the end of modern political liberty. On the contrary, under the regime of government by cabinet, it continued to progress. This is because a new separation arose to replace the separation of powers while fulfilling the same function. This is the separation between the majority and the opposition. Of course, the opposition does not constitutionally share power with the majority, but at any moment, in any case at the next election, it *can* return to power, and this perspective exercises a considerable moderating action on the government and its majority. Thus, between the time of Montesquieu and our own, the content of the separated powers has been greatly transformed, but what has not changed is the fact of the separation between two great powers. One could not conceive of a more striking confirmation of the decisive role of separations in modern liberty.

This organization of separations, this "system of liberty" according to the expression of Montesquieu, presents two somewhat opposed characteristics that explain the difficulties and slow pace of its establishment at the same time as its extraordinary stability once it is established. On the one hand, it is precisely a "system," a mechanism and even a simple mechanism. Once such a mechanism is set up, it is extremely robust. But on the other hand, in order for it to function, this mechanism requires an array of conditions that are hard to assemble, namely the prior existence of a "civil society," of a common life that does not depend or depend much on command. Thus it requires the prior development of what in the eighteenth century was called "commerce," that network of relations that members of society knit freely, that is to say, not in obedience to a command but in search of their interest.

We shall return at a later point to this most important matter of commerce. I would like for now to evoke a more specific and more political condition that falls under what might be called political psychology. In the system of which we speak, each party wants power in order to accomplish a program it sees as necessary and beneficial. But it will only be able to achieve this program up to a certain point. In practice, it will only truly attempt to do so in the early days of its mandate, during what is so well called a "honeymoon." Soon, waffling voters will be disappointed or irritated, will perhaps steer toward the opposition, and the government's maxim will cease to be "satisfy the party members," to become "don't displease anyone." These phenomena are altogether familiar to us. But inevitable as they may be, they entail consequences that can become very negative. These consequences could be designated by an expression of Stendhal, who sees in "impotent hatred" a specific trait of democratic society.

Allow me to explain. To function well such a system requires a rigorous and efficacious separation between the majority and the opposition. Thus it needs a certain vitality of partisan spirit. Such a system excites the partisan spirit it needs in order to function. At the same time, it forever frustrates partisan passions since it is organized to prevent their having an open field and being able to achieve what they desire. In psychological terms, one could say that this organization of separations excites the desires and wills of the members of society in an extreme way and frustrates them in a way that is just as extreme. Wills are mobilized since they form the link between the citizens and the party they favor. What the party wants is in principle the sum and the result of what its members want, while inversely the party incites its members to take sides more and more resolutely. At the same time, the party members know, or at least they come to know, that their wills will have very little effect and that their desires will not be satisfied. Thus such a system nurtures a will that wants to be partisan and knows that it is powerless, and perhaps wants to be more partisan the more it knows it is powerless. No one cares about being impartial since it is the system's job, not the individual's, to be impartial; but the system is not impartial, it only neutralizes each party by the other. A society that is so organized tends to present a very specific mixture of agitation and immobility that wears souls down all the while it discourages great undertakings.

Let me cite a recent example. The impeachment proceeding against President Clinton was to an important extent the result of such an exacerbation of partisan spirit, but a partisan spirit that does not resign itself to impotence or that even revolts against its impotence and has recourse to an extraordinary step to satisfy its hatred. I am not saying that those who denounced President Clinton lacked serious motives. And I do not reproach them their partisanship. They simply experienced and expressed to a more lively degree than usual the partisan passions that the system needs in order to function. But they wanted to enforce their will at all cost, at least at the cost of an extraordinary measure that put a dangerous strain on the system.[4] This contemporary example draws our attention to the psychic cost of the representative system: How can I reconcile myself to the fact that this person whom I detest for what he represents is *my* representative?

No doubt it is weariness with regard to partisan passions that explains why the French approve so overwhelmingly of what is called "cohabitation," that is, a situation in which the president and the cabinet belong to different parties. The widespread feeling that the left or the right in power have just about the same policies has made it acceptable, and for some desirable, to see a president from the left preside over a council of ministers from the right, or a president from the right preside over a cabinet from the left. At the same time, one must not close one's eyes to the fact that this arrangement, popular as it is or seems to be, is absolutely contrary not only of course to the spirit, the raison d'être of the present French Constitution, which was the strengthening of the executive, but also to the logic of the representative system itself, founded on the clear-cut separation between majority and opposition. Why then, it will be asked, is political life not completely paralyzed? Simply because the logic of the representative system, which entrusts the *government* to the side that has won the last election, transforms the French Constitution into its opposite by considerably reducing the powers of the president. Considerably, but not entirely, for the logic of the majority does not win in an absolute fashion, and the duality of the executive is not simply an appearance. This cohabitation constitutes an extremely bizarre phenomenon in the history of representative government.[5] Should we rejoice that we have thus come to efficaciously moderate the partisan logic of the system, or should we on the contrary deplore that we have grievously distorted it?

The organization of separations thus produces the system of modern liberty, that is to say, the most stable, therefore the most satisfactory putting into practice of political liberty that humanity has ever known. At the same time, this system brings separation and division into the members of society. They will and they cannot; they recognize and they reject their representative; they are omnipotent since power rests on their will, and they are powerless, since their will is shackled, limited, checked by the will of the other party. It is very tempting then to distinguish between a good democracy, one that would have only the advantages of democracy, and a bad democracy, which would be called by another name no doubt, or that would be termed decadent or corrupt.

Certainly, all democratic political regimes are not of the same worth; some are better organized or show more civic virtue than others. But it must be acknowledged, I believe, that essentially the drawbacks as well as the advantages of our regime are inseparable systemic traits. Both flow with the same necessity from the "system of liberty," that is, the organization of separations. The practical consequence of this whole discussion, a disappointing consequence, is that instead of doing battle against the innumerable windmills that our partiality likes to choose, it is more judicious to keep an eye on the systemic order and to preserve it by preserving the integrity of the partisan logic I have tried to bring to light, and, for the rest, to bear patiently with its inevitable drawbacks.

CHAPTER 2

The Theologico-Political Vector

WE HAVE DEFINED our political regime, the regime of modern liberty, by the organization of separations. I have proposed a list of six principal separations as constitutive elements of this regime. These separations frequently overlap and reinforce one another. They are built one upon the other; they are inseparable. Can one among them be called the principal separation, the original separation from which all the others flow? Several appear to be candidates for the title. One could deduce all the separations from the one between civil society and the State, for example, or the one between the represented and the representative.

There is, however, one separation that is charged with a particularly dramatic intensity. As soon as we mention it, a host of historic images arise, memories of great conflicts that decisively marked and oriented European history. I speak of the separation between church and state. From at least the Investiture Controversy of the eleventh century between the pope and the German emperor, to the serious crisis in France at the start of the twentieth century between the Catholic Church and the Republic, European history turns on the complicated, often conflicted relation between the political and the religious jurisdictions. Nowadays, we have the feeling that the problem raised by this conflicted relation was resolved in any near satisfactory way only with the separation of church and state. France, for example, only attained its stable and definitive form with the secularization law of 1905. Conversely, we think that if this separation were to be called into question, the French Republic itself would be called into question.

Yet, in recent years, a certain number of unprecedented developments have appeared precisely to challenge or at least to weaken the system that was established in France by the secularization law of 1905. Certain writers and public figures have even cried out that secularism and thus the Republic are in danger. The growing presence in France of believers in Islam, a religion that rejects the separation between church and state, and between the spiritual and temporal realms, confronts the Republic with a difficulty it thought it had already resolved.

But is it the same difficulty? If some, as I alluded, think it is, and recommend that the same separation be imposed on Muslim citizens as was imposed on Catholic citizens nearly a century ago, others are much more hesitant. They fear that to impose on Muslims rules that they can obey only with difficulty would be to hurt them seriously and, under the pretext of defending secularism, to attack their "identity." They point out that in other democracies, in the United Kingdom for example, there is more tolerance shown for displays of community identity. In the French version of secularism, an implacable line of separation cuts citizens in two if they are also religious believers. On one side of the line, they are believers, as fervent as they wish to be; on the other side of the line, they no longer have religion, they are citizens and nothing but citizens. In the English version of liberalism, its partisans claim, the coexistence of diverse communities is organized in such a way that each person can quietly express his or her religion in public without fear of being accused of endangering a separation that is conceived with less rigor than in France.

I spoke first of the problem posed by Islam, for this is the problem that set in motion the debates to which I have just alluded. But the relations between the state and religion long present in democratic countries are not without their own difficulties. The principal one, of course, concerns abortion. In most democratic countries, abortion is legal under varying conditions. The Catholic Church, which by the number of its faithful and its organization constitutes the most influential Christian church, maintains that this act is forbidden by the commandment, "Thou shalt not kill." How can one guarantee both what the law of the state considers a right—to secure the termination of an unwanted pregnancy—and the church considers a duty—to protect all human life from the moment of conception?

It is clear that, in our regime founded on separation, the law of the state prevails over the law of the church, and a woman can freely terminate an unwanted pregnancy, at least at the early stages. But it is just as clear, and also an effect of separation, that a doctor is not obligated to perform an abortion if such an act goes against his conscience. In that way a pregnant woman is by right entitled to an abortion that a doctor has the right to refuse to perform. The difficulties entailed by the separation affect all the parties involved. The religious institution itself must reconcile its absolute refusal of abortion with its active participation in a society that legalizes it.

In Germany, for example, the Catholic Church has until now worked with counseling agencies providing services to women seeking abortions, with the intent of course of dissuading them. The Vatican asked the German Church to abandon this practice and to take no further part in the workings of the law authorizing abortion, since such participation constitutes, in the Vatican's view, a way of consenting to this law. The majority of the German Church seems to be hostile to this injunction from Rome.

The debate can also concern questions that are much less serious but that, as soon as the principle of separation is at stake, nonetheless give rise to intense passions. In the United States, for example, in certain cities protesters have succeeded in obtaining court orders to remove traditional Christmas nativity scenes from public places, on the grounds that nativity scenes, as displays of a particular religion, violate the principle of the separation of church and state. Their opponents or critics have underscored the danger, in their view, of what the quest for a total separation of the public and private realms represents. The public square risks becoming an absolutely empty, naked place.

These are a few examples of the difficulties encountered in the application of the principle involving the separation of church and state. Of course, if this principle remains one of the foundations of our political regime, it does not mean that the political sphere or the religious one does not evolve. One needs therefore to take into account the recent changes in the political and religious spheres each in itself and in their reciprocal relation.

I shall take as my starting point the recent evolution of religion, with help from Marcel Gauchet's *La Religion dans la démocratie: parcours de la laïcité* (*Religion in Democracy: The Advance of Secularism*). This essay is a continuation and an illustration of a much more ambitious book, *The Disenchantment of the World*, published in 1985. It will suffice for us to recall the heart of Gauchet's general thesis. In his view we have gone beyond religion, not religious faith—there still are believers—but a world where religion was a major "structuring" element, where it commanded the political form of societies and where, more generally, it defined the organization of the social bond. Gauchet writes: "The emergence from religion is the passage into a world where the religions continue to exist, but within a political form and a collective order that they no longer determine."[1] What was decisive in this process, according to Gauchet, is Christianity, the religion that made the end of religion possible. I will say nothing more about his general thesis regarding the meaning of human history as a whole, since what interests us here is Gauchet's description of our politico-religious, or theologico-political situation. Instead, I will extract from his recent essay a few ideas important for our discussion.

For Marcel Gauchet, secularism's current trouble is inseparable from religion's current trouble. What is the "current trouble" of religion? First, it is the weakening of the churches: the decrease in religious practice, the decline in vocations, and the weakening of the authority of the magisterium. The decisive point for Gauchet is not in changes that can be measured from the outside, but in the transformation of the meaning of religion for its practitioners themselves. It is not so much that they are less numerous, but that they are *different*. In the eyes of the faithful themselves, the churches no longer truly have the authority to determine belief, and even less to guide political choices or regulate morals. It is not only a matter of taking stock of what English sociologists have called "the unchurching of Europe," but, more deeply, of observing that the intimate meaning of belief is changing or already has changed. A shift has taken place from toleration to "pluralism." Gauchet uses the term "pluralism" in a precise sense.

> By pluralism I do not mean the simple resignation to the *de facto* existence of people who do not think as you do; I mean the believer's integration of the fact of the legitimate existence of other beliefs in his relation to his own belief. To state matters in more direct terms, pluralism as a given and a rule of society is one thing; pluralism in the head of believers is another. The principled pluralism of confessions in America, to take the extreme example, was for a long time able to accommodate especially rigorist forms of adherence within the different confessions. Everyone acknowledges the other's freedom, but does not hold any less to a style of conviction of his own that excludes the idea that other convictions are possible. Herein lies the whole difference between toleration as a political principle and pluralism as an intellectual principle. This intimate relativizing of belief is the characteristic product of our century, the fruit of the penetration of the democratic spirit into the very soul of the spirit of faith. The metamorphosis of religious convictions in religious identities constitutes its outcome.[2]

Gauchet believes that contemporary believers do not see religion as an objective universal truth, that is, a truth that is true for all and thus one that all "ought to believe." They choose it rather to choose themselves, for the subjective definition it provides them, the "identity" it bestows on them. Hence, "believers" do not seek to convince or convert others, they do not even try to argue in favor of their religion (in fact, what was called "apologetics" has so to speak completely disappeared from contemporary religious discourse). But, conversely, they do not accept that anyone can argue against it, they want everyone to "respect" it. Insofar as "believers" view their religion as a personal choice that defines their identity, any critique of their religion becomes an act of aggression against their person, a "lack of respect."

This transformation of religion, this absorption of religion into democracy, necessarily entailed the transformation of its great antagonist, the Republic. According to Gauchet, until about 1970 (this date seems to me a poor choice; I would say until the Second Vatican Council that ended in 1965), religion represented collective heteronomy, that is, the institutionalization of an objective truth that people had to recognize and to which they had to submit. Facing the church, the Republic stood for collective autonomy, autonomy wrested from heteronomy, that is, won against religion. Now that religion has been absorbed by and into democracy, that it

has become an individual matter, a free matter, the republican enterprise
has lost the adversary that gave it meaning:

> One does not need to look elsewhere to explain the uncertainty that gnaws
> at our inherited political culture. It is deserted by the spirit that presided, if
> not over its founding, in any case over its last great founding moment. The
> idea of the Republic on whose capital we continue to live has lost its soul
> along with the idea of secularism that stood at its side as its most intimate
> companion. The source of meaning on which they fed has dried up. The terms
> of the rapport between religion and politics by which they defined themselves
> have been radically displaced.[3]

Gauchet sketches a parallel between the extenuation of the republican idea
and the collapse of Communism. Of course, Communism was totalitarian
and ruled in the name of the science of history, whereas the Republic was
basically liberal and ruled in the name of liberty, education, and morality.
But Communism and the republic both were grandiose projects of a human
realm—Gauchet calls it a "city of man"—where man would experience his
sovereignty. This project, in its totalitarian version as well as its democratic version, has collapsed, the former because it has failed completely and
the latter because it has succeeded too well. In other words, collective autonomy—the republic—in arraying itself against collective heteronomy—religion—has in the end produced the triumph of individual autonomy, of pure
democracy, that has finally absorbed the republic as well as religion.

Marcel Gauchet's interpretation is penetrating and powerful. It knits
together the principal elements of our present situation and of our history
in a convincing dynamic scheme. It lets us see a social world that is satisfying, since the democratic individual has won his complete autonomy,
and desolate, or sterile, since the most decisive questions, the most interesting ones for man—the questions about truth, religious or philosophical,
about political community—have been set aside, pushed back beyond social and individual consciousness, placed in parentheses so to speak. It is
as though the achievement of democracy presupposed or implied that the
questions that defined the humanity of man had to be forgotten.

I must come back to our theologico-political history. As I indicated earlier,
Marcel Gauchet sees the cause, or pivot, of this singular history in the
singularity of the Christian religion, "the religion of the emergence from
religion." I would like to consider this question briefly.

First, let me recall some elementary facts that are well known but that
are indispensable to keep very clearly in mind. A few words on the history
of religions will help us. The pagan religions, Greek and Roman religions,
were civic religions—Tocqueville nicely calls them "municipal" religions.
The gods are chiefly those of the city. There are indeed "Panhellenic" gods

in Greece, but these gods of Olympus are then "municipalized," "localized." The religious community duplicates the political community; in fact, they merge. In the famous affair of the Arginusae, the people of Athens themselves sentence to death the generals who were guilty of pursuing the fleeing enemy instead of fulfilling their religious duties to the corpses of the Athenian sailors. At the end of the chapter entitled "The Gods of the City," Fustel de Coulanges writes in his great work:

> We see by this what a singular idea the ancients had of the gods. It was a
> long time before they conceived the Divinity as a supreme power. Every family
> had its domestic religion, every city had its national religion. A city was like
> a little church, all complete, which had its gods, its dogmas, and its worship.
> These beliefs appear very crude to us, but they were those of the most intellec-
> tual people of ancient times, and have exercised upon this people and upon
> the Romans so important an influence that the greater part of their laws, of
> their institutions, and of their history is from this source.[4]

The pagan religions, which are political and local, are generally set in opposition to the revealed religions, which are spiritual and universal, which communicate a message from God, a message addressed to everyone by a God to whom everyone can convert. The contrast is very real, but one also needs to keep in mind what the revealed religions have in common with the pagan religions. Judaism and Islam reject pagan idolatry very forcefully, but like paganism they maintain the confusion or fusion of the political and the religious. They invert, it is true, the order of factors: whereas the Greek gods are the gods of the city, the people of Israel are the people of God. Whereas Greek religion is molded, if I may say so, on the political form, the people of Israel as a human community is shaped by the religious form, more precisely by the law given by God, the Torah. It was acceptance of the Law and obedience to the law—to the 613 commandments of the Law—that originally defined belonging to Israel. The Jewish law, the Torah, and the Muslim law as well, the Shariah, regulate all the actions of the members of the community, without distinguishing between the secular and the religious domains. The religious community is the political community; the political community is the religious community.

The Christian religion is different. It is defined less by a law than by a faith. To be Christian is first to *believe* a certain number of dogmas, that is, propositions bearing on the invisible world, for example, the Incarnation or the Trinity. Unlike the other revealed religions, Christianity turns away from the world, ignores the world, and so leaves the world as it is. In particular, it leaves political institutions as they are. Christians render "unto Caesar what is Caesar's and unto God what is God's" (Matthew 22:21). In order to do so, they need to distinguish between Caesar's domain and God's domain. It is this singularity of Christianity that makes many historians and philosophers ascribe to it a decisive role in the development of modern democracy, that is, a world in which man is the sovereign of the human law. If Marcel Gauchet sees in Christianity the religion that made the end of religion possible, it is because Christianity is the only religion that sets the secular sphere free.

At the same time, the Christian religion is not simply apolitical; it is not only a set of beliefs about the world beyond, and even less a set of "values," as people say today. It institutes an unprecedented human community, and thereby raises an unprecedented political problem. This community is the church, which could be defined as a "real universal community." Every human being is at least potentially a member of this community, which has its own proper principle, charity, and a specific organization, the ecclesiastical hierarchy, the head of which is the pope. Thus this nonpolitical community necessarily comes into contact and competition with all political communities, not by directly providing political laws, but indirectly, by addressing every man and every woman, claiming him or her for itself, promising him or her membership in a perfect community. The church is a *respublica perfecta* because it is *respublica Christiana*.

The specific political problem raised by the Christian religion has thus to do with the ambivalence of the church. On the one hand, she liberates the secular sphere, leaving political societies free in principle to organize themselves as they wish since the Christian church, unlike the synagogue, does not provide any political law. At the same time, she devalues political societies. By criticizing their principle—the love of self and the disdain of God—in the name of its principle—the love of God and the disdain of self—she erodes their legitimacy. The result of this ambivalence could be formulated in the following way: the church, in refusing to govern men but in devaluing those who take on this responsibility, succeeds only in preventing men from governing themselves properly. This was the conclusion, or rather the starting point, of the thinkers who invented modern political philosophy. Machiavelli, Hobbes, and Rousseau, different as they are, all agree on this point: that the spiritual power of the church introduces such confusion in the city, that it makes "any good polity impossible in Christian States."[5]

What is to be done to overcome this confusion? Clearly, the only way to cut this Gordian knot, is to separate these entities. Power must be separated as completely as possible from opinion, in particular religious opinion, in order to deprive this dangerous and in the end unintelligible notion of spiritual power of any foundation or pretext. The spiritual institution will no longer have any power except to teach whoever will be willing to listen, and the government will no longer hold any opinion, in particular no religious opinion. This idea, which will only be carried out, transformed into stable institutions in the nineteenth and twentieth centuries in democratic countries, is intellectually elaborated fully by the seventeenth century. The power that is without opinion is what we have come to know as the neutral or secular state.

But how can a human institution be radically separated from all opinion? It can be done in a very simple way. It suffices to note that, independently of their opinions about God or the Good or the world or in general about whatever interests them, human beings have irrepressible needs. They want to live, to be free, to be able to pursue happiness as they understand it. Life, liberty, and the pursuit of happiness: how would people not have a right to these goods that they cannot help but strive for? These are indeed the rights of man! Better yet, they are the *only* rights of man. The state, by separating itself more and more completely from all religious opinion, will discover more and more clearly its raison d'être, namely, the protection, guarantee, and implementation of the rights of man.

The theoretical distinction between the spiritual power and the temporal power that is impossible to institute practically will be replaced by the very separation between the power without opinion—the secular state—and the opinions without political power—society in its diversity. In this sense, the liberal state as we know it is the protector of the rights of man in civil society, thus solving satisfactorily the unprecedented problem created by the rise of the Christian religion.

Is this solution as satisfactory and enduring as most among us think it is? At the end of his essay, Gauchet suggests that our political and moral system dodges the questions of "truth" and "community." The legitimate satisfaction of living in an "advanced" democracy must not turn into complacency. To conclude this argument, I would like to make the following comments.

The modern political movement that our democracy inherits and perpetuates is a liberating or emancipating movement. Against the spiritual and temporal power, indeed against the combination of spiritual and temporal power that characterized the ancien régime, Europe and North America established a new type of power that does not give us foreign commands but that *represents* us, that represents our necessary and legitimate desires by guaranteeing our rights to life, liberty, and the pursuit of happiness. This new type of power is the modern representative state, defined by the separations we have at length discussed.

Thus, in order to find expression and be implemented, this self-affirmation of liberty must pass through the mediation of separations. This way of speaking is abstract, but when we describe our political regime we are necessarily dealing with abstract concepts. The citizen who is a believer, must, in order to be a good citizen, *abstract* from his or her religion. Moreover, the critiques of modern democracy whether from the right or the left both denounce its abstraction and formalism. Edmund Burke and Karl Marx are in agreement on this point.

This self-affirmation of our liberty involves two aspects: civil society and the state. Each one of us is an actor, or agent, in civil society, and each is represented in and by the state. Civil society and the state are the two faces of the same coin. In this sense, the liberals and their opponents are both correct, at least in what they affirm, if not in what they deny. The liberals affirm that each must be able to exercise freely in society his right to life, liberty, and the pursuit of happiness. Their opponents affirm that only a strong and truly representative state is a sufficiently robust instrument to prevent social powers, above all the "power of money," from inflicting a new form of domination and alienation on the members of society.

Historical experience seems to confirm what this reasoning suggests. From nationalizations to privatizations, from regulations to deregulations, there is a rather regular oscillation between periods when the dominant social movement seeks and obtains the increased intervention of the state and periods when the dominant social movement seeks and obtains the emancipation of civil society and the withdrawal of the state. One could say that from the New Deal to the oil crisis of the 1970s, the state was viewed with confidence as the great regulating and ordering agent of social life. For some twenty years now, it has been on the defensive. Often accused of all the dysfunctions that affect society, the state seems in any case unable to maintain or to regain its hold on the movement of the world.

This current discredit of the state must not mislead us. The critiques directed against its practical functioning are often justified, but their cumulative effect suggests almost irresistibly that the state is only useful as an instrument or that modern liberty needs the state only as a town needs a policeman. The most modern state would necessarily be the most modest state. In reality, the modern state has a spiritual or symbolic function. It is indispensable to my becoming conscious of being a citizen. In the scheme of representation, the state constitutes the neutral place, abstract and raised above society, to which I can turn as a citizen so that it can represent *me*. The state is indispensable for modern liberty to be able to see itself as it is. Under Louis XIV, says Bossuet, "France learned to know itself." These words hold the key to understanding the modern state.

On the other hand, the separation between the state and society, indispensable as it may be, produces certain negative effects, as we saw in studying the mechanism of the separation of powers. One could say very simply that living at once both in civil society and the state, I am never quite whole anywhere. Half bourgeois, half citizen, I am forever uncomfortably and at times painfully divided. In any case that is the critique voiced by Rousseau and Marx. For reasons that we shall see more precisely later, in his critique of the rights of man in *The Jewish Question*, Marx maintains that the separation between the state and civil society must be overcome if modern humanity is to achieve its fulfillment. Communism attempted to do this. The results of the attempt were catastrophic, but seen in its own light the project was understandable. In an extraordinarily primitive and brutal manner, Communism answered a real difficulty of our political regime. A regime that is founded on separations, which have in them something abstract and artificial, naturally invites projects aimed at abolishing these very separations. The totalitarian movements of the twentieth century can be considered in this light.

The social and moral movements that I described previously with the help of Marcel Gauchet can be interpreted in this same light, that is, as an effort to overcome the abstraction of the modern regime, but without going against modern liberty. Today the state as well as society are no longer called upon to guarantee human rights simply of human beings *in general*, separated from all their particularities: personal qualities, opinions, morals, but of *concrete human beings* with all their affiliations and qualities: cultural identity, religion, sexual orientation, among others. All the "identities" of an individual must be validated by the state and society as soon as that individual declares them to be his or hers, and an unconditional "respect" is due them. Instead of a power separated from opinion and neutral among opinions, instead of the secular power I have tried to describe, there is a call for a state and social power that actively approves and warmly embraces all opinions and lifestyles.

That is the negation or inversion of the movement that led to the separation of church and state. Yet, at the same time, it is the continuation of the movement. There is no leaving behind the individualistic order and even the bourgeois order. Everyone is seen as an owner whose property the state and society must respect, but that property no longer consists only of goods, even including, as does Locke, life and liberty. It consists also of opinions, "values," "identities," and "orientations." I am the legitimate owner of all that I am. The state and society must recognize and declare that. They must explicitly approve all that I am.

The old order, or rather the old disorder, relied on a spiritual power that sought to govern only "indirectly." It was a power that wanted to govern without governing. To counter the disorder and institute a more humane and rational order, men strove to separate power from opinion. This attempt, along with its corresponding regime, is modern democracy itself. To counter the corrupting effects of a religion that imposed its truth, the question of liberty was separated as completely as possible from the question of truth. That meant that human beings were defined by liberty or that truth was declared to reside in liberty. The idea of liberty prevailed completely over the idea of truth. Yet, this victory was perhaps too complete. Deprived of its conflictive relationship with truth, liberty tends to collapse. Instead of being a thrust toward autonomy and government of oneself by oneself, it became the acceptance and declaration of the self, along with the demand that others recognize and respect this acceptance and declaration of the self. Having conquered truth, or having absorbed it, liberty is conquered by property, or absorbed by it.

CHAPTER 3

The Movement of Equality

E VERY SEPARATION in the organization of our political regime appears—by definition—to endanger the unity of the body politic itself, as the opponents of democratic institutions have underscored with concern in the course of modern history. If the legislative power and the executive power are separated, if the supreme power is thus divided, critics hold, society is deprived of its higher principle of unity and condemned to paralysis, anarchy, and dissolution. If church and state are separated, division permeates the soul of every member of society; the citizen is separated from the Christian. The political bond and the religious bond, instead of reinforcing one another are separated, and instead of union, sundering prevails. Joseph de Maistre or Louis de Bonald, who voiced these concerns, were called reactionaries or counterrevolutionaries, but revolutionary writers such as Rousseau or Marx were also doing battle against the separation of "bourgeois" and "citizen." In any case, these fears were refuted by experience, since, as it turned out, our regimes did not crumble and became even more stable and coherent by virtue of the way in which they organized these separations. At the same time, the questions posed by the reactionaries and by some revolutionaries are legitimate: How did our body politic succeed in preserving its cohesion in spite of these separations? What holds it together? What is its unifying principle?

In analyzing the English constitution, Montesquieu sees the raison d'être or at least the effect of the separation of powers in the preservation of liberty. England's constitution, he says, is the first in history whose principal goal is political liberty. As I argued, the idea of science and the idea of liberty are invested with a particular authority. In this sense, liberty can be said to be a unifying principle of our societies. At the same time, its effects can be and often are "separative." For example, economic freedom, even though its effect is to increase global wealth by raising the average standard of living, often favors an increase in the gap between rich and poor. Moral freedom tends to erode if not dissolve the unity of the family and thus of the social unit that has always been considered essential to the cohesion of the social whole. Liberty, thus, has social effects that are unquestionably disruptive.

One of the major reasons why our freedom is less disorganizing and more ordered than one might suppose is that it is understood to be a liberty of equality. Our liberty is defined as *equal* liberty; our equality is defined as equal *liberty*. "Men are born and remain free and equal in rights," states the first article of France's Declaration of the Rights of Man of 1789. Likewise, "All human beings are born free and equal in dignity and rights," says the first article of the Universal Declaration of Human Rights of 1948. Now, equality indeed seems to be a principle of cohesion and concord, at least of homogeneity. The miracle of modern liberty derives no doubt largely from the fact that it seeks to be an equal liberty, that the idea of equality penetrates all aspects of free society. In the eyes of some observers, equality, not liberty, is the true principle of our democracy. Since liberty seeks to be an *equal* liberty, it is the insertion of equality in liberty that defines modern liberty.

Let us consider as an example a recent economic and social proposal: a universal allowance. This radical proposal is put forth by serious authors who developed complex arguments in its favor. I shall consider it in the version given by Jean-Marc Ferry in a work by that title.[1]

Ferry proposes a universal allowance of citizenship defined as follows: "Primary social income is equally distributed in an unconditional manner. It is a genuine income of citizenship." Ferry argues that,

> Even if there is a recovery, economic growth will not create any more jobs than unemployment. By itself, it will not bring any solution to social exclusion.
>
> The crisis calls us to reflect on a new paradigm of distribution: to distribute a base income to all citizens, regardless of the part they play in production: rich or poor, working or unemployed, students or retirees.
>
> It is by developing an independent right to income, which would also favor the impetus of a "quaternary sector" of personal, non-mechanizable activities, that the right to work will cease to be a hypocrisy.[2]

I shall not enter into a technical discussion of the technical arguments advanced by Ferry, nor shall I examine whether the project can be accomplished. What interests me is the structure of the proposal itself. In the name of equality, the proposal boldly introduces a new *separation* between compensation and labor. The link between labor and compensation was and still is, in spite of increasing complications, the material and spiritual knot of modern economy and society. It is both the principle of action and movement—members of society work to be compensated, society gives incentive to labor through compensation—and the principle of legitimacy—of wealth, first of all, and of the social structure, which is founded on productive labor.

On this point socialists and liberals agree, however much they might disagree on other issues. Locke, no less than Marx, found value in labor. In our regime—whether we call it "capitalist" or "liberal" or "industrial" or some other name—the economic system separated itself from the social whole, and in doing so made itself into a system, but it became the locus where the social synthesis takes place, that is to say where contributions to society gain recognition and reward. Of course, the locus of social synthesis is, at the same time, the locus of social struggle: individuals and groups have different ideas of social justice. By proposing to radically separate compensation from labor, at least by proposing to institute a compensation that is radically separated from any labor, Ferry introduces a new separation in the heart of modern social unity.

In doing so, Ferry and his supporters are only proposing a return to an earlier order, in which compensated labor was but a part, and the least esteemed part of social life, since "honorable" people, those who "set the tone," lived without working, for example, by collecting seignorial rights or income from property. But this return to the past is not the point here since Ferry extends the condition of "noble," the status that allows one to live without laboring, to all citizens equally. With this proposal, the aristocratic condition would be completely democratized.

In the system of a universal allowance, the problem of social exclusion is resolved through a novel and extreme separation and through an extreme equalization. What is striking in Ferry's book is the lack of a reflection on justice since, indeed, the fundamental link between labor and compensation is derived from the requirements of justice, for Marxists as well as liberals. Ferry simply asserts: "The distribution of global income, in a given collectivity, national or supranational, can no longer and must no longer seek to express the respective contribution of each individual to the production of social wealth." For sure, he gives two reasons that can evoke the principles of justice: one, that misfortune, market fluctuations, technological changes, etcetera, do not justify that a member of society be deprived of income; two, the impossibility of measuring exactly the just remuneration of an individual contribution.[3]

These are interesting remarks, calling into question the principles of justice in our current society. But Ferry, content with having cast doubt on these principles, makes no effort to explain why the society of a universal allowance would be more just than ours. Ferry's argument is simply that since the link between labor and compensation is problematic, it should just be eliminated completely. And to answer the traditional "democratic" objection that to live without working or without having worked is unjust, Ferry decides that a universal allowance would open this unjust possibility to all. By equalizing this injustice, one would transform it into something essentially just. I am making a conjecture here, since Ferry does not pro-

vide any explanation. He deals with the very real problem of social exclusion by applying the procedure by which the modern regime has always
resolved its difficulties, the procedure of separation. Thus, this proposal
extends and exaggerates the two principal processes of our political and
social regime: separation and equalization.

One can rightly argue that the inequalities in our present society are enormous, even scandalous, in that the small percentage of individuals en-
joying extravagant incomes increases, while a growing section of society is
not only poor but also tends to drop out of the social bond. They are precisely the "excluded." Conversely, we can argue that our society is the most
equal that has ever existed. The inequality between men and women, in
the family or in the workplace, has been lessened considerably; in the family the distance between parents and children has been reduced; in institutions of learning the prestige of the teacher or professor has greatly
declined. More generally, respect for various "superior" sectors has diminished considerably. Hierarchies mix and disappear in a public space where
everyone is equal. On television, the Nobel Prize winner in physics presents
his favorite culinary recipe while the three-star restaurant chef discusses
the latest philosophy book he has read. In short, it seems that the last
barriers between people and activities are in the process of disappearing
and that we live henceforth in one world only, in a homogeneous and unified world. *We are the world*.

It is beyond question that just when economic inequality is increasing
after a long period when it had greatly diminished, general social equality—human equality—also grows. In other words, while quantitative inequality is growing, qualitative equality continues to advance. How can
this strange phenomenon be explained? Is equality an illusion? Or is inequality? If both are real, how can a society contain within itself two movements so contrary? This is not the first time modern society has shown such
an oddity. During the Great Depression, Joseph Schumpeter remarked in
his 1942 book, *Capitalism, Socialism, and Democracy*, the number of servants has continually diminished while mass unemployment ought to have
brought, it seems, an important increase in their number. It seems that
even during the economic crisis, social equalization went on.

Let us assume then that against a backdrop of increasing social equality,
economic inequality sometimes increases and sometimes decreases. How
do we explain this social equality that develops in a sort of sovereign independence in relation to economic inequality? What is this equality that
cares nothing about economic inequality? Tocqueville made this observation the center of his reflections in *Democracy in America*. In his introduc-
tion, he claims that,

Among the new objects that attracted my attention during my stay in the United States, none struck my eye more vividly than the equality of conditions. I discovered without difficulty the enormous influence that this primary fact exerts on the course of society; it gives a certain direction to public spirit, a certain turn to the laws, new maxims to those who govern, and particular habits to the governed.

Soon I recognized that this same fact extends its influence well beyond political mores and laws, and that it gains no less dominion over civil society than over government; it creates opinions, gives birth to sentiments, suggests usages, and modifies everything it does not produce.

So, therefore, as I studied American society, more and more I saw in equality of conditions the generative fact from which each particular fact seemed to issue, and I found it before me constantly, as a central point at which all my observations came to an end.

And a little further: "The gradual development of equality of conditions is therefore a providential fact, and it has the principal characteristics of one: it is universal, it is enduring, each day it escapes human power; all events, like all men, serve its development."[4]

Thus, for Tocqueville, equality is a generative fact, a causal and formative principle of modern society in *all* its aspects. But what kind of equality? The kind he calls "equality of conditions," that keeps on progressing regardless of what men do or will? It is tempting to say that Tocqueville meant the social equality that gives citizens equal rights in civil society, and is distinct from political as well as economic equality. There is no doubt that Tocqueville sometimes speaks as if this were the case, as if equality would be limited by two of the constitutive separations of the modern regime: Economy—Society—Politics.

In reality, "equality of conditions" is an all-encompassing notion. It is something more than economic equality, more than political equality, more than social equality. Nor is it the sum of the three. What then is it? The answer is nevertheless simple. The equality Tocqueville speaks of, what he calls democracy, is ultimately something moral, a human disposition: it is *the sentiment of human likeness*.

One can write a history of equality in the West. Tocqueville sketches one several times without ever developing it, beginning with the Middle Ages. In the Middle Ages, we find the equality of men before God, with the corresponding institution, the church, in whose eyes and within which the inequalities of the material world are in principle without worth. But this interior and invisible equality had little effect on the social and political inequalities, which the church tended to reconfirm by declaring them in conformity with the order of Providence.

Then one can distinguish this period that Tocqueville calls "the golden age of kings." Kings, in becoming "absolute," raised themselves decisively above all the sectors of society, be they religious or secular. They subjected them all. Nobles, bourgeois, and prelates must, like the people, obey the absolute sovereign. This new inequality produced an unprecedented equality. Under the hand of the king, all tended to become equal subjects and the extreme social heterogeneity of "feudalism" was considerably reduced. Tocqueville wrote, "In France, the kings showed themselves to be the most active and constant levelers."[5] This new equality was nonetheless limited by the fact that the king, by virtue of his superiority, still stood by the old social inequalities. At the decisive moment during the French Revolution, when the monarchy's fate hung in the balance, Louis XVI did not want to sacrifice or betray his "dear nobility."

But the equality and homogeneity produced by the golden age of kings were sufficiently advanced for society to sense that the body politic, the *nation*, was capable of existing without the monarchy and without social inequality. *Opinion* circulated through all the parts of French society like blood in a living body; it could no longer be contained, in both senses of the term, in the officially authorized bodies. At that point, a third period could begin, in which the French acted upon their sense of belonging to one homogeneous body, by striving to change their old status as subjects of the king into a new status as citizens of their nation. This moment, the moment of the Revolution, was indeed decisive, and not only because it signified the irruption of political and social equality. Something happened that reverberated over all aspects of exterior as well as interior life. Henceforth, the community of citizens no longer recognized anything outside or before itself. The complex body constituted by the old social classes and the king, a body composed of *parts*, was replaced by a homogeneous body without parts, consisting of equal citizens, a unified body that was the source of all its differences and internal inequalities. The first article of the Declaration of 1789 goes on to state: "Social distinctions may be founded only on the general good."

This homogeneous body is destined to become ever more homogeneous. Why? Because men *desire* equality. But have they always desired it? Do they not have different and contradictory ideas of equality? Do some men not desire inequality as well? They do, yet it seems that there is something stronger than the ideas and desires of men. It was after the establishment of the nation as an unified body that the desire for social homogeneity became an irresistible pressure. The more homogeneous society is, the stronger the desire for homogeneity. One could say that henceforth the true sovereign is democracy itself or equality itself, the likeness among citizens and, beyond that, among men.

In *Democracy in America*, Tocqueville analyzes how this truly absolute sovereign exercises its power. I shall consider two particularly striking chapters in Part III of Volume II, the first, "How Mores Become Milder as Conditions are Equalized," and the fifth, "How Democracy Modifies the Relations of Servants and Masters."

Tocqueville first observes that in aristocratic societies the nobility is generally insensitive to the suffering of common people, not because nobles are uncaring or amoral, but because it is difficult for them to form any vivid idea of these sufferings. In the strict sense of the term, they cannot imagine them. This is so to speak a problem of social epistemology more than morality. To illustrate his point, Tocqueville cites a letter of Madame de Sévigné in which she evokes in an amusing way, with a lightness that seems us atrocious, the brutal repression of a fiscal rebellion in Brittany. Tocqueville comments:

> One would be wrong to believe that Madame de Sévigné, who wrote these lines, was a selfish and barbaric creature: she loved her children passionately and showed herself very sensitive to the distress of her friends; and one even perceives in reading her that she treated her vassals and servants with goodness and indulgence. But Madame de Sévigné did not clearly conceive what it was to suffer when one was not a gentleman.

Tocqueville continues:

> In our day the hardest man, writing to the most insensitive person, would not dare engage in cold blood in the cruel banter that I have just reproduced, and even if his particular mores would permit him to do it, the general mores of the nation would forbid it to him.
>
> How has that come about? Do we have more sensitivity than our fathers? I do not know, but surely our sensitivity bears on more objects.
>
> When ranks are almost equal in a people, all men having nearly the same manner of thinking and feeling, each of them can judge the sensations of all the others in a moment: he casts a rapid glance at himself; that is enough for him. There is therefore no misery he does not conceive without trouble and whose extent a secret instinct does not discover for him. It makes no difference whether it is a question of strangers or of enemies: imagination immediately puts him in their place. It mixes something personal with his pity and makes him suffer himself while the body of someone like him is torn apart.[6]

Thus the citizen of the democracies is naturally more compassionate. By the same token, compassion tends to favor democratic institutions.

Tocqueville then examines the fate in a democracy of the most unequal social relation, that between master and servant. He observes that it is radically transformed. Between master and servant, there is henceforth a contract. The relation, being voluntary, is no longer hereditary, necessary, or "natural." In principle, the servant can become master in his turn. Tocqueville writes:

> At each instant the servant can become a master and aspires to become one; the servant, therefore, is not another man than the master.
>
> Why therefore does the first have the right to command and what forces the second to obey? The temporary and free accord of their two wills. One is not naturally inferior to the other; he only becomes so temporarily by the fact of a contract. Within the limits of this contract the one is the servant and the other the master; outside of it they are two citizens, two men.
>
> What I beg the reader to consider well is that this is not only the notion that servants form for themselves of their state. Masters consider domestic service in the same light, and the precise boundaries of command and obedience are as well fixed in the mind of the one as in that of the other.
>
> When most citizens have long since attained an almost like condition, and equality is an old and accepted fact, the public sense, which exceptions never influence, assigns in a general manner certain limits to the value of man as above or below which it is difficult to stay for long.
>
> In vain do wealth and poverty, command and obedience accidentally put great distances between two men; public opinion, which is founded on the ordinary order of things, brings them near to the common level and creates a sort of imaginary equality between them despite the real inequality of their conditions.[7]

It is clear that Tocqueville is struggling to find the right words. He speaks of the real inequality of the conditions of master and servant while he ordinarily defines democracy by the equality of conditions. He speaks of "a sort of imaginary equality" when he has just made a list of its real effects. The fact is that the phenomenon he has in mind eludes the polarities by which one usually endeavors to understand the social world, in particular the polarity between what is in fact and what is by right, or the real and the imaginary. The equality that concerns him is not simply a juridical or moral equality that is by itself invisible; it is also not an "objective" equality that offers unquestionable visible signs for all to see, so that one could say with assurance that they *are* equal. What concerns him is an equality that takes effect in the element of representation, in the self-awareness of the citizens. They look upon one another as like beings; they cannot help looking upon one another as like beings.

Thus the characteristic separations of the modern regime are much less disruptive than might be feared because they separate people who already feel they are alike, or activities of people who feel they are alike. They are steeped in the bonding element, the conjunctive tissue of likeness. In a democratic society, the members recognize each other in spite of any existing disagreements and differences.

Tocqueville's is the most complete and subtle analysis of the phenomenon of democratic equality. Does it explain the contradiction we pointed out at the start between the advances of general or qualitative equality and those of economic or quantitative inequality? Interestingly Tocqueville also observes a similar contradiction in his own time. In the last chapter, entitled "How Aristocracy Could Issue from Industry," he describes, "Thus as the mass of the nation turns to democracy, the particular class occupied with industry becomes more aristocratic. Men show themselves more and more alike in the one, and more and more different in the other, and inequality increases in the small society as it decreases in the great."[8]

After taking stock of the new inequality, Tocqueville attenuates its importance. Precisely because it is atypical in democratic society—it is "an exception, a monster, in the entirety of the social state"—economic inequality could not develop to the point of jeopardizing democratic equality. Nonetheless Tocqueville ambiguously concludes:

> I think that all in all, the manufacturing aristocracy that we see rising before our eyes is one of the hardest that has appeared on earth; but it is at the same time one of the most restrained and least dangerous.
>
> Still, the friends of democracy ought constantly to turn their regard with anxiety in this direction; for if ever permanent inequality of conditions and aristocracy are introduced anew into the world, one can predict that they will enter by this door.[9]

One has the impression that Tocqueville vacillates. On the one hand, he is confident that industrial inequality, being contrary to the logic of democratic equality, is not a dangerous threat. On the other hand, he envisions that its development could lead to a reestablishment of the permanent inequality of conditions, and of aristocracy. His whole work is marked by the conviction that democracy is irresistible and irreversible. (After all, we can understand Tocqueville's hesitation when we recall the prodigious growth of stock market capital in recent years as reconstituting the class of the *rentiers* that the advances of industry and democracy have condemned.)

The new modern economic inequalities are more diffuse, more spread out in the social whole than the manufacturing enclaves of Tocqueville's time. At the same time, they are even more devoid of the social effects of domination than the ones that worried Tocqueville. Today, a golden boy, a creator of a start-up company is so to speak a free electron, whereas the nineteenth-century capitalist—for example, a silk manufacturer of Lyon—exercised a direct power on numerous aspects of the life of his workers. The deployment of economic activity is today as lively as it has ever been; yet, the inequalities to which it gives rise are more narrowly confined to the economic sphere than they have ever been.

Perhaps one should see in this an effect of that logic of separation that has been the leitmotiv of our analysis from the beginning. The more the economy becomes detached from the rest of social life, the more it abandons itself to its natural bent toward inequality; but at the same time, this inequality fails to influence people's views on life. This is, I suppose, what underlies the debates about "the end of labor."

Finally, the recrudescence of economic inequalities no doubt has multiple causes. The one I have sketched is not the only one. Another fundamental cause resides in the current weakening of the nation in Europe. This political form was the framework for the unfolding of democracy, and thus the sentiment of likeness and the desire for equality that Tocqueville studied. One could think that when this framework becomes weak, economic inequalities have more latitude to spread. This consideration comes down to relating the democratic fact as Tocqueville analyzes it, and the national fact about which he has little to say in his great theoretical book. Tocqueville presupposes the national fact; he does not analyze it. That shall be our next area of inquiry.

CHAPTER 4

The Question of Political Forms

ALL THAT we have observed about our political regime, the organization of separations, the separation of powers, and democratic equality, presupposes the framework of the nation. For at least two centuries, our political life has done so without giving the matter much thought. It is a given and not viewed as an object worthy of interest.

In addition to this long indifference, the nation as a political form has fallen into disrepute, at least in Europe, which for centuries has seen itself as the political *avant-garde* of the world. The two world wars of the twentieth century much discredited the notion of "nation." World War I was born of national rivalries in Europe. The second cannot be understood if one does not consider the economic and political consequences of the Versailles Treaty, which laid down the law for the new Europe by redrawing its political map according to the principle of "nationalities." These facts explain how many Europeans equate war with the nation.

Beyond that, the economic, technical, and moral developments in the aftermath of World War II have made the notion of humanity immediately obvious, with the conviction that we are now all "citizens of the world," and conceive a world "without borders." At a time when humanity seems on the way to becoming unified, the nation, with its parochial character, its preference for itself, seems painfully archaic, vaguely ridiculous, probably immoral, in any case destined to fade away. Thus the notion of a nation appears to belong in the past. There is no greater condemnation in our eyes, since from the start of the modern era, we see our life as situated along the vector of progress and we orient ourselves by it, indeed it is what defines "modernity." Under these conditions, how can we be seriously interested in the nation?

At this point I must caution that what I have observed applies only to Western Europe, in any case to the fully developed countries of Europe, those ripe to participate in the construction of the European Union. Outside Western Europe national construction can be meaningful. In Bosnia certain European as well as American officials openly admit to engaging in the enterprise of nation building. These two situations are not contradictory, but rather complementary. The "peripheral" nations, whether old or new, must first achieve a satisfactory national life before being judged worthy and capable of taking part in the construction of Europe, that is, worthy and capable of disappearing as nations.

It may be more appropriate to speak of the discredit of nationalism instead of the discredit of the nation. We are touching here for sure on a crucial question that is very difficult to clarify. What is nationalism? Where does one draw the line between a "good" nation and "bad" nationalism? Is it a feeling, a doctrine, a political pathology, or a mixture of the three? In any case, a rational appreciation of nationalism presupposes that one has first achieved a somewhat clear idea of the nation. Whatever nationalism may be, it is just one aspect of the phenomenon and a phase of the history of the national form. Contemporary works on the subject are so to speak obsessed with nationalism, as if nationalism was both the destiny and the truth of the nation. It suffices to mention a few recent books that are worth reading: *Nationalismes et nations*, by Raoul Girardet; *Nations and Nationalism*, by Ernest Gellner; and *Nationalisms: Five Roads to Modernity*, by Liah Greenfeld. Only Dominique Schnapper's *La Communauté des citoyens: sur l'idée moderne de nation* avoids the fascination with nationalism.[1]

The question of nationalism is clearly an important historical and political question. But unless one is to equate nation with nationalism, it is necessary to know something about the nation *before* nationalism or *independently* of it in order to understand what nationalism is. Some pin their hopes on a comparison or typology of nationalisms. Liah Greenfeld, for example, distinguishes three types of nationalisms: the individualist and civic nationalism of the Anglo-Saxons; the collectivist and ethnic nationalism of the Russians and Germans; and lastly, French nationalism, which, being both collectivist and civic, is in some way intermediary between the first two. These comparisons are very interesting, but they lead irresistibly to ranking the various types of nationalisms on a scale of values.

I do not question at all that such value judgments may be well-founded, but the enterprise leads to heightening the differences and thus to blurring the common character of the national form. Comparing nationalisms is not enough. If we wish to understand what the nation is, we must compare it to other non-national political forms. Even if we believe and welcome the idea that the national form is destined to disappear, it still behooves us to know what it consists of. How can we knowingly go beyond the nation and build something superior to it, if we do not know what it is?

Some argue that the question is unanswerable because the number of political forms is indefinite. Every human group has its own political culture: so many groups, so many different cultures. In France, to the scholarly term "culture"—scholarly, but now in common usage—has recently been added the deliberately popular and very trendy term "tribe": so many groups, so many tribes. Everyone has his own tribe! It is worth pausing a moment to consider how the term "tribe" is used in France today. In a deliberately provocative way, the most archaic political form and traditionally the most despised, becomes the generic name for all political forms and human groupings. One can understand the motives for the provocation—it is precisely a reply to the disdain—but the results are unfortunate. It blurs the understanding of political forms. First of all, there are a finite number of distinct political forms. On top of that, it makes one incapable of understanding the tribe itself as a political form.

In his book *Démocraties*, Jean Baechler considers the notion of a tribe in relation to the first political form, the *band*, a group of twenty to twenty-five hunter-gatherers that constituted the fundamental collective organization of Paleolithic men. The band gave way to the *tribe* when demographic pressure became too strong, the occasions for conflict more numerous, and broader protection was needed than the band was able to provide. The tribe is the collective form that assured this protection. It is defined by a twofold permanent movement of fission or division, when danger is distant; and fusion or coagulation when it is near.

What does it matter to us what happened in the late Paleolithic? What does that have to do with the contemporary debate? It is the fact that there is no indefinite political form. The tribe, the most supple political organization, was already perfectly defined thousands of years ago. It is qualitatively distinct from other political forms, above all from the band that precedes it and the city that follows it.

Thus there are a finite number of political forms. This is one of the most important "theoretical" propositions of political science. Inasmuch as the human world is political, it does not present an indefinite variability. It is structured and ordered. As soon as people live politically, they live in a political form, or in transition from one form to another. This theoretical proposition is heavy with "practical" consequences. Let us consider for instance the structure of the European Union. If we decisively abandon the nation form, we shall have to enter another form for one cannot live politically in an undefined way. What are these forms? We have started from the nation, evoked the band and the tribe, and alluded to the city. Baechler links the city to the band and the tribe in the following way: "The city recalls the band and the tribe by the primordial importance of personal relations and physical contact among members of society, but it separates itself radically from them by a firm distinction of the private from the public and a very advanced institutionalization of the political that is found again only in the nation."[2]

The starting point of any political reflection is indeed the city. It is the original home of European and Western politics, which has derived its very name from *polis*, the Greek word for the self-governing city. In the moments of France's political history, reference to the city comes naturally.

The French revolutionaries dreamed of Sparta and republican Rome. More recently, in less dramatic circumstances no doubt, when in 1968 the protestors shouted, "Elections, trap for idiots!," they appealed to direct democracy, which had its most prestigious achievements in Athens and to a lesser degree in republican Rome. And even after the French Revolution, a liberal author like Benjamin Constant maintained that ancient citizenship was no longer possible or desirable in the modern world, and defined modern liberty with reference to the ancient *experience* of politics. The ancient city is not just a memory, a shining image, a prestigious reference. It is rooted in a founding experience, in the discovery of what men can and must do to attain *justice* and *happiness*. We need a brief description of the city which is, along with the nation, the most political of the political forms.

For the Greek philosophers the city is the form of political life par excellence. According to them, the citizen's life "in the city" is the only way of life that is fully "according to nature." This is the meaning of Aristotle's famous phrase, "man is a political animal"—political, that is, made to live in a city. But why, or in what way, is the city especially natural? It is so because it corresponds to the human ability to know and to love. The power to know: the citizens know one another because in the first place they see one another. They know one another at least "by sight" since the city is finite. The assembly makes decisions after public deliberations and thus all the political structures of the city are so to speak visible. The city is "synoptic."[3] The power to love is linked to the power to know, since the citizen identifies easily with a community that is so immediately present and familiar to him. One can notice how the natural character of the city makes itself visible in that male and sometimes even female citizens go naked in the gymnasium. This nudity distinguishes Greeks from barbarians.

The natural character of the city shows itself in a dynamic way in that citizens affirm themselves, in the flesh, without any political "representative" or "civil servant." Regarding external affairs, a citizen is himself a soldier and the city is often at war. In internal affairs, he himself takes part in sovereign deliberations and magistracies. In sum, the city knows only face-to-face encounters. There is no voting booth! Nor is there any filter, only a sort of permanent incandescence. The beautiful unity of the city, the "beautiful whole" Hegel speaks of, is a misleading expression. As Plato writes, "each of them is very many cities but not a city . . . there are two, in any case, warring with each other, one of the poor, the other of the rich."[4] In its natural dynamism, the city is animated by two types of conflicts: external war against other cities, and internal war between rich and poor. These two tended to phase into one another, which led to a *megiste kinesis*—the gravest crisis of all history, in Thucydides' phrase—the Peloponnesian War, in which the Greek cities spent their strength. They soon had to submit to Macedonian hegemony. The truth about the city is liberty and war, inseparably.

It is a sad truth. For that reason, despite the unparalleled prestige of Athens, Sparta, and Rome, despite the dissatisfaction with, or even at times the revolt against, the illiberal constraints of the feudal order and the monarchy, the city will not appear again as a seriously desirable political possibility until the eighteenth century. But by then it will be a fundamentally transformed city. In the eighteenth century the traditional hierarchic order has been definitively discredited. As we recall, it was founded on the principle of obedience to temporal and spiritual powers. Liberty is what people want to institute now. But the only known free forms are cities. Yet cities are the rule of factions and permanent warfare. Thus the dynamic of the city has to be transformed, by separating liberty from the disorders that accompanied the city in the ancient world. This was achieved through two great reforms.

The first reform is the institution of *representation*. A representative republic replaces direct democracy, making it possible to filter the wills and passions of the people. This is the great merit of the English Constitution, as Montesquieu remarked: "A great vice in most ancient republics was that the people had the right to make resolutions for action, resolutions which required some execution, which altogether exceeds the people's capacity. The people should not enter into government except to choose their representatives; this is quite within their reach."[5] Of course, no sooner was this said than a great debate regarding representation arose. Where Montesquieu sees a judicious filter that tempers the people's fits of anger or enthusiasm, Rousseau sees a betrayal of the general will: "As soon as they [the representatives] are elected, it [the people] is enslaved, it is nothing."[6]

The second great change is the *multiplication of interests*, the despair of Rousseau. Rousseau saw very clearly that the difference between the ancient city and the modern states was not so much that Greek or Roman citizens were individually more virtuous than the French or English of his time, but rather that in the ancient city, "there is much less private business," as he says in the same chapter. It is precisely this visibility of private interests that makes opposition between the poor and the rich so obvious, so prominent, and thus so dangerous. To mitigate this opposition, it was necessary, against Rousseau's wishes, to multiply private interests, or "factions." This idea is set forth with perfect clarity in one of the fundamental texts of modern politics, the one that makes explicit the political philosophy at the founding of the United States of America. This is *The Federalist Papers*, which were penned chiefly by Alexander Hamilton and James Madison in 1788.[7]

Modern politics, as one can see, which seeks to reestablish liberty without bringing back war, directly contradicts the logic of ancient politics. The ancient city called for a small and homogeneous population, so that it could remain "synoptic." The modern state, if it wishes to be free, requires a large and diverse population. It appears then to be a city that is deliberately and artificially spread out and diluted. Moreover, so that the dynamics of the citizenry do not entail the conflicts that destroyed the ancient cities, two barriers are imposed: the filter of representation and a legislation that favors individual liberties, particularly commercial liberty. In the modern community, citizens are hardly ever just citizens. They are first and foremost the agents of their private "moral," no less than "material," interests. To the extent that they are citizens, they need the mediation of their representatives. One can say, like Rousseau, that they are free only "during the election of the members of Parliament," but in this way one can have freedom without having war.

Surprisingly, the establishment of modern politics within the national framework by the American and the French revolutions unleashed a new cycle of wars. Not only just military wars, but internal wars with the crystallization of a general opposition between rich and poor, which was now framed in terms of class struggle or class warfare. Just as the war among the cities of Greece had phased into a war between the rich and the poor within each city brought about the Peloponnesian War and the subsequent irreparable weakening of the cities, the war of the nations in Europe phased into the class struggle to bring about the two great wars of the twentieth century, which spelled the end of the independence of the European nations. Just as the Greek cities had had to submit to Macedonian hegemony, so the European nations had to submit to American hegemony (not to mention those that had to submit to Soviet tyranny). Thus one is tempted to say that the European nations, who were devised precisely in order to not repeat the most egregious faults of the ancient cities, ended up by making precisely these same faults.

It can be said assuredly that the catastrophes of the twentieth century flowed from the rivalry between the democratic nations and other nations that were not or were hardly democratic, and that the latter, in particular Germany, was chiefly responsible for the disaster. There is much truth in this common assertion, as in the remark, also common, that there has never been a war between two fully democratic nations. At the same time, the dangerous strength of the national dynamism of the democratic nations themselves—a dynamism that is not illuminated when termed "nationalistic"—suggests that the artifices of political science have shown themselves to be of limited effectiveness in certain circumstances. The modern nation was at once the critic and the imitator of the ancient city—its negation and its continuation.

This analysis has roughly juxtaposed, as Albert Thibaudet and Arnold Toynbee among others had done previously, the cycle of the Greek city and the cycle of the European nation, as if the founders of modern politics had directly worked on the ancient city and reformed it. Now, between these two cycles, twenty-two to twenty-four centuries have passed. Surely this very long period of time was filled with other political forms.

After the Greek cities had been exhausted in the Peloponnesian War, there came the hegemony of Philip of Macedon, followed by the empire of his son, Alexander the Great, that covered the east all the way to the Indus. Thus the Greek world passed from city to empire. The transformation was even more striking in the western Mediterranean, since on that side of the world the ancient city itself, Rome, became the heart or head of the new empire (whereas the old Macedonian state was located at the periphery of the Greek world). In spite of its extraordinary brilliance and fruitfulness, Alexander's empire did not survive its founder. The Roman Empire lasted five centuries in the west and fifteen in the east. The city signified war and liberty; the empire signified peace—the *pax romana* (war was pushed back to the distant frontier)—and property, or private right. Ancient politics, whether Greek or Roman, was thus deployed between the limits and concentration of civic life in the city and its extension and dilution in the empire. But after the Greek and Roman cycles, this rhythm was interrupted. Then modern politics began.

Why did this rupture in the "natural" rhythm of politics take place? Montesquieu believed that the Roman Empire severed the roots of liberty throughout the extent of its dominion. Another reason, perhaps linked to the first, was the appearance of an unprecedented community, a new Rome, namely, the church. As I stated in chapter 2, the church introduced an extraordinary political innovation by offering a "real universal community" of which all men were potential members. Its empire is thus more extended than the largest empire. Furthermore, its internal principle, charity, promises an even closer union than civic friendship can produce. From its appearance, the city and the empire, the two pagan political forms, were overwhelmed by the Christian church. These pagan institutions did not disappear; they were even revived in the guise of the cities of Flanders, Germany, or northern Italy, and the Germanic Holy Roman Empire, but without ever going beyond a certain level of strength and influence.

The most efficacious defender of politics and of secular life against the church was the work of a new political agent, the "Christian king." The "Christian king" was a historical operator of extraordinary complexity and importance; he was simultaneously the summit of feudal allegiances, and the sovereign rationalizer, modernizer, and nationalizer. His person could be very mediocre, but by virtue of his theologico-political role, he joined the past to the future and assured the historical continuity characteristic of the European political bodies. Through him, the nation entered the world and became the dominant and almost exclusive political form of the Christian world.

As for the political form of empire, it never again enjoyed in the Christian world the esteem that it held in the pagan world. But it did not cease to contribute to our history. In order to limit the discussion I will overlook the history of the Germanic Holy Roman Empire, which did not die officially until 1806 under the shock of Napoleon's empire, as well as the role of empire in the formation of national monarchies and the colonial empires of the European nations. However, I will distinguish three types of empires: a real empire, a possible empire, and a virtual empire.

In the present day, real empire is obviously the American empire. The United States not only holds the throne but it is the insurer, consumer, and guardian of last resort in the world as was Great Britain in the nineteenth century. It exercises a truly imperial government, much more than Great Britain ever did, not only by its direct financial, diplomatic, or military interventions, but because it sets the rules by which most citizens of the planet consent to live: American jurisprudence, rating agencies, and accounting procedures are considered by Americans *and by others* as the standard of universal norms. One of the signs of the imperial reality is that the boundary between internal and external tends to disappear. Every non-American is a potential citizen of the United States, and American jurisdiction tends implicitly or sometimes explicitly to extend to the entire world. One should add that the American empire is in most cases a benevolent and often an enlightened empire. In quite a few circumstances it even deserves to be qualified as generous. It is the only empire, along with Alexander's, to belong to this category.

Thus, it would be imprudent to justify calling the American empire as having an "imperialist" or a "unilateralist" policy. However powerful and extended the American empire may be, it naturally comes up against its limits. The most constraining limit is an "epistemological" one. Although the United States has many material interests in the world, it lacks the attention needed in the rest of the world to be able to govern it without the aid of allies and even of its rivals. One is tempted to say that the United States is a sort of "common instrument" that the world uses to govern itself. American policy can certainly legitimately pursue the particular interests of the United States, but it needs to take into account this character of "common instrument." This is why the idea of an antimissile shield system proposed by various American administrations is such a bad idea. Leaving aside considerations of feasibility and cost, we easily understand that any advance of this shield would only aggravate the epistemological deficit of American foreign policy. The complacency based upon a quasi-absolute invulnerability would rob the United States of any incentive to handle the crises of the planet, which, for now, only they alone are able to handle. It is surely too soon to evaluate the consequences of the terrorist attack of September 11, 2001 on the United States's international relationships, but the present consequences of the intervention in Iraq rather confirm my argument.

The possible empire refers to the one that Europe will constitute if the construction of the European Union is successful. This I will discuss in a later chapter.

The virtual empire is of an altogether different nature. It would be the empire with no common power, except for the weak United Nations, constituted by the whole of humanity, the human species at the present time. But does humanity as a whole have a real or at least a potential political existence? The most systematic theoretician of empire, the poet Dante, writes in his *De Monarchia* that "there is [therefore] some activity specific to humanity as a whole (*est [ergo] aliqua propria operatio humanae universitatis*)."[8] Is there such an "activity specific to humanity as a whole"? Rousseau denies it: "There is no natural and general society among men."[9] That is why Rousseau was such a vehement supporter of the ancient city, or a nation resembling the city as much as possible. Men can live decently only in a community instituted within certain limits.

One can discern the practical political import of this great theoretical question. If you think as Dante that there is a general society of the human race, you will favor one or another version of empire. For example, you will favor the current construction of Europe, including its remarkable character of indefinite extension. If you think with Rousseau that such a general human society does not exist, then you will support the nation, that is, a political order that acknowledges its own particularity.

CHAPTER 5

The Nation and the Work of Democracy

I HAVE LAID OUT in summary fashion a schema of political forms. In particular I have made an effort to sketch the dynamic relation that shaped the history of Europe: the relation of city, empire, and church that found its "solution" in the nation. Now, I would like to focus attention on the national form for its own sake. I shall begin by describing the fact or phenomenon of the nation. Then, I shall analyze Ernest Gellner's plausible and even forceful thesis on the social meaning of the nation. Lastly, I shall reflect on the relation between the nation and democracy that is not only a historical and sociological problem, but also a spiritual one.

First, in describing the nation, I will take as my inspiration a text of Jean Baechler, and distinguish economic self-sufficiency, diplomatic and strategic self-sufficiency, and lastly affective self-sufficiency,[1] which constitute elements of the national form, essential to its existence. Because these self-sufficiencies are nowadays in the process of being eroded, we see more clearly than ever how they were elements of the national form, we understand things better when they stopped being taken for granted, that is, historically, when they are threatened with disappearance.

Let us first consider *economic self-sufficiency*. To speak of economic self-sufficiency today is almost redundant, since the primary meaning of the word is for us the economic meaning. To be self-sufficient means to live on one's own resources, without needing to import goods or services or to engage in commerce or trade. The term today evokes unpleasant ideas and images, for example, war economies. During World War I, Germany's chemical industry multiplied ersatz materials intended to replace products that could not be imported due to the Allied blockade. Or totalitarian regimes, like Albania until recently, or North Korea. North Korea's self-sufficient regime has ruined the country. It survives only thanks to foreign food aid, chiefly American. The idea of self-sufficiency evokes a closed path of narrowness, when we would rather be open.

Until fairly recently, however, a certain amount of self-sufficiency was the desire and the law of all political bodies, except of course those for whom commerce was the principal activity, like the cities of northern Germany long ago or Hong Kong today. Commerce for a long time developed much more within nations than between nations. In an important book Karl Polanyi underlined that the "great transformation," that is, the development of the modern market economy, was inseparable from the building up of *national* markets. The market was at first and for a long time principally the *national* market.[2] Only one country, Great Britain, deliberately renounced self-sufficiency as soon as the mid nineteenth century. Beginning with the Corn Laws of 1846, Great Britain consented to depend on foreign sources for its basic food supply. That country's sense of security rested on its general industrial and financial superiority and its control of the seas. Of course, control of colonial possessions allowed certain European nations to enjoy a wider self-sufficiency.

It was only after World War II and in reaction to the "protectionism" that had marked the period between the two world wars, which was thought to contribute to the development of belligerent nationalism, that domestic markets (national markets) were truly and systematically opened: "The opening of the European markets to one another and even more their opening to the Atlantic and world markets dates essentially from the great and intense growth period from 1950 to 1974."[3] The anxiety arising today from outsourcing does not stem only from the conviction, justified or not, that competition from countries with low wages contributes greatly to unemployment in developed countries. Globalization is worrisome because it diminishes the feeling of economic self-sufficiency that until recently was inseparable from what defines a nation.

The second kind of self-sufficiency to consider is *diplomatic and strategic self-sufficiency*. This ordinarily refers to national independence and sovereignty. Each nation—and this is what defines it as a nation—determines its external actions in sovereign fashion: chooses its alliances, wages war, or makes peace.

It is often said that the European nations lost this independence in the aftermath of World War II, when the European continent was divided in two and the Iron Curtain was lowered on the line of demarcation defined by the meeting points of the Soviet and American armies. Yet one could rightly date the end of this diplomatic and strategic self-sufficiency to an earlier time, namely, in 1917, with the arrival of the first American troops that tipped the balance of World War I. It was the Fourteen Points of President Wilson that set the spirit in which the Treaty of Versailles was drafted, although the United States declined to participate in the League of Nations as President Wilson had wanted. In any case, from 1917 onward the United States was a full-fledged member, at times a decisive member of the European concert. America's isolationism, beginning in 1919, had many consequences, most often unfortunate ones, but its participation after 1945 had consequences that were most often felicitous.

The last "independent" foreign action of the European nations, that could be called their last attempt to maintain or recover a certain diplo-

matic or strategic self-sufficiency, was the Franco-British intervention in
the Suez in 1956, when the Franco-British expeditionary corps seized the
Suez Canal zone in response to the nationalization of the Suez Canal by
Colonel Nasser. A complete fiasco, the operation was quickly stopped
under American pressure, and the expeditionary corps recalled.

The erosion of this self-sufficiency is thus a long story that goes back to
the final phase of World War I. When the European nations are accused
of "abandoning" or "transferring" their sovereignty to the European
Union, the statement certainly has not much meaning for diplomatic and
military sovereignty, which was in great part abandoned, or lost, long ago.
In this sense, the construction of the Europe European Union is a consolation for diplomatic or strategic impotence. It gives each nation the impression of carrying out a "foreign action." While it is a consolation, it is not
yet a remedy. The sum of the infirmities of the European nations has up
to the present only produced an infirmity on a grander scale. We shall
speak of this again soon.

The third kind of self-sufficiency, that according to Baechler defines the
nation, is the one he calls *affective self-sufficiency*. The phrase is a bit awk-
ward but it articulates something very important:

> The *affective self-sufficiency* means the possibility of concentrating on the pol-
> ity every affective identification with a community and of focusing all negative
> feelings of hatred, spite, and fear on other polities. . . . In concrete terms, for
> France to exist, the French had to feel that they existed, as Frenchmen, over
> against the English and Germans, and vice-versa.[4]

This "affective identification" is something more than a "national feeling,"
even if the latter has a part in it. It causes a nation to fuse into itself and
subordinate all other identifications that a citizen might otherwise feel.

In the traditional, prenational order,

> the feeling of belonging is tied on the one hand to local entities—the parish,
> the manor, the countryside—and on the other to the person of the king as the
> transitory representative of a dynasty. To a certain extent, the French exist as
> the respectful subjects of the king of France, but France is only the domain
> where this dynasty exercises its power. For the nation to appear, the French
> and France had to come together. That meeting took place in two stages. The
> first occurred in the fourteenth and fifteenth centuries and was directed
> against the English. The second and decisive meeting took place against the
> reigning dynasty itself, under the Revolution.[5]

The first stage is illustrated by the extraordinary action of Joan of Arc.
But the second stage gives the notion of affective self-sufficiency its full
meaning.

The Declaration of the Rights of Man and Citizen of 1789 decrees that
"the principle of all sovereignty resides essentially in the nation" (article

3). Yet the idea and the sentiment of the nation already permeated the body politic of France even before the Declaration. When the deputies of the Third Estate met at the Estates General, they unilaterally decided by themselves, without the privileged orders, to verify the mandates that initiated the transformation of the Estates General into the National Assembly. How would the representatives of the Third Estate call themselves? Did they constitute an assembly of the representatives of "*le peuple*," that is, of a *part*, however much a majority, of the body politic, the other part being constituted by the privileged orders, or an assembly of the representatives of the totality as a whole and without parts of the body politic, hence of the "nation"? Mirabeau proposed the first formula, Sieyès the second. Sieyès's motion carried the day.

Since common verification is a right of the indivisible nation, the representatives of the Third Estate cannot be only the representatives of the Third Estate, of the people, that is, always a part of the nation. They are the representatives of the entire nation.[6] Prior to this moment, the body politic called "France" was structured by the division into three orders. From this moment on, it no longer had any internal partition but rather it was unified and indivisible. The national fact permeated the political space. Anywhere in the nation, there is only the nation, or a representative of the nation.

This fusion of all the elements in the crucible of the one and indivisible nation is something much more than the traditional national sentiment. But why would this particular fusion determine the meaning of the modern European nation? The national fact is certainly not reducible to the revolutionary fact. But the ordinary national reality and the revolutionary moment have in common the affirmation of internal unity and homogeneity. The nation is distinct from the political order that preceded it in that it is a body politic whose content is homogeneous or tends toward homogeneity.

In order to understand this homogeneity better, we will now turn to Ernest Gellner's brilliant work, *Nations and Nationalism*. Gellner defines "nationalism as primarily a political principle, which holds that political and national unity should be congruent. . . . Nationalism is a theory of political legitimacy, which requires that ethnic boundaries should not cut across political ones, and, in particular, that ethnic boundaries within a given state . . . should not separate the power-holders from the rest."[7] One is tempted to say that formulated in this way the nationalist principle is but an application or a version of the principle of representative democracy. If the rulers do not belong to the same ethnic group or "nationality" as the mass of the people, the latter will take themselves to be oppressed or, in any case, poorly represented. This is true, but Gellner has in mind the type of society that corresponds to this principle, that is, a society that is unified and homogeneous within, rather than the democratic, or representative, or even nationalist principle of legitimacy.

It is this novel social idea that interests Gellner. He delineates its specificity by recalling some characteristics of the prenational order, the ancien régime (although Gellner does not limit his references to Europe).

In the ancient order, most people lived at a subnational level: in the parish, the manor, the "countryside," using again the terms from Baechler. Those who govern them live and think at a supranational level. This is eminently true of the clergy when it belongs to a supranational and even "universal" church, in the case of the Catholic Church. It is also true of the aristocracy whose genealogical trees trace a network that is largely indifferent to "national" political borders. Even the heads of the "nations" are often foreigners or whose wives or husbands are often of another "nationality." The fact that the queen of France was Austrian, thus a "foreigner," was in itself something very banal during the ancien régime. It was only because the national reality was already intensely strong by the end of the eighteenth century in France that Marie-Antoinette was designated with hostility as *the Austrian* or *the foreigner*. Thus, in the prenational order, there were only subnational and supranational people; in the national or "nationalist" order, there are only "nationals," either governed or governing.

What happened? According to Gellner, it was the "industrial society." The notion of "industrial society," as opposed to "military and theological society," originated from the sociological tradition of Saint-Simon and Auguste Comte. Gellner deduces the national aspect from the "industrial society." In chapter 3 of his book, he explained that an industrial society is first a "rational" society. The notion is the main basis of the work of Max Weber, but Gellner gives it a more radical sense, following the philosophies of Descartes, Hume, and Kant. Our society presupposes, or sees itself as a coherent, homogeneous, comprehensible world by means of a language that in principle is accessible to all. All the facts of this world, all the "social facts," are susceptible to being put in relation to one another. Being thoroughly comprehensible, such a rational society can be transformed and improved. It is considered as having-to-be-improved-without-end. The industrial or rational society thinks of itself within the horizon of progress. Thus, the ancient stability of social roles is replaced by what is suggestively called "social mobility," which is necessary for optimal social output.

But what happens when such changes are constant and permanent, when they become the main trait of a social order? "When this question is answered," Gellner writes, "the major part of the problem of nationalism is thereby solved. Nationalism is rooted in a *certain kind* of division of labor, one which is complex and persistently, cumulatively changing."[8] In order to function, this division of labor requires a central and standardized system of education that gives the greatest possible number of children and adolescents a common and standardized education that makes them precisely capable of participating in this division of labor. Such an education can no longer be provided by the family or the local community that used to oversee education in times past.

Gellner summarizes his analysis as follows: "Not the guillotine but the (aptly named) *doctorat d'état* is the main tool and symbol of state power. The monopoly of legitimate education is now more important, more central than is the monopoly of legitimate violence."[9] In Gellner's eyes then, the national form was established because it alone is capable of providing the political framework of an industrial and rational society. It alone provides a framework that is vast and homogeneous enough for such a society to function.

Such is a summary of Gellner's thesis. It is one of the most interesting theses of political sociology on nationalism. It ties together a good number of factors in a convincing way. That is what one expects from a scientific thesis or hypothesis. But as with any scientific thesis or hypothesis, two questions arise. The first is whether it does not omit, without satisfactory explanation, some very important aspects of the phenomenon it claims to explain. The second is whether another thesis or hypothesis would not better account for the phenomenon that it explains.

Thus Gellner's thesis about nationalism does not account for a major phenomenon that is linked to nationalism, namely, national rivalries and conflicts among nations. Worse yet, it seems to make this phenomenon particularly unintelligible. Why did these industrial societies that were homogeneous cause, and become victims of, the greatest conflicts that the world has ever known? Nothing in the social functioning, that Gellner describes so well, explains conflict between the "industrial society" that was France and the "industrial society" that was Germany. In Gellner's industrial or rational society, the members of society only live so to speak *within* their society. What then would give rise to the conflict between two industrial societies, which, on the contrary, presupposes that the members of one society have their gaze on the members of the other? Herein lies, I believe, a great difficulty for Gellner's thesis.

Does another hypothesis not provide an account of nationalism that is just as good or even better than Gellner's? There is no doubt that at every step of Gellner's demonstration, we are tempted to speak of a "democratic" society wherever Gellner speaks of "industrial" society. A society where no one occupies a fixed place but can in principle move into all levels of society thanks to education, where no public separation can hamper social communication, where those who govern and those who are governed are essentially the same—in short, where men are equal. Is this society not what is ordinarily called democratic society? Does a change of term matter?

Whether you call "democratic" the type of society Gellner calls "industrial" matters little. What matters is to agree on the phenomena designated by those words.

But the notion of democracy is richer than the notion of industrial society. While it accounts just as well for the phenomena covered under the notion of industrial society, it also accounts for some aspects of the national form that the notion of industrial society leaves unexplained, such as national rivalries and wars. Democracy is not only equality; it is also liberty. Liberty, for the group as for the individual, is the idea of self-government. "Self-government" for one body politic in the midst of other bodies politic that also want "self-government" envelops the possibility and the probability of frictions, conflicts, and wars. Moreover, to govern oneself is to want to *be oneself*, to assert oneself, and that necessarily includes rivalry with other bodies politic that also want to assert themselves.

Gellner takes forceful exception to another philosopher, Elie Kedourie, who sees Kant as the father of nationalism. It is very difficult to make Kant a nationalist author. Kant is a "universalist," perhaps the most universalist of philosophers. On this point, I agree with Gellner. But, in speaking of the Kantian notion of self-determination, Gellner writes: "What connection, other than a purely verbal one, does it have with the self-determination of nations, which so preoccupies the nationalists? None. It is individual human nature which is really sovereign for Kant . . . it is universal and identical for all men."[10] Gellner here introduces an untenable separation between the individual and the collective, a separation that Kant himself, who was a "republican," disavows. In any case, how can one deny that once it has been brought to light, the idea of self-determination, of autonomy, has its logic, its own movement and its own force?

Gellner moreover cites with approval Lord Acton, who wrote: "Then began a time when the text simply was, that nations would not be governed by foreigners. Power legitimately attained, and exercised with moderation, was declared invalid."[11] This means that after a certain moment, even legitimate power exercised with measure—for example, that of the king of France at the end of the eighteenth century—appeared unbearable. One is no longer content with *being governed* in a tolerable way, one wants to *govern oneself*. And to govern oneself, the distinction within the body politic between the part that commands and the part that obeys has to end. All the parts of the body politic have to fuse together; a homogeneous body animated by a common will has to be produced. One could say that since only an individual can govern himself then, in order to govern itself, a body politic must become as much as possible like an individual; and the nation is this *individual* body politic. Like all individuals that are aware of their own individuality, who want to be that individual and no other, the nation is proud, in any case vain, often irritable, and at times aggressive.

Thus, from one point of view, the modern nation is an expression of the modern democratic project. Thanks to the national form, "self-government," which, in the civic form could concern only a small number of citizens, now includes and embraces millions. This fact helps to explain and legitimize the extreme pride of the great European nations in the nineteenth and first half of the twentieth centuries. In Great Britain, Germany, and France, the feeling was widespread that a summit in history had been attained, that the avant-garde of the Europeans had elaborated the ultimate political form of civilized life. It is not enough to say that democracy and the nation are two ways of expressing the project of self-government. The social dynamism induced by both nationalism and democracy are superimposed upon and reinforce one another. Democracy and the nation are both factors of internal homogenization. Social and religious differences, differences between town and country, all these diversities tend to fuse into the nation—France—or into the democratic republic. The peasants become "Frenchmen" at the same time they become "citizens."

However, nothing is simple. Democracy and the nation are not only allies, but also adversaries. As the nineteenth century advanced and democracy progressed and the nation asserted itself, "nationalist" parties were developing, for example *l'Action Française* in France. Now, these nationalist parties were most often antidemocratic parties. Of course, they declared they had the people's welfare at heart; *L'Action Française* maintained that representative democracy represented the French poorly and that the "legal country" did not express the "real country." In this sense, it came within the logic of representative democracy in spite of itself. *L'Action Française* wished to reestablish the differences, the internal articulations of the body politic that had been fused and mixed together in the democratic republic. Surely it sought a good government, but this good government had as its prerequisite condition the end of the "self-government" of the democratic republic.

More generally, as the nineteenth century ended the individuals and groups that, for one reason or another, were hostile to the democratic movement, joined in swelling the ranks of the nationalist parties. In the name of nationalism, they sought to preserve or to reestablish the independence of the institutions of command, their independence from democratic control. Among these institutions of command, the first and the most prestigious is the army. Thus the nation is at once the condition and expression of democracy and also the source and focus of the enemies of democracy. It is both the framework of self-government and the great fact that is opposed to self-government. Being French (or German or Italian) is the exercise of liberty, but it is also opposed to liberty. Therefore, if you are French, your first concern should be the honor of the French army, and if your first concern is the honor of the French army, you cannot doubt that Captain Dreyfus is guilty . . . so goes the logic.

The ambivalence of the nation with respect to democracy is very troubling for the citizen. It contributed greatly to the violent eruptions that marked the political and spiritual life of the European nations at the end of the nineteenth and the beginning of the twentieth centuries. The opposing parties did not know what they were doing because they cannot perceive what they have in common with the adversary—namely, the intimate bond between democracy and the nation. The logic of the struggle leads the "democratic" party to become not only the sworn enemy of the nation, but also the effective enemy of democracy, while it leads the "nationalist" party to become not only the sworn enemy of democracy but also the effective enemy of the nation.

This was seen in those national and trans-European political groupings after World War I, which gave rise to totalitarian movements. At the same time, if the ambivalence of the nation with respect to democracy is very troubling for the citizen, it loses much of its mystery once we realize that this ambivalence is itself the ambivalence of the individual. The human individual presents indeed this same ambivalence. His or her nature as an individual—to be this person or that person—is the condition of the exercise of his or her liberty. At the same time, the individuality of each person, their individual nature, can come to oppose their own liberty. One can say to individuals: "Be free! Do what you will!" But one can also say: "Be yourself! Become what you are!" In the political context, "Be free!" is the "democratic" injunction; "be yourself!" is the "nationalist" injunction.

These considerations shed light on Ernest Renan's lecture, precisely entitled "What is a Nation?," given at the Sorbonne on March 11, 1882.[12] Since this lecture, the French conception of the nation—as a free choice, "a daily plebiscite"—is commonly opposed to the German conception of the nation as a community of language and race. This opposition is very real. It is still to be felt today in the difference of legislations concerning the naturalization of foreigners (even if this difference has been reduced by the new German legislation). But they are two distinct, opposite versions *within* the *same* form. One can prefer the French conception to the German, as Renan does. What is the crux of the problem of the nation precisely is that it encompasses both the German and French ideas. The nation is always the difficult amalgam of birth and liberty.

CHAPTER 6

Europe and the Future of the Nation

I HAVE INSISTED on the ambivalence that characterizes the relation between the nation and democracy. My critique of Ernest Gellner underscored the modern nation as an expression of the modern democratic project. Thanks to the nation and the national form, the natural human desire for self-government that once could be only satisfied in the city form—a political form capable of embracing only a small number of citizens—can now be fulfilled in a form that encompasses hundreds of millions of citizens.

It was thanks only to the representative regime *and the national form* that democracy could be embodied in large states. At the end of the nineteenth century, Great Britain, France, Italy, and the United States all saw national pride largely fused with democratic pride. Public education contributed crucially to the progress of the nation and the progress of democracy as well as to homogenization. A nation takes part in a common adventure that joins the democratic present to the monarchic past, and promises a future of national and human achievement. The bond between the nation and democracy is so essential that some philosophers still are convinced that the modern democratic *regime* is inseparable from the national *form*. This conviction motivates those who are hostile to the construction of the Europe Union, or at least question about the form it has taken. Thus, Paul Thibaud writes: "Can the original rapport between the nation and democracy be undone, and on what conditions?"[1]

Conversely, the national idea became more and more, as the nineteenth century drew to a close, the reference point and source of the enemies of democracy. The objectivity of national belonging—as manifested in *birth* and *language*—becomes something that can be opposed to the subjectivity of the democratic will. It is not what you want that matters, but rather who you are, thanks to your national origin! The nationalists therefore favor "salutary" institutions, institutions that command, like the army, or that embody the age-old nation, and despise the institutions that, in their view, generate disorder, by representing the momentary and superficial will of the population, such as the National Assembly. Europe was ravaged in the twentieth century by the unleashing of nationalisms, so it is altogether natural that the project of a European Union is expected to put nationalism definitively behind us, to sever its roots by progressively abolishing the national form, by overcoming it, by merging European nations into a new body politic.

The ambivalence of the relation between democracy and the nation is such that the "construction of Europe" can be seen under very different lights. Those who are sensitive to seeing a link between democracy and the nation will view the "construction of Europe" with a great deal of caution and apprehension. They will tend to see in European institutions an oligarchic machine that is foreign to the life of the people, depriving them more and more of their self-government. In contrast, those who witnessed the antidemocratic and belligerent form that nationalism took in twentieth century Europe will tend to see national sovereignty as the final obstacle that needs to be overcome in order for European democracy to flourish.

The two sides must be considered with respect. This is not the case in France. The opinion of the media and respectable political parties is nearly unanimously in favor of Europe, almost without reservation. The other alternative, the defense of the nation, is left to the extreme parties that are not quite as respectable: the Communist Party (although it is more and more "European" as it gains respectability), the National Front, and other small nonconformist parties and groups. Yet, the Maastricht Treaty was approved in a referendum by a very weak majority, which suggests that the French population as a whole is more ambivalent to the European idea than its political leaders would lead us to believe. In any case, this problem is so crucial that we have to examine it calmly, without letting ourselves be intimidated by the proclamation of the inevitability of the European Union. After all, the Communists too believed in the inevitable "construction of socialism," by asserting that history was on their side: what history did show is well-known.

If the debate is often so confused, it is because the two sides can rightfully lay claim to democracy. Or, to put it another way, the notion of democracy contains an ambiguity, or a duality, that cannot be overcome. Democracy is the guarantee of the protection of individual rights; and so of personal autonomy, yet it is also the ordering of self-government, and so of collective autonomy. The two aspects are not separable, but are distinct. In the language of contemporary political philosophy, the first aspect concerns the *individual*, the second concerns the *citizen*.

There is no doubt that the "construction of Europe" signifies an extension of the rights of the individual, of the possibilities open to him, and therein lies part of the attraction of Europe for the citizens of the European nations, at least for those who feel they are capable of taking advantage of these new possibilities. Yet, the "construction of Europe" means—for the moment at least and assuredly for a long time to come—a diminution of the powers of the citizen.[2] Life for the European citizen is determined more and more not by the familiar national debate, as conflictual as it may be, but by the outcome of a European process that is much less comprehensible.

Not only does this process empower nondemocratic institutions such as the Brussels Commission, but the democratically elected government of each country must more and more take into account the wills and desires of the democratically elected governments of the other countries; countries whose number is increasing. Thus the decision-making powers are more and more heterogeneous and foreign to the citizens of *all* the countries concerned. The "construction of Europe" thus involves a continual diminution of the feeling of civic responsibility.

Today a twofold pressure toward conformity weighs on every European nation, one of which is inseparable from globalization and the other from Europeanization. This forced march to uniformity, however, is not synonymous with deepening friendship. The very rapprochement of the nations in the European framework tends to multiply frictions, among nations as among individuals. In coming closer they can indeed discover their similarities with pleasure, but they can also feel their differences with spite or pain. The citizens of the democracies often feel poorly represented by their officials, a feeling of alienation that is inseparable from the institution of representation. This feeling is inevitably reinforced when each European government is subjected to the growing pressure of a "European opinion" that does not correspond to any European civic debate but results from an inscrutable random process. Recently, when the Austrian government included members belonging to a far right wing party, it created an uproar in the European parliament. This uproar then subsided inexplicably. Why? Did anyone understand?

Many Europeans welcome a process that, according to Paul Thibaud, increases the individual's opportunities and restrains the citizen's powers. The reasoning goes: while we are necessarily individuals, it does not follow that we are necessarily citizens. It is imperative that our individual rights, our "human rights," be guaranteed and the widest possible avenues of freedom be open to us, but whether it is good for us to be part of a collective will, whether it is good that the civic and political should take precedence over all other groupings, is doubtful.

Why shouldn't national affiliation be on a par along with other affiliations, such as membership in a neighborhood or profession? Each individual then would have a portfolio of identities, among them national identity, just as he or she has a portfolio of stocks. Or a palette of identities as a painter has a palette of colors. This reasoning is very seductive because it flatters the individual by making him believe that he is the sovereign master of his affiliations. It fulfills democracy by simplifying it. Instead of emphasizing the tension at times between individual and citizen, one emphasizes the rights and opportunities of the individual. However, this democracy of the individual becomes so unilateral that it is not certain that the term "democracy" still fits. A European Union organized on these foundations would be a vast space of *civilization*, subject to rules, offering immense possibilities to individuals capable of acting to their own advantage in accordance with uniform rules, but not a body *politic* that affords its citizens a common adventure, a "community of destiny."

Is such a European civilization desirable? Is it first of all possible? These questions point to a more general question. Can human beings live fully without belonging to a body politic that claims their allegiance? Can they live only as economic and moral agents, free and mobile in a space of civilization? Whatever the answer to these questions, the "construction of Europe" has rested on this ambiguity, which has not been formulated nor understood between Europe as civilization and Europe as body politic.

Does "Europe" mean the depoliticization, through denationalization, of the life of the European people, that is, the systematic reduction of their collective existence to the activities of civil society and the mechanisms of civilization—to just economics and culture? Or does "Europe" mean the construction of a new body politic, of a large, enormous nation? The "European construction" may therefore mean something prosaic and useful—like the Common Agricultural Policy in its time, but also a sublime European federation, the United States of Europe that would fulfill the dream of Charlemagne. This ambiguity has no doubt been welcomed in the first stages of European construction, but the longer it lasts the more it risks becoming dangerous. Those who want to "make Europe" will have to come to the point of saying just what they mean to do in making it.

If this ambiguity has lasted so long, it is not only because politicians are necessarily calculators. Some of the most considerate supporters of a "political Europe" have thought that such a Europe could not be accepted by the European voters, who could only be led to the promised land through the gentler road of an "economic" Europe. If this ambiguity has lasted so long, it is that many Europeans believe that the notion of "Europe" has a clear meaning. It is not a matter of "constructing" this Europe, but rather of awakening a Europe that is already there beneath the appearance of diverse nations. Henceforth it matters little how one proceeds, at the end of the day we will hold Europe in our hands. A Europe that will be political if politics still exist, or apolitical and postmodern if in the meantime the end of history has arrived. In brief, Europe is the substance that lies beneath the national accidents, the thing-in-itself present behind the national phenomena. But does this Europe really exist? Does it exist in this manner, that is, beyond all political form?

Certainly, Europe is a geographic notion. And the logic of its development corresponds to this characteristic, since up to now it has been a law of *expansion*. Everything takes place as if Europe, born from a small cluster of six nations, embraces an ever growing number of European nations and is destined to encompass *all* the nations belonging to the geographic space. Of course if this were truly so we would soon be faced with comic results, since Europe would have to include Russia, but only as far as the Urals, and Turkey, but only as far as the straits, so that the greater part of Istanbul would be in the European Union, but not Anatolia! Surely no one has in mind such absurdities. Yet to evoke them has the merit of drawing our attention to the problem of borders, and also of proving that Europe is not to be defined solely in geographic terms.

What other definition of Europe can we have? The most common answer is that the true identity of Europe is cultural. The notion of "culture" is one of the most treacherous in contemporary political vocabulary. When we break down the notion of "European culture" into its various elements, we see that either the element in question divides Europeans more often than it unites them, or else that it unites Europeans but along with many peoples who live beyond Europe.

Religion is an illustration of the first point. Since the tenth century, religion has divided Europeans much more than united them. Moreover, the modern European States were constructed to overcome religious divisions. And even if we posit that the Christian confessions today are reconciled, which doesn't seem to be the case entirely, how could the "Christian culture" of Europe form the basis of the unity of Europe when Muslims as well as atheists and agnostics in Europe are more and more numerous?

An example of defining European culture so broadly as to encompass non-European nations is to emphasize "democratic culture" or democratic mores. Several countries have been placed on the waiting list for entry into the European Union because their democratic performance was not satisfactory. Turkey is the most important case. On can agree with the hesitation regarding Turkey's admission, but the point is that democratic mores do not suffice to define a European identity. If that were the case all democratic countries would be members by right of the European Union, beginning with Japan and Australia.

Thus the idea of a "cultural identity" of Europe is at the very least confused, perhaps even a hollow idea. At the same time, it is difficult to renounce the idea that "Europe" signifies something important in the history of humanity. But what is that? Jean Baechler writes that from 1492 onward, the Europeans discovered the rest of the world and imposed their law on it, directly through colonization or indirectly through the diffusion of cultural traits that had universal value, beginning with technical and economic traits, but also scientific, political, ideological traits. . . . Through the intermediary of Europe, natural histories and local or regional histories came into contact with one another. This contact marks an . . . irreversible threshold after which we have, not a planetary history but a history *unified* by Europe.[3]

Up to the discovery of America, everything happened "as if humanity had split into several species that ignored one another just about completely, except to meet in passing or to fight on the margins."

These very simple reminders are very judicious. Baechler points out that the Europeans saw themselves as the avant-garde of humanity. This he writes without reveling in the feeling of European superiority, but also without the anti-European tinge that so marked the "anticolonialist" reaction to European domination. In fact, by all sorts of means, some of which were admittedly inhumane, Europe brought together all the parts of the human race, making them share a history that was henceforth common. In the history of the human spirit, Europe represents indeed something very specific and very precious, nothing less than the creator of the "universal": the universal of philosophy that was of Greek origin and that developed only in Europe; the universal of the Christian religion that sent its "missions" to the ends of the earth; the universal of mathematical sciences and other "exact" sciences; the universal of democracy founded on the "rights of man." How then can the idea of an "identity of Europe" be confusing or hollow?

Europeans certainly have a right to be proud of themselves. They can place their contribution to human history very high without incurring the reproach of complacency or, one says these days, ethnocentrism. At the same time they have to admit that they cannot own the universal, precisely because it is universal. A Chinese person can without contradiction consider that the Middle Kingdom is part and parcel of the Chinese civilization, whose superiority over other civilizations is clear. Europeans cannot consider that only Europe is entitled to the universal because, if they did so, at that very instant the universal would cease to be universal! Europe cannot lay claim to the Christian religion that has now spread to the two Americas, Africa, and Asia, where it is perhaps more alive than in Europe. They cannot consider that Europe controls mathematical science and the other "exact" sciences, when Indians, for example, show themselves to be such good mathematicians and authors of software programs. Finally, they cannot consider that Europe owns democracy when it is the United States of America that, since 1917, has preserved or reestablished democracy on the European continent. In fact, in recent decades, Europeans have lost the enviable title of being the avant-garde of a unified human history, of representing both the Universal and the New to the Americans. One thus does not see how the idea of the universal, whether it is a matter of philosophy, religion, science, or democracy, could define European identity.[4]

There is also another consideration. The discovery of the universal by Europe was not the doing of a united Europe but, much to the contrary, of a Europe divided into rival nations. Shockingly, Europe discovered the unity of the human race at the very time that its own divisions were exacerbated. But the character of these divisions needs to be specified. Europe divided itself into a relatively small number of political bodies, each having about the same power, in such a way that none was able to impose a lasting domination over the other, of establishing, what in the seventeenth and eighteenth centuries was called, a "universal monarchy." The age-old law of Europe was the law of an unstable equilibrium, the product of competition, rivalry, and often war. It seems that this political formula—the competition of a limited number of comparable political bodies in the same zone of civilization—is particularly conducive to historic creation.

Earlier, following Albert Thibaudet and others, I compared the war of 1914–1918 to the Peloponnesian War. If the comparison of these two catastrophes is justified, perhaps the comparison of the successes of Europe and the accomplishments of Greece is also: the same political formula begets its fruitfulness in both cases. Why such a fruitfulness? Jean Baechler makes the following suggestion: "Any innovation could be diffused almost instantaneously in the cultural area because it met the conditions common to all diffusions: that the recipients were so well equipped to receive it that they had the impression of having awaited it or even of being its discoverers."[5]

These enlightening historical considerations are also extremely disturbing. They suggest forcefully that Europe's fruitfulness finds its major source in Europe's divisions, in particular Europe's division into nations. If there is such a thing today as Europe, we owe it, paradoxically, to its divisions. To end the rivalry of the European nations would then not be to prepare the conditions of a flowering European Union but, on the contrary, to drain Europe of the age-old wellspring of its vitality. Baechler, who, so far as I know, supports European unification, has some sad commentary on this point: "The political unification of Europe would destroy this dialectic. . . . It would be for the philosophers of the future a paradox to contemplate if the decadence of the European genius should result from the solution that was proposed in order to save it from the rise of barbarism."[6]

We have now acquired a sharper awareness of the political problem of Europe but we are certainly not in a position to propose a "program for a political Europe." We have become aware that a body politic is first to be defined politically, and not economically or "culturally." We are also aware that Europe is suffering from political languor or indetermination. To constitute and give life to a body politic is to put some things in common. Men are political animals because they "put things in common." We must thus put things in common to concretize human universality, which otherwise would remain undetermined, pure potentiality.

What must we put in common? Aristotle employs a striking expression. In the city, he says, the citizens "put words and deeds in common."[7] In other words, they act and deliberate *together*. The problem of the Europeans is that they do not know what they want to put in common. To get around the difficulty, to avoid putting anything in common while giving its due to the necessity of community, the Europeans *create* new common institutions, like the Brussels Commission or the parliament of Strasbourg; but as the old institutions, the national governments and parliaments subsist, one is faced with a juxtaposition of old and new institutions, of national institutions and common institutions, whose division of jurisdictions is unclear. The text of the Maastricht Treaty is on this point impenetrably opaque.[8]

It is true that some countries of the European Union have created a common currency. This is assuredly a crucially important initiative, although fraught with consequences of all sorts. Thanks to the euro, trans-European economic and social players will multiply. Will this move bring the onset of common political institutions, announced but never established, or will it, on the contrary, aggravate institutional confusion by underlining the growing inadequacy of the means of government, whether national or communitarian? No doubt if a political player as important as Great Britain continues to remain outside the common currency zone, the hope for a political fruition of the monetary union would be seriously dented.

These uncertainties would be much less grave if the political regimes were not exclusively democratic. The European Union could then resemble the empire of the Hapsburgs, an aggregate of very diverse political or quasi-political bodies, held together by their allegiance to a dynasty that was their only commonality. This possibility is no longer open to them. In order to belong to the same body politic, democratic peoples must "put in common" many more things than were required of the peoples of the Austro-Hungarian monarchy.

It must be emphasized that the uncertainty of the European Union bears particularly upon one factor that must absolutely be determined so that a political form, whatever its form, would be viable. This is the territory. As we have seen, Europe is prey to expansion, which is in fact unlimited. If it is not expanding further still, it is because of budgetary constraints and the unsuitability of potential members. This law of indefinite expansion corresponds to Europe's inability to define itself politically. The more it expands, the more its further expansion is technically difficult and destined to absorb the bulk of its common energy. As more nations enter the European Union, the more resentful are those who wait at the door and view their exclusion as an unbearable offense, as is the case today with Turkey.

Europeans at heart would like the democratic principle to be sufficient unto itself, sufficient to define democratic Europe as a body politic. But this is not possible. The democratic principle is not sufficient to define the political framework within which it is exercised. The democratic principle is the principle of consent. Individuals or groups can legitimately obey only a law or an institution to which they have first given consent, by themselves or through their representatives. This principle can be carried out in the most diverse communities: in the family, the village, the city, the nation. But the principle does not give an answer to the question: obedience to which law? The European democracies developed in nations that were first established by nondemocratic regimes, the monarchies.

France, for example, had first to be made by "the forty kings who made France" as the monarchists remind us. The French people first had to be *defined*, so that it could undertake to govern itself, as it did during the French Revolution. The monarchist argument against the democratic republic was weak since the republicans could reply that although it was perhaps necessary for France to be under the tutelage of the kings in childhood and youth, the French nation had reached adulthood and could succeed without the monarchy. Indeed it would be shameful for France to want to return to her infantile condition. This republican argument has the merit of pointing out that democracy, in order to become a reality, needs a *body*, a population marked out by borders and other characteristics, namely a *defined* realm.

The difficulty of democracy is that, in relation to the principle, the body is arbitrary, meaning that there is no link between the principle and any particular configuration of the body politic. One can of course say that in certain cases at least, the link is supplied by the principle itself. All those who wish to belong to the same body politic must govern themselves together. But the principle of self-determination is often difficult to apply, as we saw in Europe after World War I, and currently in the former Yugoslavia. In addition, this principle is not very helpful in the construction of the European Union since all the political bodies bordering on the European Union seem to want to belong to it. Where does one stop? It seems that democracy, in the European construction, is striving to escape the sad necessity of having a body. So it gives itself a body without limits, this Europe with indefinite expansion, a Europe defined paradoxically as an indefinite expansion.

This cannot go on indefinitely. Europe will have to end up by defining itself. Three efforts at definition seem particularly urgent. Europe will have to soon determine first its frontier. A border is not only a line on the map, it is also a spiritual limit that expresses a spiritual decision—with respect to the east, that is, to Ukraine and Russia, and with respect to the southeast, that is, to Turkey. There are plausible arguments for all the courses it can take: welcome Russia, exclude Russia, welcome Turkey, exclude Turkey, but it must in the end draw a line and these demarcations will define Europe.

Europe will also have to determine its relation with the United States. Its economic, and perhaps soon its monetary weight, besets it with an extremely difficult political choice, since neither of the two extreme possibilities appears acceptable: either to continue being the giant who cannot tie his shoes, or to actualize its potential strength. In both hypotheses, relations with the United States will be more and more difficult, but in the second a confrontation of an unprecedented kind seems inevitable. In short, the dream of leaving politics behind through European unification will remain a dream. How it addresses its political choices will determine the success of the European Union, whether it will become a new body politic with territorial limits and a spiritual physiognomy, or it will fail. If Europe fails too often and too long in the political domain, it is not certain that it will be able to survive as an economic and monetary community.

CHAPTER 7

The Wars of the Twentieth Century

THE INDEFINITE territorial expansion of the European Union is in part the expression of their strong indifference to borders. Now borders most often result from wars or peace treaties. Indifference to borders therefore expresses a new attitude toward war. We assume that war is inhuman or immoral, but also that it no longer has any political meaning or validity. War for territory, territory defined as the result of war—appears to us as an aspect of bygone politics, a residue of the past that is to be overcome once and for all.

These feelings have been with us for a long time and they found a striking confirmation in the fall of the Berlin Wall in November 1989. The Wall, the border separating West from East Germany, both symbolized and concretized the line of demarcation drawn by the meeting of American and Soviet troops at the end of World War II. The peaceful collapse of the Wall made it clear that the greatest war in history had lost its power to define borders. In a few days, its most important, visible, and most inhumane political result vanished into thin air, not just without violence, but in a celebration.

This most striking event was the confirmation and acceleration of the process by which Western Europe had erased its borders. The Rhine had long lost its political and military significance. Now the Elbe had lost it, and even the Oder and the Neisse! These geographic names, which only recently contained the memory of a war, had become merely geographic terms. We could therefore confidently believe that war would soon disappear and a new order of politics would dawn—a new order in which war would no longer be the recourse of politics.

However, other recent events suggest that it is premature to declare that war is ended, that it is imprudent to bid farewell to arms. At the very moment when traces of war disappeared in the center of Europe, and that the establishment of the European Union had made war among member nations of the European Union inconceivable, a sort of state of war was spreading in southeastern Europe in the Balkans. Nearly all the successor states of the Yugoslav Federation found themselves engaged in military actions and violent measures great and small. The Kosovo crisis was only brought under control by the massive intervention of the most advanced military means of NATO. If the democratic revolution in Serbia had interrupted the process of destruction that, for nearly ten years, had engulfed this region and given the hope of peace and lawfulness to its people, the current situation still remains extremely precarious since the status of Montenegro and the fate of Macedonia are uncertain. Bosnia and Kosovo are in fact under foreign administration and occupation; the peace rests on the presence of thousands of American and European soldiers.

Our reaction to the state of war in the Balkans was very understandably dominated by humanitarian considerations. The violence and cruelty were all the more horrible since they were often perpetrated by people who had previously lived peacefully and at times even amicably alongside their future victims. But if it is easy to agree in seeing in these events a human catastrophe, there can be differing opinions on their political significance. Some believe that the Balkan crisis was peripheral and that it will not spread to the rest of Europe. Others hold that this open wound on the southern flank of Europe risks expanding and calls into question the optimistic hypotheses on which the current European construction rests. The pessimistic school has let the tragedy of Sarajevo resonate, suggesting that, just as the assassination of the Archduke Ferdinand of Austria-Hungary at Sarajevo lit the fire that gradually engulfed Europe in the summer of 1914, so the present Balkan crises risk spreading and enveloping Europe.

The events in Serbia invite one rather to hope, but the crisis in Macedonia arouses concern. I shall remark that, as tempting as the connection "from Sarajevo to Sarajevo" may be, the circumstances in the Balkans today are very different from what they were in 1914 and that is precisely in great part the consequence of the 1914–1919 war. In particular, Austria-Hungary has disappeared. It was the fragility of this multinational empire that felt threatened by the same Serbian irredentism that incited the government of Vienna to an intransigence that, given the system of alliances at that time, unleashed the Great War. Those conditions no longer exist.

Yet, the Yugoslav and Balkan crisis today perhaps holds a more subtle threat. As the crisis stands, it produces political effects that affect all of Europe and the very validity of the "European" idea. It raises an urgent question for everyone: Is the European Union capable of assuring a decent political order on its geographical perimeter? More generally, is the European Union a creator of order, or only a consumer of the order established and maintained by the United States?

If it does not succeed in founding a satisfactory order in the Balkans, this "external" failure will have grave "internal" consequences. Every political ambition of Europe will appear as an illusion, even as an imposture. As this feeling of inauthenticity spreads, it will erode the currently considerable credit of the European ideal. It is not certain that the United States will accept to be the guarantor of European order indefinitely while the European Union vaunts its wealth and power, and demands parity with the United States. In any case, the experience of the recent Kosovo War proves that the maintenance of a decent political order in the Balkans must still rest on the availability of military means that, by their quantity and quality, are on the scale of war and not of the "maintenance of order" or "humanitarian intervention." In brief, Europe is not yet done with war. The Europeans of the European Union, the Europeans of "advanced" Europe, do not have the leisure to unilaterally decree that "war is ended." However appealing that thought might be, they must understand that, as Péguy puts it, "military realities have an importance of the first order."

I could at this point end the reflection on the wars of the twentieth century. But Europe is only a part of the world. If great wars threaten today, they do so much more in other parts of the world, such as in Asia. Whereas in Europe the consequences of World War II and of the Cold War are essentially finished, this is not the case in Asia. The political division of Germany is now only a memory, but the division of Korea remains both acute and permanent, above all because of the atrocious and aberrant character of the North Korean regime. Moreover, unlike what took place in Germany, a long war was fought in Korea over the line of demarcation from 1950 to 1953.

Neither has Japan, unlike Germany, fully acknowledged its primary responsibility in the Pacific War, nor especially the scope of the crimes committed by the imperial army in occupied Asia. By the constitution drafted under General MacArthur's supervision in the aftermath of the war, Japan has no right to an army, but only to a self-defense force whose budget must not surpass one percent of the government's budget. In brief, the Japanese are still an American protectorate.

Finally, since Hong Kong and Macao have been reabsorbed by China, Taiwan's fate is left hanging. China continues to assert its "sacred right" to bring the island back into the lap of the mother country, including the use of force. More generally, China engages quite boldly in a policy of fait accompli by installing troops on disputed islands or islets of the China Sea, despite the protests of other adjoining countries. Not to mention the permanent tension between India and Pakistan, which are now officially nuclear states. In brief, unlike Europe where disorders are limited to the territorial edges, Asia is today still essentially unstable: armies are on the alert, and scenarios of wars that would have global effects are just as plausible in this part of the world as they are unlikely in Europe.

It is useful, I believe, to recall all these facts of which the newspapers are full, to highlight them in a synthetic fashion. Every reflection on politics encompasses the reality of war, which is a crucial and permanent aspect of politics.

However indispensable war may be when studying the political order, two motives often prevent one from considering war seriously. These two motives are distinct, but they tend to get mixed up in the minds and hearts of the citizens of democracies.

First, of course, war is considered an evil, in the eyes of some, even the greatest evil. Thus to study war as an aspect of the political phenomenon seems to betray an indifference to the evils of war, if not even a dubious satisfaction, a taste for war. After all, some writers and philosophers have praised war. Hence, the study of war cannot avoid becoming an encouragement to the evils of war.

This is a serious objection that cannot be overcome by distinguishing between facts and values, by saying for example, that one studies war scientifically as a historical fact, but making a negative value judgment on it. This escape is not possible because the different value judgments fit different wars. Certain wars are criminal, others altogether justified, like the ones undertaken to stop the criminal wars. To arrive at such a judgment, it is necessary to place war in its context, to seek out its causes, to analyze the opposing regimes and the war aims they pursued. Such a judgment thus presumes a political analysis. If we truly take seriously the moral gravity of war, we must provide a political analysis, since it is only in the political context that war is meaningful or meaningless and has its moral tenor. Those who limit themselves to merely condemning war do not really condemn it since they ignore what it is.

The second motive that prevents us from studying war seriously postulates that "there should be no war," but not as much because it is immoral as because it is anachronistic. It corresponds to a barbarous state from which humanity is supposed to have emerged long ago. Modern war is the conduct of still barbarous peoples, or, by civilized peoples regressing to barbarity. This idea held sway during much of the eighteenth and nineteenth centuries; it was of course much shaken by the great wars of the twentieth century, but without ever disappearing; and today it has regained popularity.

It was the Saint-Simonians who proposed a philosophy of history according to which industrial society comes after military society, with the exploitation of nature replacing the exploitation of man by man. Whence Auguste Comte formulated categorically: "All truly philosophical minds must easily recognize, with perfect intellectual and moral satisfaction, that the age has finally come when serious and sustained warfare must totally disappear among the elite of humanity."[1] Then again:

> All the diverse general means of rational exploration, applicable to political investigations, have already spontaneously concurred in observing, in an equally decisive manner, the inevitable primitive tendency of humanity to a chiefly military life, and its no less irresistible final destination to an essentially industrial existence.[2]

If this idea finds its most systematic expression in the work of the Saint-Simonians, it is, however, a commonly accepted thought of most philosophic schools and political parties. Benjamin Constant, a liberal author, made the transition between the eighteenth and nineteenth centuries, and was formed by Montesquieu and the commercial optimism of the eighteenth century, which predicted that commerce irresistibly softened and pacified mores. Yet, Constant witnessed the violence of the Revolution and the wars of the Empire that demonstrated the vanity of the Enlightenment's hopes and the falsity of their predictions. He reconciled his own hopes and his experience by asserting that war was an anachronism in modern Europe, that it presupposed a political regime that was itself anachronistic, in this case, Bonaparte's "usurpation," and that neither usurpation nor war could endure in contemporary Europe. He developed this idea in "The Spirit of Conquest and Usurpation and Their Relation to European Civilization," an essay published in 1814.

Constant writes,

> We have finally reached the age of commerce, an age which must necessarily replace that of war, as the age of war was bound to precede it.
>
> War and commerce are only two different means to achieve the same end of possessing what is desired. Commerce is simply a tribute paid to the strength of the possessor by the aspirant to possession. It is an attempt to obtain by mutual agreement what one can no longer hope to obtain through violence. A man who was always the stronger would never conceive the idea of commerce. It is experience, by proving to him that war, that is, the use of his strength against the strength of others, is open to a variety of obstacles and defeats, that leads him to resort to commerce, that is, to a milder and surer means of getting the interests of others to agree with his own.
>
> War then comes before commerce. The former is all savage impulse, the latter civilized calculation.[3]

Constant gives a fascinating account of an age-old process. He rather summarizes a *necessary* history. He is just as much a determinist or necessitarian regarding the general movement of human history as the Saint-Simonians and the Marxists will be later. Why does history obey necessity? Because all men always pursue the same end, "that of possessing what is desired." History is thus a succession of the means elaborated by men to obtain what they desire, means that are ever more complicated

as men gain experience. They begin with war, a brutal means with immediate, but uncertain effects; they end by having recourse to commerce, a
slower but softer and surer means. War is "all savage impulse," commerce
is "civilized calculation."

Is Constant's analysis convincing? Constant moves war and commerce
closer, making them resemble one another more perhaps than they do in
reality in order to make the transition more plausible, more natural, and
finally necessary. Do they truly have "the same goal"? One might say that
Constant "commercializes" war at the same time as he "bellicizes" commerce, perhaps even "commercializing" war more than the reverse. "Possessing what is desired" can in effect be the general formulation summariz-
ing the goals of commerce. But is the same true of war? War does not
consist only in pillage raids or material conquests. It encompasses a moral
element that is largely foreign to commerce properly speaking: the desire
to conquer the enemy, to obtain victory. Constant transforms the desire to
conquer into the desire to acquire. He adopts as a self-evident truth the
psychology of acquisitive individualism, "bourgeois" psychology.

At the same time, we must acknowledge that his presupposition is also
our own, his psychology is ours. We think that the desire for well-being
and comfort is more reasonable, more natural, and more human, than the
desire for honor or conquest. In fact, democratic societies show a passionate taste for comfort, while honor, the traditional warrior honor, is disappearing—even if one still finds a pacified form of it in sporting competi-
tions and economic rivalry. Since Constant, the Europeans have often
found themselves in the political and moral situation of Constant, namely
denouncing wars that ought not to take place, not only because war is evil,
but because it no longer corresponds to the current state of societies and
to the dispositions of democratic citizens.

For two centuries the Europeans have not ceased to wage wars that
"should not" have taken place. But how is it that our societies, more and
more completely organized around commerce and industry, and therefore
for peace, periodically cause or allow war to flare up in their bosom? Why
is their reasonable hope always disappointed in the end? Will the recent
announcement of the "end of history" be just as the analogous predictions
of the Saint-Simonians, the liberals, and the Marxists? Since the future is
unknown, the only thing that we can do is to try to assess the role of war
in our century, not because past wars would necessarily herald future wars
but because the wars of the twentieth century have largely determined the
present world in which we live, and also to preserve an awareness of the
scope of possibilities in politics and in history.

Before considering the twentieth century, the century of a "chain reaction
of wars" as Raymond Aron put it, a few remarks on the preceding period

can be useful. This period from the reign of Louis XV to the eve of World War I is marked by a very wide oscillation between largely peaceful phases of homogenization and phases of separation where war is unleashed. There are essentially two great periods of commercial or industrial homogenization: the period of the Enlightenment homogenized under the aegis of French civilization, and the nineteenth century under the aegis of English industry and commerce. The two great periods of separation and war, first the French Revolution and the Napoleonic Wars, then the "chain reaction of wars" of the twentieth century, or the new "Thirty Years War" that lasted from 1914 to 1945.

What does the term "homogenization" mean? It refers to a simple phenomenon, but rich with multiple effects. Rousseau was the first to describe it:

> There are no more Frenchmen, Germans, Spaniards, even Englishmen, nowadays, regardless of what people may say; there are only Europeans. All have the same tastes, the same passions, the same morals, because none has been given a national form by a distinctive institution. All will do the same things under the same circumstances; all will declare themselves disinterested and be cheats; all will speak of the public good and think only of themselves; all will praise moderation and wish to be Croesus; they have no other ambition than for luxury, no other passion than for gold. Confident that with it they will have whatever tempts them, all will sell themselves to the first man willing to pay them. What do they care what master they obey, the laws of what State they obey? Provided they find money to steal and women to corrupt, they are at home in any country.[4]

"There are only Europeans." Rousseau wrote this in 1770 or 1771. Less than a generation later, the French, Germans, Spaniards, and English were to experience a national crystallization of extraordinary intensity, thus belying Rousseau's diagnosis but perhaps fulfilling his wishes. War played a role in the crystallization of the nation. The revolutionary war of the French, or the war of liberation of the Germans from Napoleon's domination, contributed decisively to the homogenization "from above" of the French and German citizens. A great number of people raised themselves to the level of nobility, assuming the mission of waging war that had been reserved to the nobles. In doing so they elevated themselves above the nobility. The particular privilege of a caste became a right and common duty for all. Through the virtue of war, to be a man became something nobler than to be a noble.

Kings roll in the dust and people raise their heads to the heavens. Such is the virtue of revolutionary war that it both equalizes and ennobles.

During the Enlightenment, the upper class was distributed across national borders in horizontal layers: the clergy, the nobility, and the learned were homogenized by a common language and common mores. In addition, these men were homogenized, according to Rousseau, by a common psychology: beneath the lofty and brilliant aristocratic or ecclesiastical appearance, they craved the same bourgeois comfort and tastes. When Rousseau declares, "there are only Europeans," that means there are only the bourgeois, there are no more citizens.[5] The wars of the Revolution and the Empire produced a new homogeneity and a new heterogeneity. The Europeans now came together and resembled one another within the national framework. They differentiated themselves and wanted to differentiate themselves among nations. Rousseau said: "All have the same tastes, the same passions, the same morals, because none has been given a national form by a distinctive institution."[6] Well, all these countries strove to give themselves a national form through a distinctive institution. First the Germans rose up not only against the Napoleonic armies, but also more deeply against French language and civilization. They sought refuge and roots in the German language, which they often wanted purged of Gallicisms or romanisms.

When Fichte delivered the *Addresses to the German Nation* during the winter of 1807 to 1808, after the collapse of Prussia at Jena in 1806, he formulated the project of the germanization of the Germans. Fichte took up Rousseau's analysis and predictions and transformed them into a project. More precisely, Fichte passionately embraced Rousseau's project of reform designed for Poland—a project moved by a general human benevolence—and sought to apply it to his own people: "I speak for Germans simply, of Germans simply."[7] Fichte's analysis of the contemporary situation is more radical than Rousseau's, if that is possible. He claims that selfishness ruled the day and all bonds have been dissolved by calculating reasoning. The Whole had lost its power. The social bond needed to be reconstituted beyond the calculation of pleasures and pains. The remedy to the current malady is the constitution of a general and national "I" through national education. The previous education is partial in two senses. It was addressed to but one part of the individual *and* to but one part of society. An education is now needed that emphasizes all that is German, that erases natural and social differences. Fichte's project is, at the same time, radically democratic and radically nationalist. It is explicitly separatist. It is not essentially bellicose (Prussia had just been crushed at Jena), but the aptitude and the resolute disposition for war carries out and completes the separatist project.

Thus, in a short time Europe passed from the "horizontal" homogeneity of the civilization of the Enlightenment to homogenization through vertical separations, among nations that from then on were passionately desirous to be themselves. In this sense, Europe passed from homogeneity to heterogeneity. But the phenomenon was complex and presented contradictory aspects. Nineteenth-century Europe, the Europe of national separations, was also a Europe that homogenized itself on new foundations. The principle of nationalities was obviously separatist, but to the extent that it tended to prevail everywhere in Europe, it was at the same time a principle of moral unity. And the European peoples, engaged in a process of democratization and nationalization, indeed tended to distinguish themselves but also to resemble one another, to produce new differences but also new resemblances. Peasant children schooled in French schools became Frenchmen, peasant children schooled in German schools became Germans, and so where there were peasants who were very much alike in that they were peasants, they were Frenchmen and Germans who were and who wanted to be different. At the same time they came to resemble one another in a new way, as educated and active citizens, as voters in a modern representative State.

That is why the nineteenth century, born from a long and terrible war, was in Europe a remarkably peaceful century. And, of course, this peace of bourgeois Europe nurtured the Saint-Simonian idea that Europe had left behind the era of war. Each people was turned inward, either to forge its political unity if it was dispersed into several states as the Germans or Italians, or to forge its social unity as the French people. The European nations were thus not particularly expansionist or bellicose, within Europe at least (outside the European continent several were much occupied with carving out empires for themselves). But the processes of national unification upset the status quo and gave rise to occasions of war. Thus after 1815, with the exception of the Crimean War (1854–1855), the conflicts in Europe were born of Italian unity (the Franco-Austrian War in 1859) or of German unity (the war between Prussia and Austria in 1866 and the Franco-Prussian War in 1870). These wars were brief and did not bring much destruction. To the extent that they were linked to the furtherance of the principle of the nationalities, the common principle of the Europeans, they had a stabilizing effect. If we then situate them in the framework of nineteenth-century Europe, we see a rather coherent and peaceful order establishing itself and we can understand the optimism of the Europeans of the end of destructive wars, an optimism that was so puzzling, so unforgivable even for us who know what followed in history.

This common principle of the nationalities took different forms in different countries, particularly in France and Germany, the two most powerful countries in continental Europe. This difference came to the forefront in the dispute over Alsace-Lorraine and froze France and Germany into a stance of mutual hostility from 1870 onward. I do not want to suggest that there was a difference of nature between French and German nationalism. They were both legitimate in principle and they could be equally odious, or absurd, in practice. The nation always encompassed both the French idea and the German idea. At the same time, a particular danger was attached to certain ideological justifications of German nationalism. For German-speaking populations dispersed between the Rhine and the Volga, the argument of a common language and race, although very natural, detached the national principle from the democratic principle. The alliance of these two principles, as we have seen, alone contained the promise of a tolerably peaceful new European order. Finally, this argument tended to transform the national principle into something other than itself, into an imperialist and at least implicitly racist ideology.

At the end of the nineteenth century, this dangerous outcome was only a possibility; potentially dangerous ideas do not always necessarily produce all the calamities with which they are laden. Moreover the Germans were not the only ones to speak of "race"; it was the common idiom of the time. War itself actualized this perverse potential, actualizing a scourge that could have forever remained in the realm of possibility. The political and ideological conflict between France and Germany, their existential conflict one might say, crystallized around the question of Alsace-Lorraine. Yet painful as was the loss of the eastern provinces, France was not ready to unleash war to recover them. World War I was not born on the banks of the Rhine, but at the edge of Europe, in that unstable zone of the Balkans where the new principle of nationalities wore down the old multinational empires. In this sense, the immediate cause of the Great War was the ineptness of the empires more than national passion.

In any case one has to be grateful to Ernest Renan for perceiving clearly the danger contained in the linguistic and racial version of nationalism. In a 1871 letter to David Strauss, a historian and critic of Christianity like Renan himself, he expresses himself in a particularly eloquent and trenchant way:

> [The French] policy is the policy of the law of nations; yours is the policy of the races: we believe that ours is better. The overly acute division of humanity into races, apart from the fact that it rests on a scientific error, since so few countries possess a truly pure race, can only lead to wars of extermination, "zoological" wars let me say, analogous to those that the various species of rodents or carnivores wage in order to live. It would be the end of the fruitful blend, composed of numerous elements, all of them necessary, known as humanity. You have raised the flag of ethnographic and archaeological policy in the place of liberal policy; this policy will be fatal to you.[8]

Thus the peaceful nineteenth century that began in 1815 came to an end in 1914 and the "chain reaction of wars" that defined the twentieth century broke out. Ours is a matter of studying the causal role of war in the political, moral, and even economic development of the twentieth century, rather than a simple historical study. Such an inquiry is necessary if we want to understand ourselves. The twentieth-century wars contributed a great deal to make us who we are today. Such a search is also the occasion for more general reflections. If war played such a decisive role, produced such considerable effects in a century and on a continent devoted in principle to the peaceful exploitation of nature, this tends to prove that utilitarian, bourgeois psychology, the psychology of *Homo Oeconomicus*—the man who calculates and maximizes his interests—does not suffice to account for what there is in man. And, of course, this truth has consequences for the way we envisage the future.

For this inquiry let's look at Raymond Aron's essays on the history of the twentieth century, collected in the title, *The Dawn of Universal History*.[9] Let us first read a few general considerations of Aron that appeared originally in 1957 under the title, "Nations and Empires." At the time Aron wrote this essay, the two major issues were: American-Soviet power sharing and the process of decolonization. Aron observed that, "It took two threats of German hegemony to make the United States aware of its own enormous power. And not until the European nations were exhausted did the Soviet Union come to seem invincible both to itself and to others. Even if they did not actually create them, Europe's two twentieth-century wars revealed the forces that dominate them today." Aron continues: "The wars brought out the contradiction between the principle on which order in Europe was based and the principle on which European empires outside Europe reposed."[10]

Here Aron, without asserting a causal role of war, takes stock of its revelatory power. The experience of war brought out aspects of a global situation that were almost overlooked indefinitely by the complacency of prewar Europe. The American intervention in World War I revealed a new balance of global forces; by revealing it, it crystallized something that was previously only a potential.

Of course, war does not only reveal fact; it itself is a major determinative factor. A little further, Aron writes that "in its scale and its consequences, World War I far outstripped the events that brought it about. War itself became the main fact, for which the conflicts of nationalities merely provided an occasion."[11] Once it attains a certain scope and duration, war becomes independent of its causes. At that point, it becomes the cause of new effects, effects that have their origin uniquely in the war. The fall of Eastern Europe to Communism, for example—a fairly significant phenomenon in European history—was the direct result of the advance of the Red Army: "In the twentieth century, armies are accompanied by regimes and ideologies."[12]

Aron continues: "Wars are by nature unpredictable. But the wars of the twentieth century have been much more unpredictable than those of the past. And the way they unfold turned upside-down the situations that gave rise to them. It is the fighting itself and not the origin of the conflict or the peace treaty that is the chief factor and has the most far-reaching consequences."[13]

In Aron's 1951 essay, "From Sarajevo to Hiroshima," he explored these themes more deeply. One of the twentieth century's characteristics is enormity: the enormity of wars, the enormity of war crimes, the enormity of crimes willed for their own sake and termed at the end of the World War II as "crimes against humanity." From whence comes this enormity? The question is one of the most difficult, and it is impossible to answer with certainty. The question arises again when we study totalitarian regimes. Aron considers it in relationship to one of the decisive episodes of the century—namely, the entry of the United States into war in 1917.

Aron writes:

> The intervention of the United States alone was unprecedented and marked a historical turning point, and the full significance of its role has become clear only in retrospect. And the main cause of its intervention was technological amplification of the war.
>
> The United States entered the conflict because of the Germans' declaration of an all-out submarine war, despite assurances given to Washington some months earlier. It was the new technology of naval warfare—at odds with human rights as understood at the time (though the British long distance blockade was open to the same objection)—that precipitated the U.S. decision, making the defeat of the Second Reich inevitable.
>
> Since then, efforts have been made to minimize the importance of this motive. . . . But would the Americans have awoken to the common interests linking them with Britain if the techniques of submarine warfare had not shaken the Home Fleet and the empire to which it belonged, thus revealing Germany's naval potential and making everyone dread a peace that would, like the war itself, bring destruction?
>
> It would be foolish to underestimate the role played by feeling and ideologies. In times of crisis, the kinship between the British and the Americans overcomes minor mutual misunderstandings, resentments, and irritations. By inscribing the words *democracy* and *freedom* on its flags, the Entente aroused sympathies of most Americans. Because it echoed everyone's aspirations, the language of the Allies was understood on every continent. A crusade to make the world "safe for democracy" had meaning everywhere. What sense did a defense of German culture make outside of Germany?
>
> Ideology made American public opinion accept the war; it kindled the enthusiasm of a young people and kept the flame burning. That said, the fundamental factor had been, first and foremost, material.[14]

Aron is no doctrinaire. Along with arguments favorable to his thesis, he presents opposing arguments. He asks, Did the attack of German submarines against American commercial ships only reveal and crystallize a fundamental solidarity between the Americans and the English and French, precipitating an inevitable intervention? Or did it effectively *cause* an intervention that would not have occurred otherwise? Aron clearly chooses the second hypothesis while being fully aware of the arguments in favor of the first. And if the second hypothesis is the correct one, then the submarine as a new technical weapon was the cause of the decisive extension of the war, and of its enormity.

This use of submarine warfare was also of great interest to another skilled analyst of the political and military scene, Charles de Gaulle. In a book published in 1924, *La Discorde chez l'ennemi*, de Gaulle studies the reasons why the Germans, despite their military superiority, let victory escape them in World War I. He too attributes the turning point to the unleashing of the submarine war, imposed on Chancellor Bethmann-Hollweg by the military class, especially Grand Admiral Tirpitz. Like Aron, he thinks that this action changed the course of the American policy, since President Wilson had just said that he was prepared to mediate between the opposing sides. But, unlike Aron, de Gaulle does not emphasize the technical aspect but instead the moral aspect. In his eyes, the unleashing of the all-out submarine war expresses the spiritual flaws of the German rulers and is the direct consequence of these flaws. De Gaulle writes:

> The German military leaders, whose task was to guide and coordinate such immense efforts, gave proof of an audacity, of a spirit of enterprise, of a will to succeed, of a vigor in handling resources, whose reverberation has not been stilled by their ultimate defeat. Perhaps this study—or, more precisely, the disclosure of the events that are its object—may make evident the defects common to these eminent men: the characteristic taste for immoderate undertakings; the passion to expand their personal power at any cost; the contempt for the limits marked out by human experience, common sense, and the law.[15]

And de Gaulle denounces specifically the Nietzschean philosophy that motivated the excesses of the German rulers.

The arguments of Aron and de Gaulle are compatible, even complementary. However, they emphasize a different aspect of the same event. More precisely, they explain differently what each terms as "excess." Aron raises the general question:

> People have never stopped pondering the origins of the war. But they have not questioned why it became hyperbolical. . . . Did the belligerents set themselves unlimited objectives from the first, or only as the violence increased? Was it passionate feeling that produced technological excess or technological excess that gave rise to passionate feeling? With some reservations and qualifications, and while admitting that the two kinds of phenomena interact with one another, I am prepared to say that the locomotive of change, at that time, was change.[16]

The questions Aron raises go beyond submarine warfare in World War I, even beyond war itself in general. Does technology necessarily lead men to progress? Do men always necessarily do all that technology allows them to do? Do they always end up willing to do what they can do? The question can be applied to a wide range of issues, from weapons to genetic manipulations. As far as weapons are concerned, experience does not permit an unequivocal answer one way or the other. The atom bomb was in fact used as soon as it was available, but it has not been used since. Has the atom bomb brought with it the technical excess that triumphs, through dissuasion, over the excess of the passions and the excess of technology itself?

In any case, whatever its causes, however manifold its aspects, excess or enormity became in the twentieth century a factor acting on its own. The enormity of war entailed the enormity of the political undertakings issuing from war, beginning with Communism. It seems that, having gone through the tribulations of the Great War, the Europeans no longer had a clear idea of what could or could not be done. They no longer recognized what was impossible or what was forbidden. It was their ideologies of course that assured them that everything was possible and nothing was forbidden, that man could be remade or a "new man" be made. But doesn't ideology mean, however diverse its content might otherwise be, precisely that we can do everything and that we have the right to do everything? Then one sees the link between the hold of ideology and the experience of hyperbolic war. It was war that first taught us that everything is possible. Aron writes: "It was technological excess that gradually replaced war aims with ideologies." And the ideologies brought forth a phenomenon that is proper to our time, what Aron calls "abstract hatreds," which, he says, "ravage our century."[17]

Of course, the most massive consequence of World War I was World War II, which was even more hyperbolic. Aron writes:

> We obviously cannot tell what would have happened if a compromise peace had been concluded at the end of 1916 or the beginning of 1917. It would be a waste of time to speculate about a (necessarily unreal) past that might have been the future of a different politics. But it remains true that World War II arose out of the extreme prolongation of World War I and above all out of the Russian Revolution and the fascist response to it in Italy and Germany. . . .
>
> It is as if violence, having reached a certain degree, becomes self-supporting. In war, as in nuclear science, there is such a thing as critical mass. Ever since 1914, Europe has been exposed to a chain reaction of war.[18]

Aron mentions the interpretation that certain Germans gave to what they had just experienced in World War I. The absurdity of that war derived from the contradiction between the struggle unto death and the preservation of sovereign states. A system of independent states was compatible with limited wars, but not with total war. Thus the high cost of battle would not be excessive if the profits of victory became definitive and so to speak unlimited, that is, if empire were to be achieved. The unlimited character of Hitler's undertakings was based primarily on the nature and ideas of the Führer and his team, but it is also true that the Nazi aggression actualized a possibility that was revealed during World War I. In the spring of 1918, the German armies advanced with ease into Russian territory beyond the border defined by the Brest-Litovsk Treaty, which helps to explain the rashness with which Hitler attacked Russia in June 1941.

Aron evokes a contradiction between the struggle unto death of hyperbolic war and the preservation of sovereign states, since only the acquisition of an empire by the victor would be a gain commensurate with the sacrifices made. In a context that prefigured the one we are considering, reflecting on the Terror and the dangers of a certain interpretation of the sovereignty of the people, Benjamin Constant wrote: "There are weights too heavy for the hand of man."[19] It seems that the sacrifices and massacres of the hyperbolic wars of the twentieth century were the last exercise of sovereignty in which sovereignty was discredited and thereby exhausted itself. One could say that after the wars of the twentieth century nothing can subsist any longer or retain its validity in the political order, except the universal.

In fact, it was after World War II that the idea of humanity came to the forefront with the notion of "crime against humanity," the organization of the United Nations, the Universal Declaration of Human Rights, etcetera. What was true in the intellectual and moral order was no less true in the political and military order. For sure, after the war, humanity was chiefly divided into two blocks, but it was divided in the name of unity. The "Western bloc" and the "Communist bloc" alike both equally appealed to the universal. Democracy and Communism both were finalities that were offered to all men alike. Moreover the head of each "bloc," the leading country, was more an empire than a nation.

This was true obviously for the Soviet Union, which assembled very diverse populations under the same head and claimed to embody a universal truth destined to spread over the entire planet. The case of the United States is more complex. The United States is obviously a single nation with strong traits of empire: their dimensions, their rapid expansion from one coast to the other, their massive, permanent, and diverse immigration founded on the principle that the poor and the oppressed are all potential citizens of the United States, and their global role in the world after 1917. Thus the division of humanity into two blocs after World War II represented a sort of qualitative leap toward the political unity of the planet. Using the same logic, we shall say that humanity has just made another new leap in the direction of unity. With the collapse of Communism, one is tempted to say, the United States remains the only "superpower" and the imperial unity of the world seems to be on the road to being achieved. Thus the process that was launched in 1917 with the American intervention in World War I has come to its natural conclusion. Max Weber already wrote in 1918 that the world hegemony of America was as inexorable as that of Rome after the Second Punic War.

Of course, in the case of the American empire, imperial unity of the world is no more achieved than in that of Rome. Large parts of the planet reject unity, in particular, the Muslim world and the Chinese world. No one can foresee the direction these countries will take tomorrow or in twenty years. Islam in particular gives rise to questions and anxieties. It seems to be sliding more and more toward a general secession, as if the absence of habits adapted to democratic life, a certain difficulty in dealing rationally with the non-Muslim world, incited it to tighten into a sort of "great refusal." The current inability of Islam to bring to reason its members engaged in the enormity of unprecedented terrorist violence will only be overcome when this ancient civilization is able to find the road to self-criticism.[20]

It seems, in any case, that the increasingly exorbitant European wars of the twentieth century have led to an increasingly clear recognition of the unity of the human species. Their hyperbolic violence, hovering over all states and often devastating them, has obliged human beings to forget their particularity in order to acknowledge and to live according to their resemblance to each other. If this is the case, it seems possible, if not to give these wars a positive meaning, at least to situate them along an intelligible course, a meaningful movement for the whole of humanity. And the observer today could discern, in these "chain reaction wars" what Hegel called the "cunning of reason": through the unleashing of blind passions, a reasonable outcome progressively comes to light.

Yet, this optimistic and rationalist thesis does not convince us. Many reject it to say that the experience of the century reveals to the contrary the irremediable fragility of the human in man. In any case, whether "optimists" or "pessimists," in the tranquility and comfort of a peace of now over fifty years, we nonetheless do not cease to hesitate between the particular political bodies that are the nations, whose particularity the past wars have rendered unworthy, and a universal idea of humanity that we do not know how to concretize. In this way, the effects of the European wars still make themselves felt at the most intimate level of individual and social life. Only the effective construction of a political Europe, which as we have seen is so difficult, could prove that the Europeans have spiritually overcome the intimidation of war. This "concrete universal" would manifest to the eyes of all that war, at least the long war of the twentieth century, is truly ended.

CHAPTER 8

The Forces of Trade

IN THE PRECEDING CHAPTER, I underlined the importance of those philosophies of history, in the nineteenth century, be it Saint-Simonian, liberal, or Marxist, that described humanity necessarily progressing from the age of war to the age of commerce and industry. For Montesquieu, by the first half of the eighteenth century, the rapid development of commerce encompassed a deep political and moral meaning. Commerce is a vital part of modernity since it carries out collective action that is radically different from the one that prevailed in the ancient cities or modern monarchies. To put it succinctly, commerce replaces the logic of unequal and potentially bellicose command with the logic of equal and peaceful trade. The hyperbolic wars of the twentieth century did not destroy this confidence in the pacifying effect of commerce. On the contrary, they have given rise to renewed efforts to guarantee the liberty and increase the role of commercial trade. The founding of the GATT at Geneva in 1947 represents the institutionalization of this will.

During the period of confrontation with Communism, the West defined itself more and more by "the free movement of goods, persons, and ideas." That was natural and politically expedient since, after the end of the Great Terror of the Stalin era, the oppressive character of Communism showed itself chiefly in its opposition to this free movement. By building the Berlin Wall in 1961, Communism had set before the eyes of the world the simplest and most eloquent symbol of its inhumanity. But by insisting on the importance of the free movement of goods, persons, and ideas, the NATO countries were not only acting in terms of democratic political morality, or the conveniences of propaganda alone. After all, the critics of Communism could have emphasized some of Communism's equally horrible aspects. The emphasis placed on freedom of movement signified a shift in the perception that the Western democracies had of themselves, a more and more liberal and commercial perception, giving the word "commerce" the broad meaning that it had in the eighteenth century, which the term "trade," "circulation," or even "communications," would express more adequately today.

One reason that the last ten years have seen the prestige of trade and communications increase even further is that the end of Communism abolished the obstacles that were opposed to free movement in Europe. Technological innovations now connect everyone with everything. Thanks to the Internet, every human being can communicate with every other human, with all aspects of the life of the world. Many among us, including "decision makers," believe that these latest developments represent a qualitative leap of commerce. From now on the unification of humanity through communications appears to represent an irreversible process. Yet, although these developments are surely very impressive, the hopes that previous generations placed in commerce have regularly collapsed. It is therefore necessary to evaluate precisely what commerce can and cannot do.

I shall begin by describing the logic of commerce in its opposition to the logic of traditional politics, to analyze it as an alternative to politics and even as a "critique of politics." Then we shall consider what politics— what it holds against commerce—by analyzing some arguments of Carl Schmitt in his work, *The Concept of the Political.* Finally, I shall try to analyze some ambiguities of trade that show why trade can evoke just as much blind hostility as fanatic infatuation.

First, the changes that the development of commerce brought to the logic of collective action became visible at the start of the eighteenth century. Around 1720 the most penetrating observers became convinced that the wellsprings of the human order were in the process of changing in a radical way. Until that time, order among men rested on command. Command, more precisely the relation between command and obedience, was considered the principal aspect of the human order. Thus politics, as the visible organization of the command-obedience relation, was at the center of the human world. This was true for the Greek city and for Rome, for the feudal disorder as well as the monarchic order of the European ancien régime, however different these regimes and political orders were. In the eighteenth century a new type of order was born, an order that did not rest on command.

On what does this unprecedented order rest? It rests on what was called *interest*, with increasing enthusiasm since the seventeenth century. In the old order, members of society lived together tolerably well because those whose duty it was to obey obeyed well enough those whose duty it was to command. In the new order, citizens *live better* than they did in the ancient order; they live *better and better* because they all obey the same rule, a rule that is not a command of the ancient kind, coming from above, but a law that is rather a motive born in the bosom of the agent, the rule of "rightly understood interest."

In the old order, the motives for acting tended always to come from the outside and from above—from the orders of his "superiors," the ends of nature, the law of God. In the new order, the motives for acting are born in the individuals themselves, who use their own reason to discover what is good for themselves and their freedom to seek the most economical means to attain their ends.

This fundamental change in the motives for human action is only a tendency, it is never completed. In other words, the "vertical" command does not disappear from people's lives, but it is more circumscribed (since the members of society are more "independent") and it becomes more rational, less authoritarian, since those who command are aware that their own interest is to respect as much as possible the interest of their fellow citizens. Montesquieu writes:

> Since that time princes have had to govern themselves more wisely than they themselves would have thought, for it turned out that great acts of authority were so clumsy that experience itself has made known that only goodness of government brings prosperity.
>
> One has begun to be cured of Machiavellianism, and one will continue to be cured of it. There must be more moderation in councils. What were formerly called *coups d'État* would be at present, apart from their horror, only imprudences.
>
> And, happily, men are in a situation such that, though their passions inspire in them the thought of being wicked, they nevertheless have an interest in not being so.[1]

In the commercial system, members of society behave less passionately and more rationally, not because they have become intrinsically wiser but because they are more aware of their own interests and that the system is conceived precisely for the satisfaction of their interests. At the beginning of the nineteenth century, Chateaubriand forged a characteristic phrase when he spoke of the "material and moral interests" of society. The passions certainly never disappear completely. They subsist in traditional societies that are not clearly engaged in commercial activity, that still obey the old logic, as well as in relations between these societies and commercialized ones. But the passions subsist also within developed commercialized societies, where men continue to be moved to some degree by the sentiment of honor, by patriotism, by anger, in such a way that the vertical command does not disappear completely from modern political societies, even those most fully devoted to commerce.

The United States provides a good example. American oil companies always desire—a rightly understood interest—to obtain profitable business contracts; they therefore desire to make deals with Libya, Saddam Hussein's Iraq, Iran, all oil producing countries. The American government judges such relations to be immoral and inopportune. Such contracts would increase the resources and the capacity of regimes America deems dangerous to do harm—it designates them as *rogue states*. And so the president of the United States signs an executive order that simply prohibits American enterprises from signing contracts or otherwise doing business with these countries. Here we see a fine example of the potential conflict between the "horizontal" logic of commercial interest and the "vertical" logic of political command.

Concerning the logic of collective action and its effects in the commercial system, one of the most important considerations is obviously that the logic of commerce is radically egalitarian. Commerce *presupposes* equality: "Commerce is the profession of equal people."[2] Montesquieu observed, while analyzing aristocracy, that as an aristocratic regime the nobles should not engage in commerce since their social superiority would give them too many advantages over their competitors and would make it easy for them to establish monopolies. The contracting parties must be of the same condition, or else the unequal logic of society would irresistibly distort the logic of commerce.

Nevertheless, in certain circumstances when the logic of commerce is strong and well understood, the participation of the nobles in commercial life, instead of making commerce aristocratic, helped society become commercial and thereby democratic. Historians attribute the political "advance" of England over France to the fact that the English nobles applied themselves vigorously to commerce while the French nobles were held back by the fear of demeaning themselves. Of course, the logic of commerce, which presupposes equality, *produces* inequality since some will succeed much better than others in this activity. This inequality does not in principle contradict the basic equality, provided at least that competition is not eliminated, since a monopoly would reestablish a sort of aristocracy of a new kind. Thus we meet up with the problems examined by Tocqueville when he tried to evaluate the risks of developing an "industrial aristocracy" in a democratic society.

Leaving aside the hopes placed in the transforming effects for the whole man with the collective ownership of the tools of production, the Communist economic project consisted in substituting for the vertical command so-called "planning"—the horizontal contract between economic agents (the English speak of *command economies* whereas the French speak of "*économies administrées*"). Communism reintroduced political logic in its most summary and military form within an economic system—modern economics—that prospers only if the players are in a position to act in accord with their interest, and can, therefore, have an interest and measure it. Indeed, according to certain historians, the Leninist conception of the socialist economy was inspired less by the imprecise suggestions of Marx than by the recent experience of the German war economy during World War I under the direction of Walther Rathenau.

After the tendency to equality, the other aspect of the new logic of commerce is what could be called the tendency to "globalization." I have noted that politics, which can always develop into war, is territorial: it involves a territory with borders, a territory that it presupposes and produces. For example, the sovereignty of France extends in Alsace to the left bank of the Rhine; on the right bank is the sovereignty of the Germans. While being a condition and an expression of politics, territory becomes a hindrance, an obstacle for commerce. At the border, goods, like persons, are stopped; people are identified, sometimes searched; goods are counted and assessed, taxes paid. Of course, in periods when public opinion or governments are favorable to free trade, such barriers are lowered, customs taxes are eliminated or diminished in order to facilitate the circulation of goods and services across political borders, and nations act as much as possible as though there were no political borders. This underlines the contradiction between the two logics. The ultimate aim of free trade is to achieve one sole market for all goods and services that fuses with the globe. In the logic of commerce, "the whole world . . . comprises but a single State, of which all societies are members."[3]

This underlying and essential independence of commerce in relation to the political order can appear either destructive or salutary according to the times, the regimes, the circumstances, the public opinions. The logic of the political order is autarchical. To engage, however, in commerce is to depend on others, to lose autarchy. They can for example quadruple from one day to the next the price of oil they sell us!

Of course, the correlation is not so simple. Active commerce increases the general resources of the body politic, making it more able to face difficult circumstances while maintaining its independence. Commerce, contrary to autarchy, can often reinforce autarchy if we define the word in a less mechanical way. Yet the concern for political independence virtually always goes against the logic of commerce, even though this opposition is most often understood *retrospectively*, its truth being neither so necessary nor so evident that the responsible politician should be expected to always go against the tendency to autarchy that is proper to the political order. For most nations recently, international commerce has represented only a relatively small portion of their general economic activity. The question is whether or not the current movement of globalization is in the process of radically changing this state of affairs.

Yet one can rejoice that the logic of commerce poses an obstacle to the logic of political independence, to the extent that it legitimizes the independence of political leaders with regard to certain economic interests. One can rejoice then, as Montesquieu does, that political leaders are constrained by their own interest, defined by the logic of commerce, to refrain from violent or partisan measures that their passions or their ideology might suggest to them. The fear of a catastrophe affecting the balance of payments or the exchange rate has dissuaded many politicians from taking measures that would have done serious economic harm to society. At the same time, when the logic of politics intensifies, when political circumstances and passions crystallize, then commerce takes a back seat.

Montesquieu gives a fascinating example of the salutary role of commerce when politics is unreasonable and even deadly. In chapter 20 of Book XXI of *The Spirit of the Laws*, he evokes the sad condition of the Jews in the Middle Ages in Europe. Usury was forbidden to Christians but nevertheless indispensable. The Jews took it upon themselves and in so doing became rich. Their wealth tempted the greed of the princes who pillaged and mistreated them. Thus Montesquieu writes:

> Nevertheless, one saw commerce leave this seat of harassment and despair. The Jews, proscribed by each country in turn, found the means for saving their effects. In that way, they managed to fix their refuges forever; a prince who wanted very much to be rid of them would not, for all that, be in a humor to rid himself of their silver.
>
> They invented letters of exchange, and in this way commerce was able to avoid violence and maintain itself everywhere, for the richest trader had only invisible goods, which could be sent everywhere and leave no trace anywhere.[4]

It matters little that Montesquieu was mistaken here about on the circumstances surrounding the invention of the letters of exchange. What interests us is his general thesis bearing on the historical, political, and moral significance of commerce. Commerce, more precisely the means of commerce symbolized by letters of exchange, made it possible, by making goods "invisible," to "avoid violence." This way, princes, politicians, and those who exercise material and visible force, discovered the limits of this force. Commerce played a powerful civilizing role.

This example holds even greater meaning for the modern world than it did for Montesquieu. The modern history of the Jewish people obliges us, if not to reject Montesquieu's analysis, at least to temper the hopes we can place in the mechanism he admirably identified. In fact, what saved the Jews in the Middle Ages brought them to ruin in the twentieth century. The "invisible goods" that some among them held, the lack of their own territory, their own country, became the motive, or the pretext of a new and more terrible persecution. The Jews were accused of being *heimatlos*, homeless. Since the territory of commerce is "everywhere," and the Jews, for the reason given by Montesquieu, seemed to play a great role in trade, people imagined a worldwide and invisible domination of the Jews, an idea that became one of the principal elements of modern anti-Semitism. Anti-

Semitism turns Montesquieu's view on its head. Where he saw a sphere of activity that fell outside the logic of politics, the anti-Semite discovers a hidden politics that governs nations without their knowing it. This is of course a fantasy, but it forces us to recognize the limits of trade. In laying out the possibility of a life without territory and without political government, commerce gives rise to the reaction of those who want to *see* who commands and who obeys.

These remarks certainly do not explain how this fantasy transformed itself into the project of the extermination of Jews by Nazism, but they point to a fundamental aspect of the general situation in which Nazism developed. In any case, after the Shoah, the Jews felt the necessity and the duty to create their own body politic endowed with a visible territory with "fixed and recognized" borders. They acquired and defended every parcel of this territory by the ordinary ways of politics and war. The history of the Jewish people, which for Montesquieu meant the triumph of trade over violence, ultimately testifies rather to the necessity and the irreducibility of politics when a people want to defend their security and their dignity.

Up to this point I have spoken as if the logic of commerce and the logic of politics were foreign and even contrary to one another. Modern history—as opposed to ancient, especially Roman history—has shown, however, that most commercialized nations have also been the most powerful and influential nations politically, first Great Britain and then the United States. Accordingly commerce could plausibly be rather an expression and an instrument of political power. The logic of commerce would then in no way be contrary to the logic of politics; it would be rather the logic of certain political bodies, those whose sphere and medium of action, whose element is the sea or the skies. Hence, the opposition that we have described between commerce and politics would have its root in an opposition that is immediately and fully political, an opposition between sea powers and land powers.

The author who has defended this thesis with the most acute arguments is Carl Schmitt. For Schmitt, politics is irreducible and inescapable. The human condition is necessarily political. This is so because the human being is a *vulnerable* and *dangerous* animal. Humans can die and they can kill. Thus they seek security in the group, but the same dialectic of vulnerability and threat affects the group as well as the individual. Groups are in virtual war against one another. This is the human condition. Schmitt is not a "warmonger" in the ordinary sense of the term, but he emphasizes the *risk* of war. Schmitt explicitly takes up Hobbes's conception of the natural condition of mankind. But where Hobbes insisted on the necessity and ability of a sovereign or an absolute state to keep in check members of society who are always ready to fight, Schmitt insists more on the permanence and ubiquity of the risk, on its polymorphic and hence insurmountable character. He believes that we are continuously determined by the presence or threat of our enemy. Politics, for Schmitt, then rests on the discrimination between friend and foe.

According to Schmitt, since this is the nature of the political, liberal thought—because it places its confidence in commerce—is characterized by an incomprehension and rejection of the political.

> In a very systematic fashion liberal thought evades or ignores State and politics and moves instead in a typical always recurring polarity of two heterogeneous spheres, namely ethics and economics, intellect and trade, education and property. The critical distrust of State and politics is easily explained by the principles of a system whereby the individual must remain *terminus a quo* and *terminus ad quem*. In case of need, the political entity must demand the sacrifice of life. Such a demand is in no way justifiable by the individualism of liberal thought.[5]

Since the political exists and cannot disappear, liberalism transforms and disguises it:

> Thus the political concept of battle in liberal thought becomes competition in the domain of economics and discussion in the intellectual realm. Instead of a clear distinction between the two different states, that of war and that of peace, there appears the dynamic of perpetual competition and perpetual discussion. The State turns into society: on the ethical-intellectual side into an ideological humanitarian conception of humanity, and on the other into an economic-technical system of production and traffic.[6]

In Schmitt's eyes, economic competition and humanitarian ideology—the ideology of "human rights"—are, in fact, political instruments rather than apolitical principles. Just as in other times religion was "politicized" as a means to power and influence (for example, Catholicism by the Spanish monarchy), so today the principles of free economic competition and humanitarian ideology are employed by certain countries (most notably, the English-speaking nations), to increase their power and influence. Carl Schmitt denounces this as an imposture:

> A domination of men based upon pure economics must appear a terrible deception if, by remaining nonpolitical, it thereby evades political responsibility and visibility. Exchange by no means precludes the possibility that one of the contractors experiences a disadvantage and that a system of mutual contracts finally deteriorates into a system of the worst exploitation and repression. When the exploited and repressed attempt to defend themselves in such a situation, they cannot do so by economic means. Evidently, the possessor of economic power would consider every attempt to change its power position

by extra-economic means as violence and crime, and will seek methods to hinder this. That ideal construction of a society based on exchange and mutual contracts and, *eo ipso*, peaceful and just is thereby eliminated.[7]

After recalling Rathenau's observation that our destiny today is economics and not politics, Schmitt concludes, "It would be more exact to say that politics continues to remain the destiny, but what has occurred is that economics has become political and thereby the destiny."[8]

Schmitt criticizes from a right-wing point of view the ideology of trade, the illusion of the apolitical character of trade, in the name of the irreducibility of the political. On the left, parallel critiques, sometimes even identical in content, are made in the name of equality. The left reasons that the formal equality of the exchange relation is the mask and tool of domination, the exchange being in truth unequal. The nations who are disadvantaged by the system of trade feel dominated and harbor both right- and left-wing viewpoints. For example, the entire harvest of bananas in a small Central American country being commercialized by a single, large North American company, one is certainly allowed to speak of unequal trade!

Yet, this critical counterpoint needs to be kept within proper limits. Within the last twenty or thirty years it has become clear that the violent rejection of the system of trade, the revolutionary claim to produce economic and human development by nonmarket-oriented methods, was not successful. The upshot is the recent tendency even for the countries that considered themselves traditionally as "dominated" countries, in particular the Latin American countries, to utilize the system of trade for their own profit according to the law of comparative advantages. The results have been impressive in certain cases and disappointing in others. The recent economic crisis of the so-called "emerging" countries has revived skepticism or hostility with regard to the market.

Even Montesquieu himself, who believed in commerce, remarked that commerce does not always have positive effects, in fact, that under certain circumstances nations could become impoverished through engaging in commerce. Thus even though the effects of commerce are normally positive, a nation still has to be in a position to profit from it, to make itself capable of profiting from it. That is what trading nations know how to do. In writing about England, Montesquieu argues that: "This is the people in the world who have best known how to take advantage of these three great things at the same time: religion, commerce, and liberty."[9]

The supporters as well as the critics of commerce employ the language of economics: they celebrate the increase of the GDP or denounce the deterioration of the terms of trade. But the arguments of both are not exclusively based on economics, but rather on moral and spiritual considerations. For its supporters, commerce is the way to bring people closer, of making them be aware of their similarities:

> Commerce cures destructive prejudices, and it is an almost general rule that everywhere there are gentle mores, there is commerce and that everywhere there is commerce, there are gentle mores.
>
> Therefore, one should not be surprised if our mores are less fierce than they were formerly. Commerce has spread knowledge of the mores of all nations everywhere; they have been compared to each other, and good things have resulted from this.[10]

In this sense the development of commerce entails a progress of human universality. It is not by chance that the largest democracy in the world is the center and pivot of world trade, the insurer and buyer of last resort, as the Americans boast or at times lament.

However, the opponents of commerce turn upside down the democratic argument, in the way in which Rousseau already turned upside down Montesquieu's argument: "Everything that facilitates communication among nations brings with it other nations' crimes, not their virtues, and alters in every nation the mores that are proper to their climate and the constitution of their government."[11]

Instead of the moralizing language so far from contemporary sensibility, we would argue today that commerce destroys cultures by replacing their living diversity with an artificial and dull homogeneity. For example, the diversity of world cuisines is replaced by the homogeneity of fast foods; the diversity of languages with the homogeneity of international English that is not even any longer the English of the English or the Americans, but a basic, rough lingua franca. Indeed, the democratization that commerce induces is a superficial homogenization of ideas, mores, and tastes, contrary to a true democracy that presupposes the long and slow elaboration of a common distinct life. It makes this true democracy impossible because the appeal of commerce, of the means of communication and trade, of the signs of the new universality, of the logos of the new *logos*, is such that they, particularly among young people, come to disdain their own society and are hardly disposed to contribute to its specific development. The progress of world communications arouses, if I may say it, a sort of universal discontent with one's own particular culture. For example, how can one now take the French language seriously, how can one use it to say all that it could say about our present life, how can one be a French writer— or an Italian or German writer for that matter—when all around us are signs that the truly living language that is tuned in to the world, the language in which contemporary life is expressed, is international English?

We have here a very serious problem, perhaps in one sense the most important and most difficult to solve. If it cannot be solved, one can at least try to formulate it well. It is easy to take a partisan position, either in favor of trade, communications, the future, the universal; or inversely, to be in favor of roots, the right to be different, cultural exception. It is easy to volley arguments back and forth like a tennis ball at Wimbledon. It is more useful, however, to see how they are rooted in the human condition as a political condition. The political question is this: How do people actualize their common humanity? One could say that there are two answers that always necessarily mix in practice, but that nonetheless go in two divergent and perhaps ultimately opposite directions. There is an answer of extension and an answer of comprehension, to use the language of the logicians.

The answer of extension is the answer of commerce, of trade and communication. People have to be given the means of satisfying their general needs as easily and completely as possible. Pushed to its logical end, this leads to a search for the lowest common denominator among people. This is, for example, what happens when human beings are provided with food in the quickest, cheapest way possible, with the type of food whose appearance, texture, and taste cannot possibly displease any human being on earth no matter what his tastes, that is with the most implacably dull food that can be imagined.

The other answer, the one of comprehension, is the answer of the political community, that puts as many things as possible in common among its citizens or, as in Aristotle's formulation, as many words and deeds as possible. What the citizens of this political community have in common distinguishes and even separates them from other political communities that put different things in common. Pushed to its logical end, this answer leads to celebrating the roots and particularity, the way of life of the "locals," to narrowness and finally to xenophobia. Of course, in practice, what we dream of is a public life that gives access to a universal that is not superficial, while expressing a particular human community that is not idiosyncratic. One can say that a political form is accomplished when it gives access to such a synthesis. This is how, I believe, the problem can be phrased in an impartial way.

The answer of extension considers more people in general and human rights in general; while the answer of comprehension emphasizes the requirements of civic life. The difficulties that we seek to pin down are rooted in the duality constitutive of humanity: humans are both human beings and citizens. This tension arose before the eyes of all at the end of the eighteenth century: declaring both the rights of man and of the citizen made clear that they belonged together but were not identical.

Finally, the development of trade and communications reveals a tension between communications and the exchange of things on the one hand and the production of things or the condition of their production on the other.

When I speak of "things," this term covers the goods and services that are circulated by commerce as well as concepts and works that circulate in a different mode. The more extended the market, the more general are its rules; and thus the more abundant and rapid and satisfying is the movement of things. But what facilitates the movement of things is not necessarily favorable to their production. This becomes truer as the product is more refined. A thorough work presupposes great concentration, not only in the sense of an intense and focused effort but also in the sense that its producer must exclude other things that he has to circumscribe on his horizon. It is an idea dear to Nietzsche that man cannot be a creator except within a limited horizon. In an absolutely open world, creation would be simply impossible. To return to an example I have already used, French, Italian, German writers who want to produce the best possible work must wrap themselves in the particularities of their own language because it is in the particularities of language that the language's means of expression are found. Racine, whose verses are so limpid, employs the most specific resources of French to obtain his effects. Such an effort at thoroughness is difficult, almost impossible, when the space of expression is already occupied not only by a quasi-universal language such as international English is today, but also by literary genres that are universally and immediately pleasing because their wellsprings are simple, like the detective story. In brief, one could say that trade, as it becomes generalized and intensified, tends to erase the limited horizons that men need in order to produce the things they wish to exchange.

CHAPTER 9

Declaring the Rights of Man

THE NOTION of human rights is today the common political and moral reference point in the West. Every political party, school, and "sensibility" appeals to it. Such unanimity on an ultimate principle of morality and legitimacy is extremely rare. Perhaps one needs to go back to the fourteenth century to find a comparable homogeneity of belief. It obliges us to correct a commonplace belief according to which our world would be the stage of an explosion of diversity, of a growing medley of values and mores. That may be true for certain superficial aspects of contemporary life. But the principle of moral judgments is more homogeneous than ever. The proof of this is easy to find. Those who celebrate diversity as the most pleasant and noble trait of contemporary society always invoke what they call the "right to be different." When they celebrate "difference," they are, in fact, doing the exact opposite; they are contributing to the homogenization of society since they deal with difference using the language of human rights. To make "difference"—let us leave the term undefined since its supporters generally leave it undetermined—the object of a human right is to contribute to defining man as a being that has rights. It merges the idea of "difference" with the idea of rights and increasing the already unrivaled prevalence of the idea of human rights. Now, difference can be supported by a notion other than that of "human rights." The notion of duty, for example, is contrary to a "right." A Muslim will say that he obviously has the duty to be a good Muslim even if he lives in the midst of a population that is not Muslim. Certainly, the Muslim "difference" is better protected by the duty to be a Muslim than by the right to be one.

In any case, this unanimity is recent. The concept of human rights developed in the seventeenth and eighteenth centuries, and it won a victory that was definitive at the end of the eighteenth century with the American and French revolutions. But it has long been challenged from various sides. It was only in the 1970s and 1980s that it came to be unchallenged in the West. It was in the context of the struggle against Communism that the notion regained its pertinence and its luster, in particular as the intellectual weapon and spiritual resource of dissidents. In the face of the crushing power of the Communist regime, dissidents did not invoke the idea of another regime to draw up a political project of opposition. Instead, they demanded that the Communist regime respect a certain number of elementary principles, principles that the Communists themselves had enshrined in their constitutions.

For its part, the Communist regimes, even as they imprisoned or deported dissidents, could hardly officially declare themselves hostile to human rights. Both democratic countries and Communist countries signed the Helsinki Accords, which affirmed fundamental rights such as the free movement of persons. It is tempting to say, in retrospect, that this intellectual concession of the Soviet Union heralded its political collapse fifteen years later.

Before this recent development, the notion of human rights was relatively unknown in civic discourse. More precisely, since the Declaration of 1789 was a Declaration of the Rights of Man *and Citizen*, one could say that the rights of the citizen had superseded the rights of man. In the nineteenth and the first half of the twentieth centuries, there was greater interest in the *political* inscription of human rights within the framework of the nation-state than in the general affirmation of rights as such. Human rights were politically or socially specified: the right to vote, the right to work, the right of nationalities, etcetera.

Inversely, the insistence placed on human rights today has an incontestably *antipolitical* flavor. The notion of human being is preferred to that of citizen and there is a tendency to reject the collective restraints linked to citizenship. For example, compulsory military service, long considered to be the most necessary and noble expression of civic devotion, now seems to be no more than a nuisance devoid of meaning. When just recently the president of France decided to eliminate it purely and simply, no one protested against what would have appeared as a dismantling of the Republic at other times. So, until recently, human rights were understood in their relation to civic and national obligations. However, the sentiment of this relation seems to be weakening from day to day.

This historical sketch of our attitude regarding human rights would be incomplete if we omitted the opinion that challenged the principle of human rights. One can distinguish three main groups of opponents, who rejected human rights on religious grounds, political grounds, and social grounds. Let us consider each briefly in turn.

In the West, the most resolute opposition to the principle of human rights came for a long time from the Catholic Church. It was only in 1965, at the Second Vatican Council, with the Declaration on Religious Liberty, that the Church, in recognizing the fundamental and not merely prudential character of religious liberty, agreed with the principle of a basic human freedom, a fundamental human right. In recent years, the Church has gone even further, particularly under the impetus of John Paul II, who has repeatedly affirmed that human rights is a Christian idea, found in the Gospel, and that the Church in appropriating this principle today is only taking back what is its own. The rallying of the Catholic Church to the idea of human rights has contributed a great deal to the foundation of the unanimity I was speaking of at the beginning. But this recent rallying interests us less than the Church's long dissent. What was its justification?

In very broad terms, if the Catholic Church long rejected the principle of human rights, it is because this principle subordinates truth to freedom, whereas for the Church, the reverse ought to prevail. Since the meaning of freedom is to attain truth, the human order must first recognize the objectivity of truth. The primary duty of human beings is to recognize truth, of which the Church is the repository and carrier. In this context, the Catholic authors have often opposed the rights of truth, even the "rights of God," to the rights of man. At the same time, the Church has always affirmed unequivocally that adherence to truth is only valid if it is freely given. The Church affirmed this even in its most authoritarian times and by its strictest theologians. This ever-present second consideration, prepared and perhaps authorized before, was used later in rallying to religious freedom and human rights. One could say, in a formula that would hold for both periods, that people are called freely to the truth of which the Church is the repository and vehicle. Depending on whether the accent is placed on "freely" or on "truth," there are two divergent and even opposite political directions, the one "liberal" and the other "authoritarian."

These considerations do not have only a "historical interest." This tension is still present today. As I have already pointed out, the Church embraced liberal logic only with reservation. On several major matters of morality, particularly those concerning the relation between the sexes and reproduction—marriage, contraception, abortion, etcetera—the Church takes positions contrary to the dominant opinion and the trends of modern mores and laws. The Church takes its stand in the name of the existence of an objective moral truth, that human beings cannot alter since it defines them.

Of course, the idea of an objective moral truth is not the exclusive domain of the Catholic Church, but the Church is the collective body that publicly upholds this ideal with the greatest insistence and coherence.

The second ground for opposing human rights is political, in the broadest sense of the term, encompassing what is "social." It manifested itself as soon as the rights of man were proclaimed at the end of the eighteenth century and, in the process, founded European political conservatism. Perhaps the greatest author in this tradition is its founder, Edmund Burke, who published his *Reflections on the Revolution in France* as early as November 1790. Burke believed that the idea of the "rights of man" was a "metaphysical" idea, that is, an idea detached from the conditions of human experience, and became destructive when put into practice. What does it mean that "men are born and remain free and equal in rights," when in fact every human being is born *bound, obligated,* morally but already physically, to take his or her part in an ordered series of several "wholes" that goes from the family to the body politic and to the entire creation? To set people apart from nature as "sovereigns," and every person apart from every other as "equal," is to transform society from a harmonious cosmos into a chaos of "elementary corpuscles." Burke sees the French revolutionary "anarchy" in the process of doing just that. In a rhetorical volley that has not lost its brilliance, Burke opposes the rights of *Englishmen* to the rights of men in general. Our rights exist and have meaning only in a previously constituted body politic. They are not to be detached from the social and moral habits and political laws that give the body politic, whose members we are, its form and life.

I shall consider at greater length in a later section the third ground of opposition to human rights, which could be called "social," but in another meaning than Burke's and that finds its most trenchant and influential expression in the work of the young Karl Marx. This connection has been examined by Claude Lefort.

This brief overview of the history and criticism of the rights of man alerts us to the danger of taking human rights for granted. The present-day conviction, that this good and true idea has never had anything against it but particularistic prejudices and oppressive fanaticism, is simply wrong. The notion of human rights is a powerful and convincing idea that emerged at the end of the eighteenth century, but it is also a problematic idea that presents some difficulties, that has aroused great debates, and to which serious objections have been raised.

I have spoken until now as if we had a clear idea of what human rights are. Indeed, whether or not we have read attentively the various declarations of human rights, we have some knowledge of what they are since we participate in a democratic society whose goal is to guarantee them. The daily functioning of the institutions of our democratic society does not cease to raise questions, bringing us to the principle of human rights. For example, we ask questions about the functioning of justice. Of the seventeen articles of the Declaration of 1789, three concern justice directly, and most of the others do so indirectly. An interesting study would be the history of our institutions and how they implement the principles of the Declaration. But we would then risk losing sight of the fundamental and spiritual significance of human rights.

The spiritual significance of human rights expresses itself in the way that the rights are proclaimed. For example, in France, they appear in the form of a declaration made by the national Assembly representing the French people. Thus the highest text that rules the life of the French was drawn up and promulgated by the French themselves. We now take that for granted but until the time of the Declaration of the Rights of Man, the principles governing people's lives were understood to come from God Himself, revealing His will through His commandments, or from the ancestral customs such as the "fundamental laws" of the French monarchy.

In the human order prior to the proclamation of rights, people indeed considered themselves as free beings, but they exercised their freedom in a framework not of their making, of which they were not and could not be the authors. This framework was *received* from God or from people mysteriously close to the gods, their ancestors. People, prior to the Declaration of the Rights of Man, were free beings, but were *sub lege Dei*, under the law of God; they were free subjects, but *sub rege*, under the king or the prince or legitimate magistrate. In the human rights revolution this freedom *sub lege Dei* and *sub rege*, which was a *conditioned* freedom, was now experienced and defined as submission or even servitude and rejected in favor of an *unconditioned* freedom that people gave to themselves. They declared a freedom of which they are both the authors and the beneficiaries. One could say, with a solemnity befitting the circumstances, that the Revelation of the Law of God is replaced by the Declaration of the Rights of Man.

The philosopher Immanuel Kant gave this idea its simplest, most natural, and most striking expression. In the very first lines of a short text written in December 1784, entitled *What is Enlightenment?* Kant writes as follows:

> Enlightenment is man's emergence from his self-imposed immaturity. Immaturity is the inability to use one's understanding without guidance from another. This immaturity is self-imposed when its cause lies not in lack of understanding, but in lack of resolve and courage to use it without guidance from another. *Sapere aude!* "Have courage to use your own understanding!"—that is the motto of enlightenment.[1]

If we follow Kant's suggestion we will say simply that in declaring the rights of man, human beings declare that they have come of age.

To come of age is to become responsible for one's own acts, to become capable of doing by oneself, without needing authorization of parents or tutor. In the language of Kant's philosophy, which on this point has largely become our own, it is to pass from heteronomy to autonomy. In observing the movement of minds and morals in European countries, Kant sees more and more men passing from heteronomy to autonomy. They are emancipating themselves from all forms of tutelage and becoming free.

But men can only become free if they are already free—in the language of the seventeenth and eighteenth centuries—if they are free *by nature*.

This idea of natural freedom is contained in the French verb *naître*, as it is employed in Article I of the Declaration: "Men are born and remain free and equal in rights." What does it mean precisely that men are born and remain free and equal in rights? Is this not a statement altogether contrary to experience, almost to evidence? Is not the newborn child the least free of beings?

This is what the conservative or reactionary critics of democracy will not fail to underscore. For example, Charles Maurras, while not the most profound of its critics, has the merit of offering a clear and amusing refutation of the idea of being "born free." At the beginning of *Mes idées politiques*, Maurras writes:

> The little chick breaks through its shell and starts to run.
>
> He needs little to cry: "I am free. . ." But what about the little human?
>
> The little human lacks everything. Long before he runs, he needs to be weaned from his mother, washed, dressed, covered, and fed. Before he is taught his first steps, his first words, he needs to be kept from mortal dangers. The little instinct he possesses is powerless to procure him the care he needs, which he must receive, in good order, from others . . .
>
> The little human, almost inert, who would perish if he faced brute nature, is received into the bosom of another solicitous, clement, and humane nature: he lives only because he is its little citizen.
>
> His existence began with the afflux of external free services . . .
>
> The nature of this beginning is so luminously defined that it straightaway brings about this grave, irresistible consequence that no one has mistaken as much as the philosophy of "immortal principles," when it described the beginnings of human society as the fruit of conventions among fellows fully formed, filled with conscious and free life, acting on the basis of a kind of equality, . . . to conclude this or that surrender of a part of their "rights" in the express design of guaranteeing the respect of others.
>
> The facts dash to pieces and pulverize these reveries. [Man's] Freedom is imaginary, their Equality false. Things do not happen this way, they have nothing in them that even resembles these reveries. . . . Everything works and will work . . . , proceeds and will proceed by actions of authority and inequality, squarely contradicting the bland liberal and democratic hypothesis.[2]

Maurras here is obviously right in what he affirms; but is he right in what he denies, when he dismisses with disdain "the bland liberal and democratic hypothesis"? Would it have escaped the philosophers of democracy that newborns did not do the grocery shopping? Birth in this sense is not biological birth. The Declaration harkens back to what the seventeenth- and eighteenth-century philosophers called the "state of nature," a state "anterior" to the social state, an underlying state, immanent in the social state, in which all men are free, the autonomous and sovereign authors of all their acts.

By proclaiming the rights of man and declaring that "men are born and remain free and equal in rights," democracy gives rise, alongside the real society filled with inequality and dependencies, to the promise of another society where the seeds of liberty would blossom without obstacles. The democratic project claims to bring about this promise. Maurras, and conservative critics in general, have a sharp eye for spotting the dependencies that impede the movement toward freedom, but they lack the spiritual sense to recognize the significance of this desire for an unconditional freedom, which they reduce imprudently as injustice to a "bland hypothesis."

We see the limits of the conservative critique, but the democratic project is more than a project of freedom raised against the dependencies and inequalities of real societies. What is this human being who has such rights? What is the human being who is declaring himself or herself in the Declaration of the Rights of Man? Marx examined these questions profoundly in his youth. The young Marx's critical comments about human rights are more interesting than those of Maurras, because first of all Marx shares the democratic project of unconditional freedom and emancipation. His critique notes some intrinsic difficulties with human rights, whereas Maurras opposes it with a kind of common sense that is always and so fruitlessly right.

The essentials of Marx's critique are contained in "On the Jewish Question, *Zur Judenfrage*," published in 1844, in which Marx answers his contemporary "young Hegelian" Bruno Bauer. In a text entitled *The Jewish Question*, Bauer had analyzed the situation of the Jews in modern Christian states and sought the solution to their exclusion and their inferiority in the development of the secular state. In his reply to Bauer, Marx offers a brief but powerful sketch of his conception of modern society, as it was unfolding under his eyes. Marx writes:

> Let us notice first of all that the so-called *rights of man*, as distinct from the *rights of the citizen* are simply the rights of a *member of civil society*, that is, of egoistic man, of man separated from other men and from the community. . . .
>
> Liberty is, therefore, the right to do everything which does not harm others. The limits within which each individual can act without harming others are determined by law, just as the boundary between two fields is marked by a stake. It is a question of the liberty of man regarded as an isolated monad, withdrawn into himself. . . .
>
> Liberty as a right of man is not founded upon the relations between man and man, but rather upon the separation of man from man. It is the right of such separation. The right of the *circumscribed* individual, withdrawn into himself.

The practical application of the right of liberty is the right of private property. . . .

The right of property is, therefore, the right to enjoy one's fortune and to dispose of it as one will; without regard for other men and independently of society. It is the right of self-interest. This individual liberty and its application, form the basis of civil society. It leads every man to see in other men, not the *realization*, but rather the *limitation* of his own liberty. . . .

Security is the supreme social concept of civil society; the concept of the police. The whole society exists only in order to guarantee for each of its members the preservation of his person, his rights and his property. . . .

None of the supposed rights of man, therefore, go beyond the egoistic man, man as he is, as a member of civil society; that is, an individual separated from the community, withdrawn into himself, wholly preoccupied with his private interest and acting in accordance with his private caprice.[3]

Marx's discussion is already very condensed, but I shall try to summarize it further. The rights of man and of the citizen are in fact the rights of man inasmuch as he is different from the citizen; they are the rights of the private man, the bourgeois, the individual. Marx's purpose is of course a critique and a denunciation. He is at odds with a society that, because it is founded on egoism, separates people that it ought to bring together. This denunciation is banal today, but it was already so during the 1840s, not only among socialists, but also among Catholics and many liberals. In short, with just about everybody. Yet, this denunciation of the egoism of our society is not very interesting in itself. Are our ministers and businessmen more egoist than the ministers and financiers under the reign of Louis XIV? Are we more egoistic than our forebears (you will note that those who denounce the egoism of our society exempt themselves from the condemnation, which suggests that egoism is not universal)? Marx's important point is the link between egoism—something that we all reject in principle—and the rights of man—something that we all embrace in principle.

What Marx finds strange in modern democracy is that this political project is founded in some way on the negation of the political condition of man. The rights of man inspire or accompany an extremely vast and ambitious political project. As a political project, it intended no doubt to bind men, to gather them; but, to the contrary, it is more concerned with separating men, with establishing each man in his property. First, to establish ownership of himself, and then with protecting this property. In short, it seems there is something intrinsically *contradictory* in the modern democratic project.

One has to acknowledge that Marx's analysis of several articles of the Declarations of Rights is rather convincing. Moreover, it is perfectly applicable to the authors who inspired these Declarations of the Rights of Man, such as Hobbes, Locke, and Rousseau. These were the political philosophers of the seventeenth and eighteenth centuries who in effect hold that the body politic is born of the necessity of individual preservation. It is indeed true that for them, as Marx says, "society exists only in order to guarantee for each of its members the preservation of his person, his rights and his property." But can the matter stop there? How could a political society maintain itself durably on the basis of an apolitical and even antipolitical principle? Marx certainly believed that this contradiction of bourgeois democracy was going to give rise to a revolutionary transformation that would soon reunite the individual and the citizen. He thought that the revolution went beyond the political emancipation of the Enlightenment, that was founded on the separation of civil society and the state, and would produce the true human emancipation and reconcile the individual with his "generic being," with his universal human calling. We know that nothing of the sort took place. The contradiction, if there was one, disappeared, or men were reconciled with it. Where was Marx's error?

In his essay on "The Rights of Man and Politics," Claude Lefort severely critiques Marxist attacks on the rights of man. Lefort noted that Marx, in his "On the Jewish Question," limits himself to the *texts* of the American and French Declarations of human rights. One would certainly not deny their individualist, bourgeois, and separatist logic, but why is Marx not interested in the real social effects of these founding texts? This is all the more strange since Marx constantly opposes in his work reality and ideology, and claims to tear the veils with which the latter covers the former. Lefort writes: "Marx falls into and draws us into a trap, that on other occasions and also for other purposes, he was well able to dismantle: the trap of ideology. He is a prisoner of the ideological version of rights, without examining what they signify in practice, what upheaval they bring in social life." Thus Lefort critiques Marx's commentary on Article 4 of the Declaration of 1789: "Liberty is the right to do everything which does not harm others." Marx declared that this liberty is that of "an isolated monad, withdrawn into himself." For Lefort, Marx subordinates the positive liberty to "do everything" to the negative liberty "which does not harm others," "without taking into consideration that all human action in the public space, whatever the constitution of society, necessarily binds the subject to other subjects."[4] Thus Marx is blind to the real liberating effects of so-called bourgeois liberty: "Marx strangely ignores the lifting of the multiple prohibitions that burdened human action before the democratic revolution, under the *Ancien Régime*, he ignores the practical import of the Declaration of Rights, so captivated is he by the image of a power anchored in the individual and capable of being exercised only until it encounters another's power."[5]

Next, Lefort analyzed what Marx has to say about liberty of opinion. For Marx, the right to freely entertain one's own opinion is a modality of the right of property, the right that is "the basis of civil society." Lefort notes that Marx ignores the articles of the Declaration concerning liberty of conscience and opinion. So Lefort cites them: Article 10: "No one shall be disquieted on account of his opinions, including his religious views, provided their manifestation does not disturb the public order established by law." Article 11: "The free communication of ideas and opinions is one of the most precious of the rights of man. Every citizen may, accordingly, speak, write, and print with freedom, but shall be responsible for such abuses of this freedom as shall be defined by law." Lefort comments:

> Must Marx be so obsessed by his schema of the bourgeois revolution not to see that liberty of opinion is a liberty of relations, or as is said precisely here, a liberty of communication? . . . Assuming that the first of the two articles mentioned does not exceed the metaphor of property, the second . . . lets it to be understood that it is the right of man, one of his most precious rights, to go out of himself and to bind himself to others, through speech, writing, and thought. . . . The article lets it to be understood that there is a communication, a circulation of thoughts and opinions, of spoken and written words that, in principle, do not come under the governing authority, save in cases specified by law.[6]

One sees how Lefort and Marx give opposing readings of the Declaration of the Rights of Man and of the democratic society that it founds. Where Marx sees principally the right to separate oneself, Lefort sees principally the right to bind oneself.

Lefort's analysis also opens new perspectives on the political and human meaning of the rights of man. Lefort recalls that the revolution of the rights of man ties rights to man. This seems to go without saying, but in fact it presupposes and signifies a reversal of the relation to rights, since it was hitherto rooted in God or in ancestral custom. At first blush, it must be said that a right is detached from God to be attached to man. But this statement is in fact misleading. The human being cannot truly be considered as the subject of inherent rights, since this inherence cannot be represented. Only a particular right of a particular individual can be easily represented. The statement, "the baker's daughter inherited her father's shop," does not present any difficulty to the intellect. But how does one *refer* rights defined in *general* terms to the human being *in general*? To the extent that the rights of man are recognized, Lefort says, "modes of existence, modes of activity, modes of communication whose effects are *undetermined* are recognized." And again:

> The rights of man are stated; they are stated as rights that belong to man; but, simultaneously, man appears through his proxies as the one whose essence is

to state his rights. It is impossible to detach what is stated from the stating of it once no one could occupy a place, at a distance from everyone, from where he would have authority to grant or ratify rights. Thus, rights are not simply the object of a declaration; it is of their essence to declare themselves.[7]

Lefort's text at this point is difficult since he is attempting to convey a profound idea. The generative principle of our society, the right, is not visible in a determined and unquestionable way as it was formerly in the law of God or the person of the monarch, but neither is it susceptible to be located in man in general even though these are rights of man. These declared rights are declared by no one, or else they are declared by all; each man being at once subject and object, author and beneficiary of the rights, of all the rights. In short, in our society the indeterminate and fluid character of right gives rise incessantly to new claims to rights. Whatever the state, the administration, the social authorities may do, all these agencies of command or domination are open to what Lefort calls very well an "opposition by right."

Lefort writes: ". . . [T]he democratic State exceeds the limits traditionally assigned to the legal or constitutional State. It tests rights that are not yet incorporated into it, it is the theater of a challenge whose object is not reducible to the conservation of a tacitly established pact, but that takes form from sources that the power cannot fully master."[8] And lastly: ". . . It is from the bosom of civil society, under the sign of the indefinite demand for mutual recognition of liberties, of a mutual protection of their exercise, that a movement antagonistic to the one who precipitates the power of the State toward its goal can be affirmed."[9]

Lefort's critiques of Marx are certainly pertinent, but are they completely convincing? If Marx is blind to the binding effects of the rights of man in the new society, no doubt Lefort is not sensitive enough to the separating effects of these rights, and in particular of those he approvingly calls the "new rights." He is favorable to these new rights because in them he sees new liberties as well as an increased independence with regard to social authorities and established dominations. But how can one deny that these new liberties lead to separation? Let us consider for example, the new right of the family that has developed these past twenty or thirty years. There is no doubt it can be included under the heading of the "new rights" of women (e.g., the disappearance of the notion of "head of family," of divorce by mutual consent, of easy access to contraception and abortion). Thanks to these new rights, women enjoy an independence that had been previously only open to a small number of daring ones. But the very fact that they no longer need to tie the "conjugal knot" in order to have a place and a role in society, the very fact that they can live "unattached" without encountering the disapproval of opinion, confirms that the logic of the rights of man is indeed a separatist and "individualizing" logic. Hence, there remains something profoundly true in Marx's analysis when he defines the liberty of modern man as the liberty of "the isolated monad, withdrawn into himself."

The dialogue could go on. Lefort could respond that these new liberties are not contrary to social bonding, to human ties. They have as their only goal to guarantee that these ties be freely bound and maintained, and that they can be freely dissolved once they are esteemed as enslaving.

The discussion has no end in sight, but it is not useless. This dialogue among philosophers reflects the development and deepening of the dialogue among citizens, the civic conversation. We must try to arrive at an analysis of our society that recognizes its individualizing logic, while giving the new modalities of the social bond that appear in private and in public life their due.

Tocqueville reconciles Marx and Lefort. Tocqueville defines democracy as a double movement. There is on the one hand what he calls the "nature" of democracy, or its "instinct," and on this point, he goes even further than Marx in describing how the democratic individual wants passionately to refer all aspects of social and human life to himself. On the other hand, Tocqueville calls "the art of democracy" that set of institutions, behaviors, virtues by which the citizens of democracies knit all kinds of ties among themselves. One could say, following Tocqueville, that democratic man accepts to bind himself only if he is certain to do so absolutely freely. He must then first detach himself completely beforehand, and in doing so, he can bind himself legitimately. Even when his purpose is to bind himself, his first movement is to detach himself. Such is the ambivalence that tests our soul under the reign of the rights of man.

CHAPTER 10

Becoming an Individual

LET US NOW CONSIDER, with the help of Tocqueville, how modern democracy binds men after it has unbound them, how the art of democracy is joined to the nature of democracy.

The best approach is to begin with the word "individualism" itself. Widely used today, the word appeared in 1826, precisely to designate the problems that concern us here. A chapter entitled "On Individualism in Democratic Countries" in Tocqueville's *Democracy in America* is illuminating. Tocqueville writes:

> I have brought out how, in centuries of equality, each man seeks his beliefs in himself; I want to show how, in the same centuries, he turns all his sentiments toward himself alone.
>
> *Individualism* is a recent expression arising from a new idea. Our fathers knew only selfishness.
>
> Selfishness is a passionate and exaggerated love of self that brings man to relate everything to himself alone and to prefer himself to everything.
>
> Individualism is a reflective and peaceable sentiment that disposes each citizen to isolate himself from the mass of those like him and to withdraw to one side with his family and his friends, so that after having thus created a little society for his own use, he willingly abandons society at large to itself.
>
> Selfishness is born of a blind instinct; individualism proceeds from an erroneous judgment rather than a depraved sentiment. It has its source in the defects of the mind as much as in the vices of the heart.
>
> Selfishness withers the seed of all the virtues; individualism at first dries up only the source of public virtues; but in the long term it attacks and destroys all the others and will finally be absorbed in selfishness.
>
> Selfishness is a vice as old as the world. It scarcely belongs more to one form of society than to another.
>
> Individualism is of democratic origin, and it threatens to develop as conditions become equal.[1]

From the start, Tocqueville dispels the confusion which so captivated Marx, in analyzing modern society as the reign of the "selfish man." The epithet "selfish" falls immediately within the moral domain and in the realm of blame. Of course, Marx's confusion is tempting; how many authors and ordinary citizens in the last two centuries have denounced the "selfishness" of bourgeois society! Tocqueville notes soberly how "selfishness is a vice as old as the world." Denouncing selfishness does not contribute to a better understanding of our society, but one enters the realm of perennial morality and this denunciation is neither more nor less justified today than in the time of Molière, Aristophanes, or King David. In fact, when selfishness is denounced as a characteristic trait of our society, something else is intended, something else for which another word was soon found: individualism.

What is individualism? Tocqueville gives a very full and subtle description of it in Volume II of *Democracy in America*. He first underlines its intellectual character. It concerns a judgment of the mind, an erroneous judgment that involves emotions, an interior disposition. Individualism concerns a judgment by which each man isolates himself from his fellow citizens, wills to be independent from them, a will and an attitude of independence that are not limited to each man properly speaking but that encompass his family and friends. Of course such a judgment "dries up the source of public virtues" that presuppose that each man feels concerned with the public sphere and society at large.

Although this definition of individualism is clear and suggestive, it is not completely convincing since it is hard to see how the exclusive preference given to parents and friends proceeds more from an erroneous judgment than a vice of the heart. This is why this preference would be more marked today than in the past, in democratic society more than under the ancien régime, when it seems that men showed a lively concern for the fate of their family. Precisely, in order to understand what Tocqueville means, one has to proceed as he does, that is, to compare the new society with the old. He writes:

> Men who live in aristocratic centuries are therefore almost always bound in a tight manner to something that is placed outside of them, and they are often disposed to forget themselves. It is true that in these same centuries the general notion of those like oneself is obscure and that one scarcely thinks of devoting oneself to the cause of humanity; but one often sacrifices oneself for certain men.
>
> In democratic centuries, on the contrary, when the duties of each individual toward the species are much clearer, devotion toward one man becomes rarer, the bond of human affections is extended and loosened.[2]

Tocqueville does not underestimate our ancestors' attachment to their family; perhaps it was more intense than ours. But it had a different character. Democratic man relates his family to himself, bringing it back to himself; aristocratic man, on the other hand, referred himself to his family, tied himself to it, and in some way forgot himself in it. The vectors of the heart are opposed. But here again one runs the risk of "moralizing" the problem, of saying in effect that we are selfish whereas our fathers were devoted. That is not what Tocqueville means. He writes: "Men who live in aristocratic centuries are therefore almost always bound in a tight manner to something that is placed outside of them, and they are often disposed to forget themselves." The subjective devotion of our fathers answers to an objective situation. They were "bound in a tight manner to something that is placed outside of them." The abstract, almost geometric character of the statement is striking. Tocqueville sketches the structure of the public sphere in ancient society. In this society, the social bond, including and first of all the familial bond, is immediately inscribed in the public sphere as natural. It is immediately perceived as an objective fact outside of the subject, verified and confirmed by the duty of each person to obey his or her social superior. In the family, in society, *people are bound and they have no choice but to be*. What we see first about the social world is the set of bonds in which men find themselves, which define them, and to which they are responsible.

This detour through the old society allows us to better understand the new society and its "individualism." In this society, what all members perceive first is not the objective totality of bonds that join them to each other, but themselves as the only legitimate source of all their bonds, as *subject* with all that is *their own*—family, property, friends. Members of aristocratic societies "are often disposed to forget themselves" because what they see first is the social bond that is situated outside themselves, not because they would be less selfish than we are. Democratic people, on the contrary, rarely devote themselves to another person, not because they might be especially selfish but because what they feel first is their individuality as subjects.

Certainly, even when formulated in these amoral, sociological, or anthropological terms, aristocratic societies seem to be an advantage over democratic ones since aristocracy seems to join people to each other and thus alone to be a true society. But that would be to forget the price paid by aristocratic society. The devotion shown to those to whom one is especially bound—father, lord, king—has as its correlative and condition an indifference to humanity in general because "in these same centuries the general notion of *those like himself* is obscure." We remember what Tocqueville says elsewhere about the weak extent of pity in aristocratic societies. The comparison is thus much more balanced than it seems. In aristocratic societies, self-oblivion ("devotion") and indifference to humanity go hand in hand. In democratic societies, what goes hand in hand is the sentiment of the self (the impossibility of forgetting oneself) and the sentiment of humanity in general, of *those like oneself*.

Such in any case is the nature of democracy according to Tocqueville. When he speaks of the "passions," the "tendencies," the "instincts" of democracy, he has in mind all those social, political, moral aspects that are rooted in individualism, where each man sees himself as the source and reference point of all his bonds. That is, the democratic man relates all the elements of the social world to himself, to his own "interest," and above all, to his consent, to his capacity for identification. It is in this sense that Tocqueville believes democracy is dangerous for man's humanity. Its tendency is to enclose us within ourselves, to have us lose the sense of otherness[3] and thus the capacity and desire to go outside ourselves to encounter what is external to us, what is objective. Tocqueville concludes by affirming that democracy "constantly leads [each man] back toward himself and threatens finally to confine him wholly in the solitude of his own heart."[4]

Accordingly, this "nature" of democracy must be corrected, these "tendencies" moderated, these "instincts" regulated. How? By restoring certain aristocratic elements in democracy? Certain interpreters ascribe this conclusion to Tocqueville, who would be an "aristocratic liberal." I do not believe this to be the case. Democracy is too strong, and its principle too opposed to aristocracy for such a compromise—such a "mixed regime"— to be possible or to endure. How would the personal allegiances that constitute aristocracy survive, caught in the pincers of each person's sentiment of self and sentiment of humanity in general that are the two faces of democracy? In the language of Tocqueville, which aristocracy, as moderated as can be, would resist the "passion for equality" that keeps on growing the more it is satisfied? The dangerous tendencies of democracy can be resisted only by relying on democracy itself.

The general intent of the art of democracy is easy to conceive, since this natural tendency is to enclose each man within himself. What matters is to make man go outside of himself and to make him sense that there are "others." For that, the democratic art will make use of very diverse means. Religion, for example, will help to moderate the instincts of democracy, because the idea of an infinite being or a Creator is to conceive something that is essentially greater than us. This effort in and of itself obliges us to go outside of ourselves. But in their most general expression the means of the democratic art will be those of social and political participation. Tocqueville writes:

> The legislators of America did not believe that, to cure a malady so natural to the social body in democratic times and so fatal, it was enough to accord to the nation as a whole a representation of itself; they thought that, in addition, it was fitting to give political life to each portion of the territory in order to multiply infinitely the occasions for citizens to act together and to make them feel every day that they depend on one another.[5]

And a little further: "Thus by charging citizens with the administration of small affairs, much more than by leaving the government of great ones to them, one interests them in the public good and makes them see the need they constantly have for one another in order to produce it."[6]

In a democratic society, men are irresistibly tempted to forget that they are political animals. They need to be reminded of that, not by speeches but by institutions, by mores that compel them to be free by obliging them to participate together in the management of their affairs. Such is the art of democracy, which the Americans perfected so early.

Certainly, the analyses of Tocqueville form a definitive acquisition of modern political science. Yet, they are specific to the conditions of his principal laboratory, America. The secret of America resides in its way of administering "small affairs" rather than governing "great affairs." In America small matters are always large because of the size and vitality of the country but, inversely, most great matters remain in some fashion small because they are dealt with at the level of the states and not of the federal government. In the European nations, on the contrary, small matters are in general very piddling, but they are almost always closely joined to great matters, or rather the greatest matter, which is national government. Thus, in Europe, democracy is specified by the national context in a way unknown in America. In Europe, and particularly France, the national factor specifies the natural movement of democracy, just as it circumscribes the possibilities of the democratic political art.

In the French Revolution, the moment of nature and the moment of art, so well distinguished by Tocqueville, are in sum combined. When the French detach themselves from the bodies of the ancient régime—the parishes, provinces, domains, corporations, etcetera—they become citizens of the nation. At the same time they are separated from one another, they are attached to the same authority, the nation. And so decomposition and recomposition coincide. Of course, the moment of fusion did not last. It nevertheless had disastrous consequences, which Tocqueville deplored, because the grandeur of the new national idea and its crushing sublimity did not give the new citizens the capacity, or even the desire, to manage their "small affairs" by themselves. But this moment of fusion offered a synthetic truth that Tocqueville's analysis, well founded as it may be, risks concealing. The nation is the political form inhabited by individuals, or conversely, the individual is the one who inhabits the nation. In other words, individualism and nationalism belong to one another, as opposed to the common opinion that makes them contraries.

Nationalism is individualism in the strongest sense of the term. The body politic, the nation, has to assert and deepen its individuality, its particularity. The nation, like the individual, can heed the injunction to "become what you are" and answer it. Hence, there is a kind of affinity between the individual and the particularism of the body politic under the national form. I am not here proposing an abstract, unverifiable thesis. Take, for example, the life story of Maurice Barrès, who went from the "cult of the 'I' " to promoting "nationalism," the cult of the nation. In *Scènes et doctrines du nationalisme* (1902), Barrès himself explained the logic of this development:

> I was an individualist, and I stated my reasons without shame; I preached the development of the personality by a certain discipline of interior meditation and analysis. Having long probed the idea of the "I" by the sole method of the poets and novelists, by introspection I had gone down, down into the sand without resistance, until finding at the bottom and for support the collectivity. . . .
>
> We are not the masters of the thoughts that are born in us. . . . Human reason is chained up in such a way that we all pass through the steps of our predecessors. . . .
>
> Whoever lets himself be penetrated by these certitudes abandons the claim to think better, feel better, will better than his father and mother. He says to himself: "I am they." What consequences he will draw from this awareness! What acceptance! You can see it. It is a vertigo where the individual disappears to find himself again in the family, the race, the nation.[7]

After this digression on the nation, let us return to the twofold movement of democracy that consists of undoing the inherited social bond of inequality and of making a new bond, one that is equal and freely willed. This twofold movement follows a principle of consent that can be formulated as follows: There is no legitimate obligation for me except that to which I have previously consented; there is no legitimate bond except that which I freely entered. The life of democracy is the implementation of this principle. Democracy strives for a state of society in which there would be only free individuals, bound solely by freely contracted bonds. Democracy aims to have its citizens go from a life that one suffers, receives, and inherits to a life that one wills. Democracy makes all relations and all bonds voluntary.

Historically, the principle was first affirmed and institutionalized in the political order of human life. From there it spread more or less quickly in the different domains of social and private life. As Tocqueville states near the end of Volume I of *Democracy in America*, it is a principle that in the end concerns "most human actions." In fact, during the French Revolution, while political consent was being instituted by the national representation, private consent was being implemented by liberating children from all parental control upon adulthood, and by instituting divorce. Things went so far as the suppression of perpetual vows of religion (which seemed to contradict the principle of consent). It was indeed creating a situation so that there would be no action or condition except those freely willed. Despite temporary setbacks (due essentially to the Civil Code of Napoleon), this empire of consent did not cease to spread. Simultaneously, the empire of command did not cease to shrink.

I will use three examples to illustrate these conclusions. In the realm of the family, the law abolished the power and the title of the "head of the family," and parents found it less natural to exact obedience from their children, whom they perceived to be more their equals. On the national level, the democratically elected government no longer dared to order citizen-soldiers to die for the country. If it engages in a military operation entailing some risks, it uses military professionals—who accept as a matter of course encountering "job risks"—and *volunteer* recruits, that is, those who explicitly and specifically consent to take part in the operation. In the religious realm, according to Marcel Gauchet, the principal office leaves the established churches and "passes to individuals." As Gauchet puts it, "the very movement that brings the different spiritual and moral authorities back to center stage on the other hand subjects them to the judgment without concession of consciences that are less disposed than ever to obey them."[8]

One can discuss the significance of this or that phenomenon, but the movement as a whole is beyond doubt. The empire of consent spreads, the process of individualization intensifies, and thus the authority of the communities of different orders in which human beings hitherto found the meaning of their life—the nation, the family, the church—declines more and more each day. The nation is henceforth a community among others and no longer the community par excellence; the family is an optional, uncertain, and recomposed association; the church is the place where one tentatively looks for meaning, no longer where one receives it. The French and Catholic father of a family—the man who was defined by the communities to which he belonged—has become an individual in search of his identity. He can still be the father of a family, a Frenchman, and a Catholic, but these affiliations no longer define him as they once did, even in his own eyes.

Once again, considered in broad terms, the movement is beyond doubt. But precisely because it is beyond doubt, one is almost irresistibly brought to emphasize the specific traits of each of the two phases of the process. On the one hand, one has an old society more "holistic" and "heteronomous" than it could ever have been, and on the other, a new society, more "individualistic" and "autonomous" than it is possible to observe. The sociologists of modernity evoke the old nation, the traditional family and the church of the past, as if membership in these communities could ever have been a simple given in which freedom and consent had no part. As if there were no disobedience or indifference or hostility to national authorities; as if marital infidelity and family disorders were unknown; as if the church, immune to heresies and doubts, was then the sovereign mistress of morals and consciences. These sociologists of modernity describe modern freedom as if we had become incapable of loyalty, promise, and faith, as if devotion to country had disappeared from all hearts, as if close-knit families were henceforth nowhere to be found, as if the virtue of faith and concern for objective truth had given way completely to subjective religious sentiment.

The contrast is too sharp. There is indeed a polarity between community and authority on one side, the individual and freedom on the other. There is indeed an irresistible and multiform movement of long duration from one extreme to the other. At the same time, each pole contains the other, normally subordinated but present and at work, and capable of seizing the upper hand. In the old order, community membership was primary and by right, but it was unthinkable without the mediation of consent, which was generally presupposed. Obedience to the king presupposed an interior movement of allegiance, possibly even an explicit and formal oath. Marriage in Christian Europe had always rested in principle on consent, since consent constituted the very substance of the sacrament of marriage. And to take the most indicative example in this context, when the church took unto itself the right to impose the rule of faith, she still affirmed that the act of faith was valid, "meritorious," only when it was freely and sincerely formed.

In the new democratic order, free personal searching is now a right but it can lead to deep and lasting adherences, whether be it the formation of a couple or participation in a religious or other type of community. One must decidedly enter a bit further into the mechanism of consent and freedom.

Consent presents two important difficulties. The first is well-known, but multifaceted, and must be formulated in an overall fashion. How does consent extend over time? At a given moment, I consent to enter into such and such a political, religious, or familial community, and I accept the obligations its entails. But is this consent sufficient? Is it naturally extended through time? Or must it be renewed at every instant for it to remain valid? And if that is the case, how is it to be renewed?

Everyone sees how modern society is forever seeking compromises between the increasingly imperious legitimacy of present consent, the need to confirm at every instant that consent has indeed been given, and the impossibility of doing that. This is a practical impossibility but it is also a moral one. One is obliged to assume that over a certain period of time consent has indeed been given. For example, a democratic government is assumed to be legitimate when the electorate has cast a majority vote for it and the consent of this electorate is assumed to last until the next scheduled election. In practice, things are more complicated. In certain countries the government can call earlier legislative elections if it deems that the state of opinion is favorable. More importantly today the state of opinion, the degree of consent, is evaluated day after day through the use of polls. The solemn consent, which is confirmed every four, five, or seven years, is more and more enveloped if not replaced by consent that is continually confirmed.

Thus we are witnessing a transformation of temporality. Time is becoming for us what it was for God in Descartes's philosophy, a succession of instants distinct from one another. Just as creation according to Descartes was maintained in being by the divine will exercising itself at every instant of time as a "continuous creation," our institutions, our communities, our couples are maintained in their legitimate being by our will, private or public, which exercises itself and must express itself more and more at every instant of time. It is in this continuous creation of consent that individuals are truly authentic individuals. They become what they are precisely by actively exercising their liberty ever anew, at every instant, by refusing to take on any obligation from the past, even if that past be that of our own choice.

This often renewed liberty that accepts nothing from the past, which at every instant creates itself forever anew, is freedom as Jean-Paul Sartre defines it in his philosophical writings and novels. But it is also the dominant idea of freedom today, the socially active idea that is incessantly transforming morals and sentiments. To what extent can it really be thought or be lived?

The expression of consent necessarily opens a certain *future*, whether that future is determined by an institution or not. Even in our democracies that are governed, as was said, by polls, no one would dream of calling for the resignation of a government not long after an election even if the polls were very unfavorable. The government is still supported by the legitimate impetus of electoral consent. Thus, consent of itself entails a certain duration or *promise*. In fact, it was by the promise that consent was produced in predemocratic societies. But promise ran contrary to modern consent. It was held that one of the most specific and also most noble human traits was the capacity to promise and to keep promises, since in that way our liberty overcomes time and fortune. To renege on one's promise, to break one's oath, was the act of a soul deprived of nobility. The promise par excellence was valid for a lifetime, until death and sometimes beyond death. (Sartre, of course, would say that a promise so conceived is the death of liberty, since there is no guarantee that what one promises at a certain instant one will want to promise at the next. One is no less a slave for being a slave to oneself.) In any case, we are necessarily divided between two ideas of freedom, the modern idea of continuous consent and the ancient idea of promise.

The second great difficulty with consent is linked to the first. Consent is an act, and this act transforms the agent. The person who gives consent is different from what he was before giving consent. In the social and political context, he has become part of a whole. For example, before becoming a member of this political or religious community, or simply before marrying, the agent is if not "a perfect and solitary whole," as Rousseau said,[9] at least a whole unto oneself and in a certain way an equal to the community one wishes to enter. Consenting to enter presupposes the right to refuse consent. In this sense, one is sovereign. But once one has entered, one's condition changes radically. From being a whole unto oneself, one is now part of a whole. How would one remain sovereign after willingly renouncing one's sovereignty?

Therein lies the problem Rousseau explored in *On the Social Contract*. He wrote that in society the individual "remains as free as before," but also that the individual also disappears in the new social body. In any case, consent transforms. One cannot act toward a membership one has entered as if one had not contracted it and had not been transformed by it. The only way to avoid this difficulty is obviously to consent as little as possible. Let's therefore assume that in order to be able to consent later on, to preserve my freedom to consent, I consent as little as possible. In the language of Montaigne, I no longer give myself, I "lend" myself. To remain free, I exercise my freedom as little as possible and I restrict my memberships as much as possible. The dilemma of modern liberty—the dilemma of modern liberty as experienced by the modern individual—could then be roughly formulated in the following way. Either I enter into a community, association, membership, and I transform myself into a part of a whole and lose my liberty, or I do not enter into such a community, association, membership, and I do not exercise my freedom. In brief, this is the dilemma of modern liberty: either I am not free, or I am not free.

Naturally we wish to escape this alternative (we like to be free but we do not like to choose!). And we think that it is now possible that we no longer have to choose between belonging and not belonging. This is the extraordinary promise contained in what is today called "communications." Communications promise us all that community gave us, but without belonging, without the constraints of belonging.

To take a simple example: learning previously implied inclusion in a teaching institution, belonging to a class, the obligation of listening to a professor and note-taking to some extent of what was said. In short, all the constraints of what is called the "school system." The communications society promises us all the benefits of school, and more yet, without its inconveniences and above all without its constraints. The Internet and

CD-Rom allow us to learn without having to belong to an apprenticeship community. Communications allow us at last to be individuals, something we have not been able to be until now. We have been unable to be individuals because we truly needed one another. We needed to form true communities of learning, defense, production, etcetera. What others gave to us, we henceforth obtain from them without needing to have anything in common with them except the technical tools of communication. Even biological reproduction itself no longer requires that a couple come together, however brief the union.

It is difficult of course to judge these phenomena. What I have presented as a promise is a threat in the eyes of some. What is striking in any case is that the modern technologies of communication promise to bring about the condition that the modern political philosophers situated only in a distant past or hypothetical space, the state of nature. The state of nature is the state wherein people are truly free and equal simply because they are independent, *without ties*, the state wherein people are really individuals, "perfect and solitary" wholes. For the modern political philosophers, one had to leave the state of nature and form human ties, simply in order to survive. With modern technical means, particularly in communications, this necessity is suspended or greatly reduced. Technical ties render human ties superfluous. In this sense technology makes it paradoxically possible to remain in the state of nature. It becomes a tantalizing possibility.

There is no doubt that the state of nature haunts modern individualism. In fact, it presents itself in two versions: the rosy optimistic version of communication technology, and the dark, pessimistic version that is offered and explored by a great part of modern literature. From Proust and Céline to the theater of the absurd and the Nouveau Roman, this literature unmasks the imposture of human ties, the lie of love, the inanity or deception of language. In this way it explores what "becoming an individual" means. To become an individual is to confront a world without ties and without true human communication.

In the theater of Ionesco and Beckett, speech has ceased to bind, words have ceased to speak. Thus, whereas modern technology multiplies the means of communication, modern literature explores and sometimes denounces the intrinsic emptiness, even the impossibility of any communication. Such is how we are: endowed with extraordinary means of communication, but doubting the very possibility of communicating.

CHAPTER 11

The Religion of Humanity

I HAVE ATTEMPTED to give a coherent meaning to the common and vague notion of "individualism." I followed Tocqueville's analysis at a time when the word and the concept itself appeared, in the 1820s and 1830s. Tocqueville brought out the specific meaning of the modern democratic individualism (individualism *is* modern and democratic) through a comparison with the dispositions that prevailed in earlier, predemocratic, "aristocratic" societies. In ancient society, people were inclined or led to devote themselves to certain individuals, but they hardly had any sense of humanity in general or of man as man: "the general notion of *those like oneself* was obscure." In democratic societies, on the contrary, what people first perceive of the social world is not the objective; it is they themselves who are the subjects, they who are the legitimate source of consent, along with what belongs to them: property, family, and friends. Simultaneously, this individualist person identifies easily and willingly with another simply because he is human. Thus, in aristocratic society, self-oblivion ("devotion") and indifference to humanity go hand in hand, whereas in democratic society the sentiment of the self (the impossibility of self-oblivion) and the sentiment of humanity, the awareness of those similar to oneself, go hand in hand.

Modern democracy is inseparable from the seemingly self-evident perception that there is something called "humanity." Of course, the idea of humanity, the notion of humankind or the human species is much older than modern democracy. It was fully articulated by Greek philosophy. Precisely in order to define what is properly human, Greek philosophy elaborated the notions of *species* and *genus*. Human beings were political and rational animals. But the division between Greeks and barbarians does not contradict the notion of the unity of the human species. The Greeks did not doubt that the barbarians belonged to the same humanity they belonged to. The barbarians simply did not know how to live freely and to live in cities, so that they were less accomplished human beings than the Greeks. Thus, within the human species whose unity they articulated, the Greeks recognized great qualitative differences or great inequalities. They did so in such a way that they felt the difference almost as strongly as the likeness. This is what leads us to reproach them for having misunderstood the unity of the human species because for us, the homogeneity of humanity has become evident for two centuries albeit with some terrible interruptions. This homogeneity is evident not only intellectually but also affectively and even so to speak sensibly.

What do I mean by evidence? Nothing is harder to define than evidence, since the proper character of evidence is to be perceived immediately, to jump at the eyes, thus to be in no need of definition. Ortega y Gasset provides us an anecdote that strikingly illustrates the character of evidence that the notion of humanity has acquired from a certain time onward:

> The story is told . . . that for the celebrations of Victor Hugo's jubilee a grand reception was organized at the Élysée Palace to which representatives of every nation came to pay their homage. The great poet took his place in the reception hall in a solemn statuesque pose, elbow resting on the marble of a chimney. One after another the nations' delegates came forward from the crowd and presented their homage to the Master. An usher announced them in stentorian voice: "The gentleman representing England," he proclaimed, and Victor Hugo, his eyes in ecstasy, his voice shot through with dramatic tremolos, replied: "England! Ah, Shakespeare!" The usher went on: "The gentleman representing Spain"; Victor Hugo, in the same vein: "Spain! Ah, Cervantes!" "The gentleman representing Germany"; "Germany! Ah, Goethe!" But a short man stepped forward, clumsy, chubby, of rustic bearing, and the usher announced with flair: "The gentleman representing Mesopotamia." Then Victor Hugo, who until that moment had remained impassible and sure of himself, appeared troubled. His suddenly anxious pupils cast a broad look around that seemed to embrace the universe, searching in vain for something out there. But it soon became clear to the spectators that he had found it and that he once again mastered the situation. And with the same pathetic accent, the same conviction, he answered the pudgy representative with these words: "Mesopotamia! Ah, Humanity!"[1]

The word "Mesopotamia" did not evoke for Hugo anything real or definitive, any human *figure*. If he had been a contemporary of Louis XIV, Hugo would have found *nothing* to say. From the nineteenth century on, behind every mention of a human fact, even the most remote and opaque, the notion of humanity or humanity in general is present. It is not by chance that the anecdote concerns Victor Hugo. Of all the poets of his century, he is without doubt the one who has expressed most amply and insistently, almost systematically the idea and sentiment of humanity. In two poems belonging to the cycle of *La Légende des siècles*, entitled "Pleine mer" and "Plein ciel," Hugo shows humanity passing from division to unification, to greater and greater unification. Here, first, is how he evokes the ancient world:

Pas d'unité, divorce et joug; diversité
De langue, de raison, de code, de cité. . . .
L'Adam slave luttait contre l'Adam germain;
Un genre humain en France; un autre genre humain
En Amérique, un autre à Londres, un autre à Rome;
L'homme au-delà d'un pont ne connaissait plus l'homme. . . .
Les rois étaient des tours; les dieux étaient des murs;
Nul moyen de franchir tant d'obstacles obscurs;
Sitôt qu'on voulait croître, on rencontrait la barre
D'une mode sauvage ou d'un dogme barbare;
Et, quant à l'avenir, défense d'aller là.[2]

No unity, divorce and yoke; diversity
Of tongue, reason, code, city. . . .
The Slavic Adam fighting against the Germanic Adam;
One human race in France; another human race
In America, another in London, another in Rome;
A man across a bridge no longer knew the man. . . .
Kings were towers; gods were walls;
No way to cross so many dark obstacles;
As soon as one wished to grow one came up against
A savage way or a barbaric dogma;
As for the future, the way there is forbidden.

This world of separation and obscurity progressively gives way and now
more and more quickly to the new world of communication and clarity.
Hugo now evokes the "vessel" of the new humanity:

Il est la joie; il est la paix; l'humanité
A trouvé son organe immense;
Il vogue, usurpateur sacré, vainqueur béni.
Reculant chaque jour plus loin dans l'infini
Le point sombre où l'homme commence. . . .

Faisant à l'homme avec le ciel une cité,
Une pensée avec toute l'immensité,
Elle abolit les vieilles règles;
Elle abaisse les monts, elle annule les tours; . . .

Elle a cette divine et chaste fonction
De composer là-haut l'unique nation,
À la fois dernière et première,
De promener l'essor dans le rayonnement,
Et de faire planer, ivre de firmament
La liberté dans la lumière.[3]

It is joy; it is peace; humanity
Has found its immense voice;
It sails, sacred usurper, blessed conqueror.
Each day backing further into infinity
The somber point where man begins.

Making with heaven one city for man,
One great immense thought,
It abolishes the old rules;
It abases mountains, sunders towers;

Its divine and chaste task is
To make up above the one and only nation,
Both the last and the first,
To wave the banner in all its radiance
And to make liberty bathe in the light,
High on heaven above.

By letting us experience how the idea of humanity is inseparable from
a feeling of liberation and even a physical sensation of opening, expansion,
and bedazzlement, Hugo helps us to understand what was the irresistible
evidence of humanity when it overtook the Europeans and Americans at
the end of the eighteenth century. His poetic enthusiasm is the expression
and the proof of its religious character.

Assuredly, Hugo's poetic style no longer suits the dominant taste today.
It is easy for us to find it bombastic and ridiculous. At the same time, we
share in the poet's religious or quasi-religious sentiment. In the old order,
the gravest unforgivable crime was sacrilege—the crime against God, or
the things held sacred, which included regicide and parricide. In the new
democratic order, the gravest crime, the crime for which there can be no
statute of limitations, is the crime against humanity.

This recent notion is at the center of many of today's debates, but it is
difficult to define. It is even somewhat impossible to define precisely, to
the extent that any crime against human beings can be said to be a crime
against the humanity of these human beings. Quantitative considerations
are important, but then one senses that something is missing, something
qualitative. André Frossard has proposed a sort of definition: a crime
against humanity occurs when human beings are killed simply because
they were born and not for what they have done or would be susceptible
of doing. This definition covers the Nazis' crimes in what is most specific
to them. It also covers the genocide of Burundi, and more generally tribal
or ethnic massacres. It corresponds less adequately to Stalinist crimes or
to those of the Khmer Rouge.

That there should be no completely satisfactory definition of crime against humanity is a great embarrassment for jurists and for the conduct of certain trials. At the same time this juridical uncertainty is most often accompanied by a moral certitude. Certain crimes appear to us qualitatively different from others, they seem to wound humanity more deeply, more definitively than other crimes. They have a sacrilegious character. They bring out by contrast what one is almost irresistibly led to designate as the "sacred" character of humanity. It was during the French Revolution that we began to speak of crimes of *lèse-humanité*. We can smile at the poetry of Victor Hugo or the philosophy of Auguste Comte, but we too adhere to something like a religion of humanity.

Comte compromised his reputation as a philosopher by attempting to transform this general notion of humanity and this imprecise religiosity into a constituted and organized religion, with its feasts, rites, and calendar. I will not linger on its details, which can indeed make one smile. I would like simply to give an overview of this religion of humanity that in some way is our own, that is the natural religion of modern democratic society.

According to Comte, humanity passes progressively from the theological and military order to the scientific and industrial order, that is, from an order built on separations—the separation between God and human beings, separations between human beings—to an order characterized by unity. The fundamental tendency of humanity is the tendency to unity. (Aron says profoundly that Auguste Comte is the "sociologist of human and social unity.")[4] At the same time, if the movement toward unity is irresistible, unity will not come about automatically or mechanically. It will have to be institutionized and organized, precisely through the organization and institution of the religion of humanity. The specificity of Comte's thought rests in this last idea.

By itself, the idea that humanity tends irresistibly toward unity spread in Europe at the beginning of the eighteenth century and won over nearly everyone in the following century. Marx, for example, considered that once the last separation between people was abolished, the separation between capitalists and workers, humanity would reunite spontaneously. Many liberal economists also already envisaged the progressive unification of the world through commerce. For his part, Comte in no way believed that economic mechanisms could produce the unity of the human species, quite simply because the economic system is only a part of the social whole. Thus, left to itself, it is a separator rather than a unifier.

Today, as many await unification, indeed the pacification of the world through the mechanisms of the market, Comte's critique engages our interest. Comte accepted the modern capitalistic economy with the private ownership of the instruments of production and the concentration of capital that it implies, even though he believed it favored the capitalists to the detriment of the workers. These economic realities were essential to industrial society and could not be eliminated or transformed as the socialists and Communists wished to do. But these realities are not enough to guarantee the harmony of the world as the liberal economists believe. One must correct the economic and social system by supplementing and crowning it, not by a political organization (politics in Comte's eyes is either archaic or anarchic), but by a new religion, acceptable to modern minds trained in scientific methods. The industrial and financial power will then be corrected by the "spiritual power" of scientists, women, and workers; selfishness will have to be corrected and completed by altruism. Human unity, in order to exist, will have to be willed for its own sake; it will have to be the object of knowledge and feelings. To exist, it will have to be loved: "One tires of acting and even of thinking; one never tires of loving." This explains the central role of women in the "positive" society that is the culmination of human history.

One can smile, here again, at this society held together by the affectionate force of the feminine heart. But at least Comte raises the problem that we most often fail to raise: what can bind people once obedience has lost its power and interest deals only with self-interest? Positive religion was discredited as the invention of a sociologist and in its modalities as a faint copy of Catholicism—thus incapable of satisfying either religious or rationalist minds. Yet, Comte's religion fulfills and is defined by a social function. Can a society endure and prosper without this function of "religion" being fulfilled? Once again, what is it that binds people when they cease to obey and interest keeps them apart as much as it brings them together?

In this brief discussion of Auguste Comte, I have chiefly insisted on the unity of humanity that is the heart and so to speak the whole of his religion. Now, let us suppose Comte's hopes are achieved. Certainly the new humanity will present enviable traits if altruism effectively corrects its selfishness! But precisely because it will be satisfying and satisfied, this new humanity will no longer have any principle of movement. Human action in fact has two moving forces: the flight from evil and the desire for good. There will be no reason for any flight from evil to the extent that the evils of society will have been healed by altruism. The desire for good will be necessarily lukewarm since it will already be essentially satisfied and this reunited and reconciled humanity looks to no greater good than itself. It will be a humanity closed onto itself that is a prey to an immense or sublime selfishness. Could there not be in effect, besides the selfishness of the individual and of the group, something like the selfishness of humanity taken together and as a whole? That is the conviction of Friedrich Nietzsche, the great modern critic of altruism and humanitarianism.

Nietzsche had great respect for Comte, that "great honest Frenchman," but he considered that he "did in fact with his famous moral formula *vivre pour autrui*, outchristian Christianity."[5] This was by no means a compliment. The religion of humanity is Christianity and specifically Catholicism, with all the vices Nietzsche sees in it, but without the greatness of a belief in God entails, that is, in a being *greater* than humanity. Nietzsche's critique is expressed in most of his works. Particularly, in *Thus Spoke Zarathustra*, there is an impressive passage about "the Last Man." Zarathustra has just announced the Overman to the crowd. The audience laughs or jeers. Then, as a last resort to gain their attention, Zarathustra wants to offend them, provoke them to finally awaken their pride by means of disdain: "Let me speak to them of what is most contemptible: but that is the last man."[6] But before speaking of the Last Man, he tells them of the urgency in which man lives today: "The time has come for man to set himself a goal." What is proper for man is to set a goal, a goal beyond man and the human. Thus man should look up to the Overman (this idea is not a whim of Nietzsche, it is as old as the heroic and "erotic" conception of humanity). Yet, Zarathustra remarks, man is less and less capable of this overcoming and is more and more the Last Man. Zarathustra speaks to the crowd in these terms: " 'Behold, I show you the last man.' 'What is love? What is creation? What is longing? What is a star?' thus asks the last man, and he blinks."

Thus, the Last Man no longer knows the meaning of the verbs to love, to create, or to long for, verbs that express transcendence of the self. Zarathustra goes on: " 'The earth has become small, and on it hops the last men, who makes everything small . . . the last man lives longest.' 'We have invented happiness,' say the last men, and they blink."

Nietzsche has just mentioned twice how the Last Men "blink." I do not wish to discuss this verb at any great length.[7] This blinking in any case indicates complicity. The Last Men express and confirm their agreement without needing to make it any more explicit beyond the observation: "We have invented happiness." This happiness does not need to be articulated; it is a satisfaction with oneself that is enough to indicate or signify. To blink is to share a secret and to conceal it from others. Who can be excluded from their complicity when the Last Men have become the sole inhabitants of the earth, multiplying and triumphing? Possibly they themselves can be, inasmuch as they could still have "superhuman" hopes and desires . . .

Zarathustra goes on:

> "They have left the regions where it was hard to live, for one needs warmth. One still loves one's neighbor and rubs against him, for one needs warmth.
>
> "Becoming sick and harboring suspicion are sinful to them. . . . A little poison now and then: that makes for agreeable dreams. And much poison in the end, for an agreeable death.

"One still works, for work is a form of entertainment. But one is careful lest the entertainment be too harrowing."

Nietzsche describes a happiness that is almost perfect and at the same time perfectly sinister. The Last Men have as their only concern to maintain themselves by all available means, even the most artificial, in a state of subjective contentment. Reality normally appears to us, as I have said, under the form of an evil that we must confront or under the form of a good that we desire to obtain. The Last Men ignore these two modalities of relating to reality. They want to ignore reality. Zarathustra says further:

" 'Formerly all the world was mad,' say the most refined, and they blink.
"One is clever and knows everything that has ever happened: so there is no end of derision. One still quarrels, but one is soon reconciled—else it might spoil the digestion.
"One has one's little pleasure for the day and one's little pleasure for the night: but one has a regard for health.
'We have invented happiness,' say the last men, and they blink."

"Formerly all the world was mad," say the most refined. The most refined are the scholars, the intellectuals, the professors. . . . "Formerly all the world was mad" means that men formerly believed in something, in gods, or heroes, and they made war against one another, they troubled their digestion for the sake of things they did not understand. Again they "blink." They know well that there is nothing outside them, neither gods nor heroes, and that above all they must not try to transcend themselves, they must resist every temptation to transcend themselves, they must rest content with themselves.

"Formerly all the world was mad," this familiar formula, sums up the attitude proper to modern man, the attitude that elsewhere, in a more noble and philosophical style, Nietzsche names the "historical perspective." The "historical perspective" sums up the disposition of modern humanity. The modern generations willingly look behind them, they willingly look at the Roman roads, the cathedrals, the palaces, they willingly admire these works, but it is for them an occasion to observe that they are strangers to the motives that produced these works—faith in God, the desire for glory—that they hold these motives to be founded on illusions. In short, these great works are admirable undoubtedly but in the end absurd.

The modern generations—this is the mechanism Nietzsche points out here—, instead of experiencing the desire to imitate the great undertakings of the past, the desire to "create," are happy and relieved—they "blink"—happy and relieved at not having to transcend themselves. They "blink" because they experience a feeling of superiority over all previous generations. Nietzsche discerns that the principle of scientific superiority of modern man, which is, once again, the "historical perspective," produces the flattest disposition of the soul, that of the tourist. The effectual truth of the modern religion of humanity is tourism.

Comte and Nietzsche, different as they are, strive to describe the same moment when humanity becomes conscious of itself as a developing whole, unfolding in history. Instead of depending on God or nature, man now depends only on himself to the extent that everything that happens to him necessarily takes its place in the "fundamental series of the diverse human events."[8] Where Comte sees the conditions of a new piety, a piety that is at last rational and human, in particular through the cult of great men,[9] Nietzsche sees the conditions of an ultimate degradation, the historical perspective making it such that the present generation, the latest generation, simply because it is the latest, looks at those that preceded it while experiencing a feeling of radical superiority that sterilizes it and prevents it from creating anything in its turn. It is not a question of choosing between Comte and Nietzsche but of attempting to grasp a phenomenon that we no longer perceive because it has become an evidence, or rather an essential part of our self-awareness (the people of the nineteenth century perceived it with much intensity because it was unfolding for the first time under their eyes). What is this phenomenon? Precisely this gathering of humanity in a unified consciousness, a consciousness of unity that allows us to say and obliges us to say: we, we the human beings . . .

Thus, just when today's humanity seeks and is proud to exclude nothing of what is currently human, it excludes its whole past, all past generations. At the very moment when it embraces itself wholly, it ceases to comprehend itself.

There is nonetheless one point on which Comte and Nietzsche are in agreement, even though they interpret it differently. It is the essentially contemplative or passive character of this new consciousness of humanity. With Comte, the love that women bear more particularly, the admiration and veneration for great men, are sentiments that are more conservative than active. The humanity of the positive age will be more and more an object of worship, the object of contemplation more than the subject of action. Whence Comte's famous phrases that "Humanity is made up of more dead than living" and "the dead govern the living more and more."

According to Nietzsche, we are dominated by the historical perspective, which is a passive or contemplative perspective. Thus, apart from the technical progress aimed at improving our comfort, more profoundly at mastering nature and thus rendering us independent of all that is not human, apart from the technical progress aimed at creating a world that is through and through human and nothing but human—a world where everything is predictable—modern humanity is not very enterprising. It is already altogether and wholly human in its own eyes. To be human is a fact to note and even to celebrate, more than a task to accomplish.

CHAPTER 12

The Body and the Political Order

THE IDEA of "nature" when applied to human beings, that is, "human nature," is today completely discredited. It sums up all the subjections and inequalities from which democracy now has striven to liberate us for two centuries. Let us take the clearest example, the notion of "female nature." It is immediately related to a whole group of notions that are held together precisely by the idea of nature: the symmetrical notion of "male nature," that of the "natural complementarity" between man and woman, of the "couple" that they form "naturally," and in which the man is "naturally" the "head of the family." This representation of the relation between the sexes has been discredited and its legislative expression abolished. It seems clear that the foundation of this "structure of domination," or rather unequal association, resided in the idea of nature. This idea sums up all the obstacles encountered by the democratic desire, the desire for liberty and equality. This desire, it seems, can be affirmed and satisfied only against the idea of "human nature." In the matter that concerns us here, it can be affirmed and satisfied only after recognizing that, as Simone de Beauvoir writes in *The Second Sex*, "One is not born a woman, one becomes a woman." To put it in our current abstract language: female identity is not a fact of nature, but a fact of culture, a cultural construct.

The challenge to the natural character of the difference between the sexes is evident to many because it converges with the well-established democratic challenge and rejection of the inequalities traditionally conceived as natural: between races and peoples, between parents and children, between the individual considered as normal and the handicapped, or "mad" or otherwise "different." The spirit of contemporary democracy is familiar to us; it is the very air we breathe. Thus to affirm natural differences is to refuse to see the essential resemblance among human beings; it is to be viciously blind and unfaithful to the "notion of those like oneself" that Tocqueville sees as the heart of democratic self-consciousness.

The idea of nature consigned without remorse to a past of obscurantism and inequality would be settled if democracy and equality did not first assert themselves *in the name of nature*. The eighteenth century saw the idea of natural equality among men assert itself, against inherited conventional social inequality. As Figaro puts it in Beaumarchais's play, *Le Mariage de Figaro*, the count thinks he is a great genius because he is a great lord.

This natural equality is the very principle that grounds the Declaration of the Rights of Man: "Men are born and remain free and equal in rights." One is *born* human, with rights that necessarily flow from our belonging to the human species and thus with *natural rights*. One sees that "our fathers of '89," to speak like Tocqueville, could not have affirmed this equality if they had not drawn it from the realm of "nature." Imagine that they had said, in the manner of Simone de Beauvoir, "one is not born a human being, one becomes a human being." Then, the world of inequality would have been preserved, even reinforced. That would have been to say that, in order to be a human being, one must become one, by receiving education that cannot be complete and finished except for a small number of people, the aristocrats. The situation is thus more complex than it first appeared. Equality and democracy entered the world in the name of nature. Democracy and equality, in the meantime, have turned against nature, their chief enemy being the idea of nature applied to human beings, in other words, human nature. How did this reversal come about?

One has to return to the birth of the notion of nature, which came with the birth of philosophy. Nature is the very discovery of philosophy, when philosophy arose in ancient Greece. More precisely, philosophy distinguished between *phusis* and *nomos*, *phusis* being "nature" and *nomos* being ordinarily "law" or "convention," with the preference given to nature. *Nomos* is the changing rules that men or gods set. *Phusis*, nature, is what does not change, that over which neither men nor gods have any power, which cannot be modified, only understood, and which provides the ultimate intelligibility to the world. Before the discovery of nature, people believed the world was the way it was because someone did something—because Theseus chased the bandits out of Attica, or because the gods willed it so, or because of sacred custom our ancestors have passed on to us. After the discovery of nature, people understood that the universe exists the way it does because the nature of things, and of man in particular, is necessarily so. Instead of saying simply that the city of Athens was founded by Theseus who chased the bandits out of Attica, one will say that man is a political animal, an animal that naturally lives in a city. Athens is such a city with or without Theseus. A city has some fixed, essential traits that one can come to *know*. The second explanation is intrinsically superior to the first because of its universal application. It alone is scientific.

Of course, this presentation leaves aside the specific circumstances of the birth of philosophy, in this particular case, of political philosophy. Recently historians have underscored that the development of political philosophy is intimately linked to the development of civic life, in particular of democratic civic life. In order for Socrates to spend his life questioning whoever came along in the public square, there must first be a public square and the right to speak just like that to whoever comes along. The complicity of the birth of democracy of the Greek city and philosophy is most striking in the famous definition proposed by Aristotle: human beings are political animals. That means that human beings are naturally made to live in a city; they are not completely fulfilled unless they lead a civic life, unless they are citizens. In the eyes of philosophy, the human phenomenon first manifests itself in *political* life.

The relation between philosophy and the city is not only one of solidarity and complicity, but also one of tension and even hostility. Socrates was put to death by the city; Aristotle had to leave Athens. The philosopher is not a citizen of a particular city, Athens, Sparta, or Thebes, but a "citizen of the world," whereas the city as city is always particular, different from the others. The philosopher as philosopher is concerned only with the universal, and what is valid for all human beings in all cities. For the good of the city as well as philosophy, this tension needs to be reduced. Precisely, Aristotle's definition sums up the most generous effort made to reduce the tension. If human beings are political animals and the city is natural to human beings, then they fulfill their humanity and thus their universal calling by being citizens of *this particular* city. Thus the language of human nature, so shocking to us, is what allows Aristotle to find the universal in civic life.

Why then have we rejected the language and ideas of Aristotle? It is because the nature of which Aristotle speaks is intrinsically contradictory in our eyes, for, although it conditions and legitimates equality between citizens, at the same time it conditions and legitimates inequality between citizens and noncitizens, namely women, children, slaves, and resident aliens. The effect is to conceal the contradiction between civic equality and social and familial inequality.

For Aristotle not only the city is natural but associations, the diverse bonds among people that are willed by nature, are natural as well. More precisely, the city is the most perfect community, that encompasses and crowns the other numerous human communities; Aristotle's starting point is that humans always belong to a community. The first community, the original, is the family, the *oikia*. The *oikia*, which could also mean "house" or "household," is in fact the convergence of three relations, three separate and unequal bonds, all joined in the person of the head of the family. This head, the *despotes*, has a wife, children, and slaves. These three relations are unequal, but also unequally equal.

According to Aristotle they are all three founded in nature, meaning they are essentially just and in keeping with the interest of the two parties. The children obey their father, the slaves their master, but this obedience is in their interest because children need to be educated and slaves guided. (This concerns only "slaves by nature," who have enough reason to follow the master's reason but not enough to govern themselves.) The wife also obeys her husband in her own interest, but she is not comparable to the slave by nature. To the Greeks, equating women to slaves is characteristic of the Barbarians. A woman is a rational being like a man, but Aristotle believed her reason simply had generally less force than the man's.[1] (I note that Aristotle's thesis under one form or another was almost universally accepted in Europe by men and women until relatively recently.) Such is in any case the first human community, which is thus natural, that is to say both necessary and good but which ignores equality and liberty. Equality and liberty can only prevail outside the family, outside the "house." They can only unfold and prevail in the public space of the city. And the only ones who are equal and free, the only ones who are citizens, are the heads of families who, going out of their house, come into the public square to deliberate upon public affairs.

Such is the Greek city and Greek democracy sketched in light of Aristotle's analysis. Our feelings about it are very ambivalent and even contradictory. It is repugnant to us, not only because of the servitude of slaves and the subjugation of women, but also because it affirms that such servitude and subjugation are natural and hence just and good for slaves and women. The whole effort of early modern political philosophy was to refute these propositions, to radically challenge the natural character of the servitude of slaves and subjugation of women, to maintain that children are only held to obey their parents in the strict measure that this obedience is necessary for their education. Where Aristotle affirmed the natural character of the different bonds among human beings, Hobbes, Locke, and Rousseau affirmed the natural character of independence, that is, of the absence of bonds. For Aristotle, human beings are born bound; for the moderns, they are born unbound. For Aristotle, human beings are born in the *oikia*, the "household"; for the moderns, they are born in the "state of nature," where they are free and equal. These radical oppositions are the ground of our rejection of the Greek city and Greek philosophy of nature, for being unequal and justifying inequality.

At the same time, the most ardent democrats among the moderns did not cease to admire in Greek life the most accomplished image of civic life. In chapter 15 of Book III of *The Social Contract*, Rousseau makes an extraordinary panegyric of the Greek city. Among contemporary authors, Hannah Arendt has contributed greatly to reviving the political credit of Greece. She has in particular attempted to rediscover the authentic human meaning of what is so shocking to us in Greek life, the contrast between the free order of the city and the "despotic" order of the family. The *oikia* is the locus of the absence of liberty, of constraint and inequality because

it is the place of the necessity of maintaining life and the vital processes—
nutrition and reproduction. There can only be liberty outside the place of
necessities, outside the "household." This is what Hannah Arendt explains
in *The Human Condition*:

> The distinctive trait of the household sphere was that in it men lived to-
> gether because they were driven by their wants and needs. The driving force
> was life itself . . . which, for its individual maintenance and its survival as the
> life of the species needs the company of others. That individual maintenance
> should be the task of the man and species survival the task of the woman was
> obvious, and both of them were natural functions, the labor of the man to
> provide nourishment and the labor of the woman in giving birth, were subject
> to the same urgency of life. Natural community in the household therefore
> was born of necessity, and necessity ruled over all activities performed in it.
>
> The realm of the *polis*, on the contrary, was the sphere of freedom, and if
> there was a relationship between these two spheres, it was a matter of course
> that the mastering of the necessities of life in the household was the condition
> for freedom of the *polis*.[2]

And a little further:

> The polis was distinguished from the household in that it knew only
> "equals," whereas the household was the center of the strictest inequality. To
> be free meant both not to be subject to the necessity of life or to the command
> of another. . . . Thus within the realm of the household, freedom did not exist,
> for the household head, its ruler, was considered to be free only in so far as he
> had the power to leave the household and enter the political realm, where all
> were equals. To be sure, this equality of the political realm has very little in
> common with our concept of equality . . .[3]

Hannah Arendt's analysis has fascinated and perplexed many readers.
If the rigorous separation between the private inequality of the family and
the public equality of the city is the condition of political liberty, and thus
of a truly human life, Arendt ought to recommend the reestablishment of
the *oikia*, including no doubt the subordination of women and slavery. Of
course, she does not do this.

Our perplexity corresponds to the duality of the Greek city, which joins
extreme inequality and extreme equality. This duality derives from the
division between the order of the family and the order of citizenship,
which itself derives, between the order and logic of the body and soul.
What is curious is that after the Greek cities and the Roman republic,
these two logics are never again joined together, but unfold successively.
The history of Europe, or of the West, was in fact first the unfolding of
the logic of the body and the family, then of the logic of the soul and
citizenship. To understand the specificity of the present situation, one

ought to reconstitute its genesis, so that we understand that our democracy seeks to institute a political and thus a human order that is free of all "incorporation," as Claude Lefort says, a political and human order that is purely "spiritual." This idea conflicts with appearances: doesn't our society give a large place to the body and hardly any place to the soul? In reality, our society is the one in Western history that most systematically reduces the role of the body.

How can one characterize the predemocratic order: as feudal anarchy? As the inequality of orders? As the power of kings? As the empire of religion? As a combination of all these? But then in what proportion? The only way to define it with a global trait that sums up its essence is to define it as an order of *filiation*. Each person's place in society is determined by birth; one's name and property are acquired by inheritance. There are in sum only families, rich or poor, common or noble, but each governed by the head of the family. By contrast, in the ancient city family heads participate equally as citizens in the same public space. But in premodern Europe there is no public space; family heads are unequal. Instead, they constitute a chain, rising from peasant to king, as Tocqueville says.

What one ought to say is that the public sphere is based on the familial analogy, the logic of filiation and paternity, the most basic human bond, which circulates throughout the whole body politic. The poorest father of a family is king in his family, the surliest king is in principle the father of his people. Finally, what is public is the sacred person, the body of the king. The family is of course rooted in bodies, in both the general causality but also in the contingent particularity of bodies. The analogical logic of this association of families culminates in the king's sacred body that in France, heals the sick, and in France and elsewhere, provides and perpetuates the monarchy by begetting a successor. The king's body, whose fruitfulness preserves the body politic, is the heart of the body politic.

This order of incorporation seems today bizarre, barbaric, and painfully physical. One must, of course, be mindful also of the religious factor as well, given that the person and body of the king are seen as a Christlike figure. This question has been carefully studied by Ernst Kantorowicz. As I said, the modern viewpoint sees this logic as a bizarre and barbaric order. Or if we are sophisticated, we say simply that it was the cultural system of our ancient fathers, but other systems exist. Our system is altogether different, our grandchildren's will be different in yet another way, and so turns the kaleidoscope of cultures. In fact, this order of incorporation is not simply a "cultural construction." It draws its force and its quasi-universal resonance from being rooted in *nature*, that is, in the reality of begetting and of filiation. Even in our altogether different democratic order, radically opposed to this order of filiation, one still observes a lively interest in genealogies.

The logic of incorporation has another, different but important aspect to it: the expression "body politic" was for a long time used in Europe as a generic term to designate political organizations, such as cities, princi-palities, and kingdoms. This usage has been deliberately rejected, and as a consequence it has almost completely disappeared. The term "body" implies an "organicist" or "holistic" vision of political association in which the individual with his rights would be subordinated to the collectivity or "whole." In reality the notion of "body" should be distinguished from that of "organism." When one says "body politic," one can think "political organism," implying the functional subordination of the part to the whole. *Organon* originally meant "instrument," and in an "organism" the part can be said to be an "instrument" of the whole. It is thus perfectly legiti-mate to reject this representation of social existence and political life. But a body is more than an organism. In a body, the whole is present in each part; the same life animates each part because it animates the whole. This is the most significant aspect of the notion, much more than potential sub-ordination among the parts or of the parts to the whole. Thus the idea of the "body" applied to political communities is not a mechanical and crude idea. On the contrary, it is a complex and spiritual idea. It underscores the notion that, in a political community, each element is both itself and the whole. In this sense, every political community is a body of sorts: whether composed of unequal subjects or equal citizens, each member lives within it both its own life and the life of the community.

Thus we understand and can measure the force of the order of incorpo-ration that joins and mutually reinforces the physical idea of the body that begets and the spiritual idea of the body as the presence and life of the whole in each part. Nevertheless this order of incorporation has been delib-erately destroyed. Lefort formulates well the meaning as well as the enor-mity of this process:

> The *ancien régime* was made up of an infinite number of small bodies which gave individuals their distinctive marks. And these small bodies fitted together within a great imaginary body for which the body of the king provided the model and the guarantee of its integrity. The democratic revolution, for so long subterranean, burst out when the body of the king was destroyed, when the body politic was decapitated and when, at the same time, the corporeality of the social was dissolved. There then occurred what I would call a "disincor-poration" of individuals. This was an extraordinary phenomenon. . . .[4]

Why is it an "extraordinary phenomenon"? Because it has inverted the social logic. While earlier society organized itself to bind its members and was intended to represent and consolidate the social bond, our democratic society organizes itself to unbind its members and to guarantee their independence and their rights. In one sense our society wants to be a dis-society.

Earlier society, bizarre and barbaric to us, was summed up and made visible and tangible in the king's body. What would sum up in the same or a like way our society and its extraordinary or paradoxical character of dis-society? It would be the notion of the *state of nature*, a representation that is just as abstract, ideal, and invisible as the king's body was concrete, tangible, and visible. This notion was first elaborated by the philosophers, then forgotten by them. But it has penetrated our society more and more deeply in its diverse aspects and components. It is familiar to us. It is found in Hobbes, Locke, and Rousseau, the three great theoreticians of the state of nature. But it is not taken seriously. Or we see it from only a "historical perspective," as an idea that had some importance in a certain political and social context in the seventeenth and eighteenth centuries. Indeed, how can we be interested in the individual in the state of nature as Rousseau describes, eating acorns and quenching his thirst at the first stream? This animal nonetheless interests us since ultimately this individual is each one of us; he is what we want to be.

To put it in a nutshell, the state of nature is defined as a state of independence, liberty, and equality. We want to live independent, free, and equal. In this sense, the state of nature forms our horizon. The very term "nature" repels us. But we here fall victim to a kind of official illusion. When we believe we need not entertain the idea of "human nature," and believe this notion to be an impediment to our liberty, it is simply we have now formed an idea of our nature that is very different from that prevalent in predemocratic times, when it ruled supreme.

In the predemocratic order of incorporation, nature is the whole or rather what makes it so that there is a whole. In brief, it is what binds, produces, gives birth, or begets. It is rooted in and finds its model in the fruitful body. It resides more in the relation, in the bond rather than in the individuals it connects. To be a father, for example, to be in the relation of paternity, was then incomparably more important than to be *any* particular father. Our understanding of nature is today the inverse. Nature no longer resides for us in the relation; it resides wholly in each individual inasmuch as the individual is independent of others. That is why our philosophers spoke of a *state* of nature, the only way to designate a situation where there are only individuals, natural beings without natural relations. It is the individual that matters and no longer the relation. To be *this* particular father is henceforth incomparably more important than to be a father, more important than to be a part of the relation of paternity. Thus his children will call *this* particular father no longer by the name "father," which bespeaks the relation, but by his first name, which bespeaks his individuality.

Of course in our society there are also relations among individuals, bonds are forged, couples and families formed . . . but these bonds, must at every instant be willed and bound anew. As soon as we consider them as natural, they alienate our liberty, and thus our true nature as individuals. Our bonds are only consistent with our nature of independent individuals if they are continually created by our continued consent. This aspect of contemporary morality is a Sartrean liberty, which is the enemy of any human nature and which presupposes a state of nature in which at every instant the individual must be ready to begin life over again. The dilemma before which our liberty finds itself is thus: either I enter into a community, an association, a relation, a bond, and I transform myself into a part of a whole, I "naturalize" myself by "incorporating" myself, and I lose my liberty; or else I resist all association, all relation, all bond, and I do not exercise my liberty. The very idea that we have our liberty and our individuality thus places us before a potentially paralyzing dilemma.

At the same time our society, no more than those that preceded it, does not go all the way with the tendencies that characterize it. It is not dissociated, has not become a dis-society. The fear of decomposition has indeed haunted it since the democratic movement took hold of it, as Claude Lefort writes. If this fear is groundless, it is because its continuous decomposition has been accompanied by a continuous recomposition. But what is its new unifying principle since it is no longer incorporation? It is *representation*. The order of representation has succeeded the order of incorporation. This notion is familiar to us. Nearly all the peoples of Europe and America and numerous peoples of Asia live under representative governments. Since the end of the eighteenth century, this political organization seems to us the only one that is truly rational and in conformity with human rights. We know well that it has its difficulties, that sometimes we feel badly represented, but in the end, it remains not only the most satisfactory, but the only conceivable political arrangement. At the same time, it has something deeply mysterious in it.

Rousseau sensed the difficulty the most. He was radically, absolutely, almost violently hostile to the idea of political representation no matter what form it might take. His principal argument is very simple: "the will cannot be represented. Either it is itself or it is something else; there is no middle ground."[5] Rousseau's statement draws our attention to the bizarre character of the representative principle. The will of the members of society produces a new political bond, making it valid through the election process. But where is this will located? Either it is still in the members of society, and the new political bond is not yet created; or it is no longer in them but has passed into the new body politic, the political institutions, and so no longer the will of the members of society. Would one have to think that the will of the members of society in some way continuously creates the body politic as God continuously creates the world in the philosophy of Descartes? The representative principle, taken in its root, consists in wanting to produce the political bond, more generally the social and human bond, by the will alone, or from the soul alone. Our time is perhaps not very religious, but in the political and social order it is very "spiritualist." We want all our bonds, even corporeal ones, to have their origin, their cause, and their duration in a decision that is purely and sovereignly spiritual. In the political, social, and moral order, we want to be angels.

This paradox is striking. We spontaneously think that predemocratic societies gave a crushing advantage to the soul in relation to the body, that the soul crushed the body. Likewise, our societies have "rehabilitated" the body—or the "flesh," as the Saint-Simonians said—through rejecting the abusive pretensions of the soul. This is indeed true in a certain sense. But the contrary is also true. Earlier societies were societies of incorporation, rooting all bonds in the fruitfulness of the body, coming together and culminating in the king's body. They appear to us unbearably corporeal and thus barbaric.

On the contrary, our societies are those of representation and consent, where bonds are begotten by the soul alone. We go so far that we reject even the idea that the body can create bonds, or that there are bonds that are corporeal or essentially rooted in bodies. Whence the dilution or the blurring of paternity and maternity in contemporary families. Whence the fact that what was formerly called "carnal commerce" and what the English, following the Bible, called "carnal knowledge," no longer creates any bond by itself, no longer has an intrinsic meaning. It has meaning and is a bond only to the extent that the will gives it this meaning or consents to the bond. The will is obviously free to confer or withdraw the bond's validity, precisely at will. We lead our lives, would like to lead our lives, as angels that by chance have a body, and that we would be free to leave it aside and take it up again at will.

In concluding I return to politics. "Disincorporation" produces a society and lives within this society that is affected by a disturbing uncertainty, an indetermination that is both exhilarating and harrowing. Claude Lefort is the contemporary author who has best analyzed this aspect of our democracies:

> The modern democratic revolution is best recognized in this mutation: there is no power linked to a body. Power appears as an empty place and those who exercise it as mere mortals who occupy it only temporarily . . . There is no law that can be fixed, whose articles cannot be contested, and whose foundations

are not susceptible of being called into question. Lastly, there is no representation of a centre and of the contours of society . . . Democracy inaugurates the
experience of an ungraspable, uncontrollable society in which the people will
be said to be sovereign, of course, but whose identity will constantly be open
to question, whose identity will remain latent."[6]

Instead of the king's body—too tangible, too carnal in our spiritualist
eyes—we have the empty, abstract place of power, provisionally occupied
by human beings, our "representatives," but in reality by our will, by the
sovereign and elusive will of the members of society—an exhilarating situation, with an inebriating feeling of liberty, but also a harrowing situation
that nurtures dreams, or phantasms of reincorporation.

CHAPTER 13

Sexual Division and Democracy

I HAVE ATTEMPTED to contrast modern democratic society, founded on representation, and ancient society, founded on "incorporation" and the analogy of the body. What is today called the "social imaginary" is the way in which each society represents to itself its own beginning. As we have seen, in its own eyes, democratic society begets itself *spiritually*. It begets itself by the effect of the will of the members of society who, in voting, produce the "national representation." Ancient society was begotten *corporeally*, according to the fruitfulness of bodies; or it was begotten by fathers—fathers of families, the king the father of his peoples, God the father of all men, according to the analogy of the body. I underscored that compared to the ancient society our society has an "angelic" character since it does not want to admit into its essential composition anything that has to do with the body or with "blood" or "birth." (Of course, one has the right to vote—one is authorized to be an angel—if one has the nationality of a given country. However, even nationality largely depends on birth—the terms "nation" and "native" have the same root, but even this dependence tends to be loosened more and more.)

It will be said that the idea of a pure representation, founded on a pure general will, arises less from the imaginary *producer* of our society than from a political and social *convention*. But the pure general will is only the impure result of a great number of individual and collective wills, rooted in social needs and social and political passions. In short, the members of the modern society know well that they are not angels. That much is certain. At the same time, the fact remains that these wills—the wills of the voters—are, because they will themselves to be, essentially equal wills, and that consequently there are in society no essential differences, no differences of "order."

The general will, if it is convention, is an efficacious one. The society that it produces is an essentially homogeneous whole. As different as they may be by their incomes, their professions, or any other criteria maybe, the members of the modern democratic society define themselves as citizen-voters by their right to make their will weigh equally with every other citizen-voter. Whence the great discovery of Tocqueville is the power of the idea of the equality of *those like oneself* in a democratic society. The idea of those like oneself will progressively join and mix kings and subjects, masters and servants, parents and children. But under the rule of equality and likeness, under the rule of equal wills, what happens to the difference between man and woman, which is as fundamental as those which I have just mentioned and which seemed to be the *natural* difference par excellence? What happens to sexual difference in the society of individuals?

I shall begin by recalling the traditional understanding of the couple by which humanity has lived through the greater part of its history and which continues to rule today over vast cultural areas. I shall then consider the individualist critique of the traditional conception that is at the foundation of the contemporary sexual order. Finally, I shall study the way in which Rousseau's *Émile* imagines a perfectly united couple beginning with two perfectly free individuals. Not that Rousseau's theses are convincing on every point, but he is the one author who has studied the problem of sexual difference with the greatest care in modern or perhaps of all times. In other words, no one has looked at women with such intelligent attention as Rousseau.

One must attempt to understand the traditional sexual order not in order to sympathize with it, but to grasp its logic, which is a political logic. Moreover, this traditional political logic is perhaps nowhere more visible than in the way it governs the sexual order, the way it strives to bend sexual life to its laws. This logic is a logic of command. Every member of society is a commander or one who is commanded; in fact, generally, one is both commanded by a person and commander of another. If this notion of command has a military tone, let us say that every member of society is governing or governed, in general one and the other: governed by this person, governor of that one. No one is free in the sense that we speak of a "free" election. Everyone belongs to one or more communities, organized according to this relation of command or government. Whether done well or badly, the members of society are always necessarily governed. In practice it is the fathers, the "family heads," who govern. No important thing can escape the government of the fathers, when the most important matter, the marriage of children, depends very strictly on the will or consent of the fathers. The marriage of children is thus in principle decided by the father (in accord or not with the mother), not because he is necessarily tyrannical, but because he is responsible, in the eyes of all, for all the important decisions in his family. Of course the will of the father is *naturally* felt as tyrannical by the children, who in turn employ all the ruses by which one can dupe or circumvent a tyrant, so amply shown in the tradition of the Roman comedies and in many of Molière's comedies.

Additionally, in this type of society, marriage is not so much the union of two individuals as of two families. Once again, the basic unit is not the individual but the family. Since the individual is considered above all a member or representative of the family, it is natural that the union of two families should be decided by the heads of families. Such is the logic that rules the traditional familial order.

Of course, such an order gives little place to the sentiment and the desires of the heart. This sacrifice was recognized and accepted as a necessity, even a fortunate necessity. Nothing solid, people believed, can be built on passion, feeling, taste, which are fleeting, deceptive, and disappointing. Nothing solid can be built on the fragile heart of young men and young women. Because they are not blinded by passion, fathers know better what is suitable for their children. This paternal order was a rationalist order.

This order involved all children, but especially girls. The necessity of being governed weighed especially on them. Girls passed, generally at a very young age, from the tyranny of their parents to the tyranny of their husbands, who were invariably older and better educated.

This order is familiar to us through literature and has the coherence and solidity of social logic. It has social nature on its side: the group commands the individual. Of course, it is vulnerable as well as tyrannical in that it constrains and sometimes wounds individuals in what is most personal. For a long time, the critique of this order had remained mostly confined to fiction and the theater, where the complaint of the badly married vented itself or the complex, comic, and painful game between the father's will and the resistance of his children was depicted. Yet, as critical as Molière was of the tyranny of fathers, the paternal power was also a constitutive element. The spectators rejoice when young lovers are united at the end of a classical comedy, but the principle of the order of the fathers was not called into question. It will be called into question when a new principle asserts itself.

This new principle is consent, which can be formulated in various ways. The version given by Hobbes delineates perfectly the new democratic rapport with the law. There exists no legitimate obligation but the one to which I have previously consented. Since marriage entails obligations, the principle expressed by Hobbes can be very well employed to challenge the power of fathers in the matter of marriage. But another expression of the principle, also found in Hobbes and that gained popularity in the seventeenth century, is more directly pertinent. Everyone is the best judge of what concerns them exclusively, or in other words, everyone is the best judge of their interest, whether material or moral. Previously, the best judge of a person's interest was thought to be the one who governed the whole in which that person was situated: the king in relation to the members of the body politic, the father with respect to the members of the family, and so on. The best judge was the one who saw things from above. Now, the best judge is the one who sees things from within. Such a change grounds the democratic revolution in everyone's sense of self.

As an epistemological proposition, each thesis is supported by good arguments. The old thesis has the advantage of considering the whole and thus makes the modern thesis seem deliberately partial, as the choice of the part to prefer itself to the whole. Besides, what exactly concerns me *exclusively*? Is our individual interest not generally inseparable from common interests? This argument loses its force when one wants to apply it to passion, in particular to the sentiment of love. What is more individual, what is less to be shared and less communicable than love? Consent legitimates the sentiment of love, and in turn, love presents consent with natural evidence. Once the two elements are joined, the individualist order is definitively installed in the aspect of social life that is called "private life."

All this presupposes the prior legitimization of passion, hence the abandonment of the moral rationalism I was evoking earlier. In order for the personal sentiment of a child to be allowed to overcome the rational judgment of the father, passion must first be recognized, that is, one must first conclude that the sentimental life is an important or essential part of life. Moreover, it deserves to be recognized by society, that is, the public marriage should express private sentiments. Now, this idea is an idea of recent origin.

In the Greek and Roman world, the great affairs were politics and war. Love found expression chiefly on two levels: the erotic level, in the ordinary sense of the term, and the level of *durus amor*, a violent passion that was painful because of its very violence and because it is sufficiently unrequited. (For example, see Sappho's work or the unhappy love of Dido for Aeneas in the *Aeneid*.) The Christian world was more favorable to amorous passion because it was less political and less military. But it was also painful for a positive reason. The essential component of modern love, at least until recently, is the idealization of woman, which was elaborated in a Christian context. Of course, the Christian religion disapproves of the erotic, "carnal" component of love, the expression of one of the three great "concupiscences" of sinful man. Perhaps more profoundly, it condemns the idolatry that lies at the center of love. Thus it is only in a Christian world, weakened, that the sentimental life could receive all the attributes of legitimacy.

The third change that made the individualist order possible was the affirmation of the equality of women. In truth, this is a quite unclear question, for the term "equality" is very confused in this context. In previous societies, where everything was so-called unequal, the subordination of women was but one aspect of the general order of things.

In democratic society, the moral horizon is the idea of the equality of rights, but also "the general notion of *those like oneself*," which means that every inequality related to women appears as a shocking negation of the principle on which our society is founded. We find it hard today to imagine not only predemocratic societies but even the beginning of democratic society, when the equality of women appeared to be compatible with their real subordination, particularly with their exclusion from the political sphere. Yet, it must be said against current caricatures that never in ancient or Christian Europe was the idea of women's inferiority maintained. Even Aristotle, often considered to be *the* philosopher of natural inequality, sees woman as a rational being on a par with man, just not with the same force. It is not a matter of intelligence or talents or virtues, but of the force of reason, that is, of the capacity to make the judgment of reason prevail over every other consideration. On this score, traditional opinion affirmed a certain feminine inferiority, or a certain "weakness." Thus women were considered to be naturally less able than men to govern themselves, but in a world where *most men* were also considered to be unable to govern themselves. And because women were assumed to be less able to govern themselves, they had to pass straightaway from paternal to conjugal control.

A last element that appears to us today a bit bizarre was that until the sixteenth century, but extending into modern times, the conviction was that women were less apt to govern themselves rationally because their sexual appetites were unlimited and their body had more power over them. The nineteenth century witnessed this contrary dissymmetry, in the "romantic" idealization of woman.

All these considerations on the relative "political weakness" of women, their supposed lack of capacity for self-control and self-mastery, were finally brushed away by the growing sentiment of the equality and resemblance between men and women.

It is time to consider Rousseau's work. First, one is tempted to say that Rousseau proposes an early synthesis between the ancient holistic order and the new individualist order, a synthesis that one will say is utopian. In reality, Rousseau's starting point is radically individualist, thus radically modern. Why is this so? Simply because in his view the human being is by nature an individual, that is, a "perfect and solitary whole."[1] That means that everyone loves only themselves and can love only themselves. At the same time, no one can live a truly human life, encompassing the full range of sentiments and virtues, unless they extend their being, unless they love other human beings, unless they love something greater than themselves. Everyone must thus construct for themselves a second nature in which they will love themselves in loving another than themselves. This second nature can then be the new city mapped out in *The Social Contract*.

However, Rousseau no longer places much hope in politics. The circumstances proper to the modern world make the restoration of the ancient kind nearly impossible. What are these circumstances? The development of great states, the expansion of commerce, the influence of Christianity all have irreversibly individualized political, social, and moral life. Thus one must found another type of community in order to overcome the corrupting individualism wherein everyone is everyone else's enemy. Another type of community is needed, not immediately political. It is a new kind of family. The traditional family is founded on the rule of the father and subjugation of the individuality and the liberty of the wife and children. As for the new "family" that was common through the "enlightened" part of society in the eighteenth century, it placed its children with a nurse, then in a boarding house, while the spouses married each other only to be able to cheat on one another. Such a family is the opposite of a union. Rousseau wants to found a family that would be a true union in equality; in his eyes there is no true union except in equality.

But how can a true union be possible if nature has made everyone an individual, a "perfect and solitary whole?" Nature has made man and woman physically complementary of course for purposes of reproduction, but above all, morally complementary too. This idea of complementary natures is banal and even disagreeable to contemporary sensibility because it seems to be a pretext and a euphemism for the continued subordination of woman. It is an idea that can be used to this end if one conceived of it in a vulgar way. Rousseau, however, utilizes it subtly to show how the complementary natures of a civilized man and a civilized woman can create a new being more complete and richer than either of the two beings taken separately. Even if this couple has no child, it creates a third term different from each one of them, which is the couple itself.

This sexual politics of Rousseau is inseparable from his moral democratic project. Human beings naturally want to produce and to produce themselves (also to reproduce themselves), but here I am considering only the first two terms. To produce and to produce oneself is to produce a work that is reflected in the eyes of others. When production and self-production mobilize individual talents, they arouse the desire to distinguish oneself and, vice versa, the desire to distinguish oneself mobilizes individual talents. Such is, according to Rousseau, the mechanism of social corruption that is especially devastating in modern times where the division of labor motivates and stimulates talents. Rousseau believes that the formation of a family or a couple constitutes a work that fulfills the desire to produce and to produce oneself, the desire to "create." The desire to reproduce oneself does not necessarily enter into play, without engaging the fatal desire to distinguish oneself since it is the family itself that notices, appreciates, and crowns the construction of the work. This production is open to all human beings, not just the winners in the talent competition. This is a human possibility that the ancien régime did not much cultivate because of the characteristics of the traditional family, but that played a great role in the development of the democratic society, even if it is likely that few families approached the model outlined by Rousseau.

This type of family is largely discredited today under the name of the bourgeois or traditional family. The expression "bourgeois family" serves well since "family life" was one of the most characteristic expressions of "bourgeois life." But the expression "traditional family" is less suitable because it is in fact a new family, clearly distinguished from and less enduring than the unequal and patriarchal family of the ancien regime. At the same time, there is a widespread desire to escape the craze of competition. Now, the family thus conceived offers a sort of asylum where one can escape the obsession to compare. American cinema has given us touching images of this type of family life in which the man participates with the necessary toughness in the harsh ways of competition, while the woman gently looks after the home. But this possibility no longer has much meaning since women have in great numbers entered the work force and thus engage in competition. Besides, such a compromise is not what Rousseau had in mind, since he wanted the man also to escape the corruption induced by competition. Once again, Rousseau's idea of the couple and the family is a human work that miraculously escapes the corruption that is inseparable from human works. Claude Habib presents the question excellently:

> No one today would dare to consider a family as a work. Nonetheless, that was Rousseau's point of view: every family is a work. This work brings into play the essential part of feminine liberty and for this reason woman bears responsibility for it.
>
> To say that the creation of the family mobilizes the best part of feminine liberty and inventiveness is not to sterilize the other qualities with which a woman may be endowed by nature but it is definitely to subordinate them to this purpose.
>
> For Rousseau there is no renunciation or sacrifice. In a woman the desire to dominate is deceptive. . . . The eternal dilemma of modern women divided between career and private life is inconceivable in Rousseauan terms: one has to think that they feign this dilemma, precisely because they lack a private life. If they knew what it was to live the life of a sincere woman who becomes a lover and mother, they would orient themselves toward that kind of life and the conflict would be eliminated. . . .
>
> For a woman, to develop a talent for the sole purpose of developing it is to

turn her gifts to her own detriment, to utilize them for her own unhappiness. In this effort, the woman has the illusion of liberating her strengths, whereas she denatures her own being. Basically she is mistaken about her weakness, which is not to be able to make herself happy all alone, to be able to achieve it only by freely consented dependence.[2]

Of course, we can take seriously what Rousseau says only if we take seriously the thesis of the complementary natures of man and woman. Once again, this "holistic" thesis is abhorrent to our naturally "individualistic" viewpoint. But Rousseau makes this thesis plausible, as Rousseau lays out in Book V of *Émile*. But this complementarity has a primary meaning, Rousseau insists, which is that sexual desire is reciprocal, not symmetrical. The dissymmetry resides in the fact that on the feminine side modesty comes first, while on the masculine side initiative does. Nothing in this state of things can change; it is in our nature.

Rousseau forcefully opposes contemporary philosophy, the philosophy in which enlightened people reduce modesty to a "prejudice."[3] Of course, modesty can be repudiated, but to do so would repudiate the truth of desire. Rousseau does not defend feminine modesty out of love for morality and law. He detests the law, which is why he so interests those who also detest law in part thanks to his influence. He does not pretend to regulate desire from the outside, whether by the law of God or the law of Nature. If there is a law of Nature, then it is the law of desire itself. The rule of desire plays on the dissymmetry that turns on feminine modesty.[4] One consequence of this analysis is that there is no knowledge of desire, that desire cannot be mastered by knowledge or by science. In short, what we today call "sex" does not exist. And if "sex" does not exist, "sexology" does not exist either. There is no knowledge of what desire is, because desire does not know what it desires.

My aim here is not to give an account of Rousseau's thought, nor to propose him as a moral compass. There are excellent accounts and judicious commentaries, albeit quite different, in the books of Allan Bloom and Claude Habib.[5] But reading and meditating on Rousseau make us aware of a strange aspect of our present situation. Contemporary democracy stridently affirms both individuality and sexuality. It takes aim aggressively at the old authoritarian and holistic order. Individualism seeks to dissolve all authority over the individual, while sexual freedom defies the order of the Law in what is most ancient and deepest in it. But do individuality and sexuality go together so easily? After all, if reduced to their essentials, to be an individual is to be independent, to be sexual is to be dependent. One can skirt the difficulty by presenting desire as the supreme expression of individuality. That is true only when desire sincerely seeks the obscure object it ignores, that is, when desire encounters the other dissymmetrical desire engaged in the same perplexity, and the two desires discover the reciprocal accommodation that traditionally bears the name of love. In other words, when desire is engaged in the supremely individual work that Rousseau describes, which is the creation of a couple.

Individuality and sexuality can be joined only in the bond of love, which, as a bond, refutes the hypothesis of independence. If we use the somewhat crude language of today, we will say that Rousseau is not hostile to sexual freedom since he detests the law, but neither does he favor sexual freedom because it blatantly overlooks the delicate nature of desire. This desire, being instituted by nature itself, we cannot truly master or know, but can only regulate by following its own rule.

As for the question of children, for Rousseau a couple is normally and naturally fertile, but in *Émile* he analyzes the formation of a couple from the starting point of two independent individuals, while the child is but the consequence of this union. For us, the couple is not naturally fertile since it can choose to have a child or not. And this "mastery of fertility," heavily weighted with consequences, is one of the most important aspects of the "mastery" of nature that, since Descartes, shapes the perspective of the West. With the discovery of the contraceptive pill, this mastery envelops human nature itself in its most intimate aspect, in its most specific link with nature. This represents an extraordinary philosophical experience for the study of the relations between human nature and human art or artifice, as well as the evaluation of the Enlightenment project of the conquest of nature.

In concluding I shall limit myself to two quite simple remarks. The first of course concerns demographics. The mastery allowed by the contraceptive pill is of an individual order. Each couple in principle has the number of children it desires. But the global effect of all these microdecisions escapes human mastery. In practice, this means that in nearly all countries using modern means of contraception, the birth rate is not high enough to assure the renewal of its population. The deficit is considerable, in countries like Japan, Germany, or Italy. Everybody is aware of the social and economic problems—public health, pensions, etcetera, that this demographic fact entails. It is not so much that we do not know how to solve these problems but that we do not know how to formulate them since they are so new. A rapidly aging population that, even absent war or epidemic, will diminish rapidly, as is the case in Japan, is an altogether unprecedented phenomenon whose consequences no one can pretend to discern or measure.

The views of experts on the subject are even more contradictory than usual. There is a deep irony in all this. In this case, we are stronger than nature, we master it, we subject it, but we subject it to the point that it lets us down and indirectly recovers all its power over us. Formerly we had more children than we desired or can feed and raise; now we have fewer children than needed to assure the renewal and continuity of the current population. In this game between human beings and nature, there is an equilibrium that we desire and that forever escapes us. In this sense, the hopes of Descartes and the Enlightenment have until now been disappointed. In spite of our extraordinary means, we are still not "masters and possessors of nature." As the most ancient Greek philosophers already said, nature likes to hide and to elude us.

My other remark also concerns our relation to nature and the notion of the "mastery of fertility," but in a qualitative way. Of course, a couple can easily avoid having children. This is a case of effective but negative mastery. Even leaving aside the issue of sterility, a couple cannot choose the children it accepts or desires to have. The expression current in France today, "to make a child," expresses the desire for a positive mastery that is not quite within our grasp. The old and modest expression, "to have a child," remains more faithful to reality. In this sense, human beings are as blind and disarmed today as they were at the beginning of time. In spite of all the possibilities of science, their relation to nature remains ultimately a relation of confidence and faith, not one of mastery.

CHAPTER 14

The Question of Communism

ONE MIGHT QUESTION whether a study of the totalitarianisms of the twentieth century, even a quick one, should have a place in this analysis of the contemporary political situation. After all, one of the two totalitarianisms—the "brown" of the fascisms and Nazism—capitulated unconditionally over sixty years ago and no significant resurgence has been seen since. The so-called "xenophobic" parties like the National Front in France or the Liberal Party in Austria arouse some concern and the calculated provocations mouthed by their leaders justify suspicion, but in reality they bear little resemblance to fascist parties. These new parties lack the fascists' conquering ardor and violent intentions against their political adversaries. They offer no revolutionary recasting of political and social institutions; they are without ambition or hope; only aggressively defensive. A watchful vigilance on these parties is wise, but the pan-European hysteria that periodically greets their electoral successes proves only one thing: not how much we remember but how much we have forgotten what the fascisms and Nazism truly were.

The other totalitarianism, Communism, did not capitulate unconditionally but, beginning in 1989, it declared itself nonexistent. Gorbachev suggested that it had never truly existed, that perhaps it was an invention of the anticommunists and other "enemies of peace." In short, the hard-core Communist regime evaporated and liberal democracy remained as the only conceivable regime. It is true that the democratic hopes placed in the new Russia have been dashed by recent developments. The current government seems to be intent on conserving or restoring some of the more odious traits of the Soviet regime, whose personnel has largely remained in power. However, the more specific elements of the totalitarian regime are lacking, such as the one party system and the Marxist ideology. Furthermore, nothing suggests that their return is envisaged. Thus it would seem that the study of the totalitarianisms belongs henceforth to the discipline of history. On the contrary, I believe that this study is indispensable for understanding the present.

Nazism appeared and grew intrinsically linked to a criminal will whose only perspective was destruction, first of the Jews and the peoples deemed inferior, such as Slavs, Gypsies, the handicapped, and then other peoples, including the Germans themselves, deemed unworthy of the sublime ambitions of its superhuman masters. Even though it was unable to achieve its murderous goal, it did so much killing so quickly and under such conditions that it presented us with two enigmas. First: how could one of the most civilized European nations place its strengths and its virtues at the service of such an undertaking? (This historical question is one about the "corruption" of a body politic.) The second enigma is: how are such crimes, "crimes against humanity" possible? As I have noted, our contemporary perception of humanity is decisively colored by the experience of crimes against humanity, in particular Nazi crimes. The German philosopher, Adorno, asked how it is possible to write poetry after Auschwitz. I find this formulation of the problem uselessly melodramatic, but it is true that it is difficult to escape the feeling that a line was crossed that had never been crossed.

Communism appears to be different. First, it still poses a political problem, for it is still a political reality. We often speak as if Communism had disappeared. While it is true that Communism has disappeared from Europe and that the "international Communist movement," whose head, heart, and arsenal resided in the Soviet Union, has also disappeared, there remain Communist regimes in Asia, one of which, North Korea, is simply appalling.

How does one characterize the Communist Chinese regime that in the last few years has undergone "capitalist" development in its maritime provinces but is still governed by a Communist party that maintains its monopoly on power? In the former Soviet Union things are not clear either, since it is divided into some fifteen successor states. Nearly all these states are governed by former leaders of the Communist party or the KGB, often with very little democracy. In other words these countries are no longer Communist in the sense that they no longer aim to "construct" the Communist utopia, but they remain largely governed by the old Communist elite or *nomenklatura*. This was still the case until 2000 in Serbia, a European state.

This strange death, or strange survival of Communism, is worth considering. Unlike Nazism, which was concentrated in time and space, Communism occupied nearly all the twentieth century and spread in all parts of the world. Unlike Nazism, that was frontally and frankly opposed to the modern developments, to democracy and equality, but embraced technology with enthusiasm, Communism wanted to be the fulfillment of modernity, the culmination of progress in all its aspects. It knit a powerful synthesis, some of the great ideas elaborated in the nineteenth century when the democratic movement became fully aware of its strength and formulated all its hopes: humanity conceived as a collective subject capable of transforming and mastering both nature and human nature, the perspective of a world freed from domination and exploitation—including Saint-Simon's man's exploitation of man, which gave way to the exploitation of nature, and lastly, "real" equality as opposed to only "formal" or "by right."

In this sense, Communism as an idea belongs to the democratic world; and when seen under a certain angle, the Communist idea and the democratic idea seem to merge. That is why most democratic societies were indulgent towards Communism.

The success of the "Communist idea in the twentieth century"[1] was surprising in that the regime in charge of making the idea a reality revealed extremely shocking traits that were altogether contrary to the idea: instead of abundance, penury; instead of equality, the "special treatment ration" of the *nomenklatura* and the dominant "new class"; instead of fraternity, generalized suspicion and denunciation; instead of liberty, the most meticulous, the most absurd, and most humiliating constraint. Worse yet, the regime at certain times deployed unprecedented violent measures and committed mass crimes comparable only to those of Nazism.[2] Indeed, these two enemy regimes in the end resembled each other to such an extent that historians had to elaborate the notion of totalitarianism as the genre whose species were Communism and Nazism.[3]

To better understand these remarks on Communism, I shall like to first consider the controversial question of the *nature* of the Communist regime. Then, I shall attempt to describe what François Furet called "the Communist illusion," with its mysterious capacity to endure in spite of experience. Finally, Claude Lefort's analysis raised the question of the relation between Communism and democracy.

The Greek philosophers understood that the principal instrument for analyzing political life is the notion of *regime*. The true political changes are the changes of political regime. According to whether one lives in an oligarchic or a democratic regime, for example, life in its various aspects takes on a different character. I say *life*, not only political life. The political regime entails or has consequences for all aspects of life. In this sense, as Rousseau says, "everything is related to politics." The political regime is not only the organization or the constitution of powers, but also the general tonality of common life, as determined by those who govern, who precisely "set the tone." Thus the work of political philosophy culminates in drawing up a *classification* of political regimes.

Now, with the development of the great "sovereign" states and modern civil society, the question of political regimes seems to lose its importance for two main reasons. First, since the structure of the great states became defined by the distinction between the state, with its administration, and civil society, the complex plurality of regimes analyzed by the Greeks is replaced by the simple opposition between states with a representative government and those with a nonrepresentative government. Second, social transformations involving the emancipation of society from its political and religious commands tend to devalue politics and reduce its importance. The feeling grows that politics is an oppressive and archaic superstructure that should be abolished or restrained. The way to the future seemingly does not pass through politics.

But Bolshevism and Fascism surprisingly gave back to politics all its previous importance, even more importance than it ever had. They "politicized" life as perhaps never before. In short, the phenomenon of the *regime* again occupied center stage. At the same time, it seemed impossible to rigorously define these regimes. No place could be found for them in the available classifications. It was for that reason that they were called "totalitarian regimes," since the new reality called for a new term by which to designate it. Besides, the term had been employed first by the Italian fascists to designate the regenerative ambition of the fascist State that wanted to be "the form and interior norm, . . . the discipline of the whole person."[4] The term then quite quickly acquired a chiefly critical, even denunciatory coloring. But the term that was used matters little. What concerns us is to attempt to grasp the specific form of these regimes, in this case the Communist regime.

Alain Besançon does just that in a text that confronts this particular difficulty, "On the Difficulty of Defining the Soviet Regime."[5] The text begins with the following sentence: "The Soviet regime nimbly evades the classifications of Aristotle and Montesquieu." Aristotle's well-known classification distinguishes three types of good regimes—monarchy, aristocracy, and polity. They are good because these regimes govern, whether by one alone, a small number, or a great number, in the common interest. It also distinguishes three "deviations" from these good regimes—tyranny, oligarchy, and democracy. They are bad because these regimes govern (whether one alone, a small number, or a great number) in their own interest.

Besançon shows that this classification is in the end of no use in defining the Soviet regime because if one considers what the regime says about itself, it merges with the three good regimes, and if one notes the facts, it merges with the three bad regimes. According to the doctrine, the regime resembles a monarchy, in which the Secretary General wills the interest of the people; in reality, it resembles a tyranny (the Secretary General is chiefly concerned with his power). But it also resembles an aristocracy (of the competent and devoted Party) that otherwise appears as an oligarchy (of the incompetent and selfish party). It also resembles a good democracy, a "polity," in which the people govern for the good of the people, that otherwise appears as a bad democracy (for the poorest and the most uncouth oppress those who have some ease or education.) In short, all the keys of Aristotle fit the Soviet lock, but none opens the door. The regime assuredly has traits that are or appear to be tyrannical, oligarchic, and democratic, but its specific form lies elsewhere.

Besançon then examines Montesquieu's classification that distinguishes among republics, founded on virtue, monarchies, founded on honor, and despotism, founded on fear. Does not the Soviet regime belong to this third species or genre? Besançon acknowledges that the thesis has some plausibility. But he notes that "Oriental despotism" is described by Montesquieu as the despotism in which only the upperclass has cause to fear; as for the people, the despot in general leaves them alone just as he leaves traditional institutions untouched. The Communist regime was different. He will seek out the lowliest citizen to make him obey, to transform him into a "good Communist," into a "new man." Thus, both the most famous ancient classification and the most famous modern classification fail to grasp what is proper to the Communist regime.

The pivotal point of the Aristotelian analysis, the opposition between the common interest and the particular interest of the governing body or person is of no use because the Communist regime does not set its sights on either the general interest of the population or the particular interest of those who govern. What then was its aim? Besançon replies that it aims at what the Communist ideology enjoins it to aim at. The Communist regime hangs on the Communist ideology of which it is but the tool. Besançon writes:

> The absolute originality of this regime in relation to all known regimes, what makes it impossible to imagine or to understand as long as it has not been tested by experience, has to do with the position occupied by ideology. It is the principle and the end of the regime, to which totalitarianism is ordered as a means. . . . Rather than "totalitarianism" the word "*ideocracy*" would fit better. . . . Let us simply say . . . *ideological regime.*[6]

This thesis, according to which the Communist regime was above all or fundamentally an "ideological" regime, is rather widespread among the best observers and analysts of this regime. Besides Besançon, who gives the most radical and most suggestive version of the thesis, Hannah Arendt, Raymond Aron, and Alexandr Solzhenitsyn give similar insights. These authors invoke ideology as the decisive factor, because they are struck by the fact that some of the most absurd and most criminal actions of the regime derived directly from ideology. For example, the collectivization of farms by Stalin was contrary to all economic, political, and even military prudence. The regime nonetheless mobilized all its forces to bring it about. The only rational explanation of this irrational behavior is that it was driven by the ideology according to which the abolition of private ownership of farms would by itself produce an unheard of development of Soviet agriculture. Stalin believed that the new human being, an incomparably prosperous and perfectly just society, would result from collectivization. He believed this because he was certain of the absolute truth of Marxism-Leninism.

The way in which the ideology and the regime are linked remains enigmatic. These men accomplish absurd actions or commit enormous crimes because they believe in an ideology that dictates these actions and crimes. The question then arises how they can believe in an ideology that leads them to accomplish absurd actions and commit enormous crimes? And if they adhered to this ideology *before* coming to power, why didn't they abandon it when it drove them close to the absurd and criminal? Instead of ideology being the cause of crime, one can inversely conceive of crime as the cause of ideology, more precisely of the project of totalitarian power as the cause of the invention of ideology, at least of the ideological use of ideas that were first elaborated to serve other ends. Ideology may have given rise to tyranny; but tyranny may have given rise to ideology at a time when every politics had an ideological or abstract component.

Mostly everyone is in agreement on two fundamental points: one, tyranny is a phenomenon as old as politics, belonging to the human political condition, and second, modern totalitarian and ideological tyrannies represent an unprecedented phenomenon. To understand the Communist phenomenon, one would thus have to understand how the new phenomenon is linked to the old. No one has yet succeeded in describing this link in a completely satisfying way. Leo Strauss has in any case formulated the problem in a particularly clear and forceful way: "Present-day tyranny, in contrast to classical tyranny, is based on the unlimited progress in the 'conquest of nature' which is made possible by modern science, as well as on the popularization or diffusion of philosophic or scientific knowledge."[7] This general definition is particularly applicable to Communism which, on the one hand, wanted to be the avant-garde of humanity for the conquest of nature (the Soviet Union devoted enormous resources to carrying out technological feats intended to demonstrate the superiority of the regime) and which, on the other hand, transformed Communism as a gigantic *experiment* of social science where the party conducted the experiment and the rest of humanity was the object of the experiment.

What many authors call "ideology," Leo Strauss characterizes as the popularization of science or philosophy. In fact, Marxist-Leninist ideology did incessantly proclaim its absolutely scientific character, according to a conception of science that was in effect more "popular" than rigorously scientific. Moreover, this characterization has the advantage of situating modern tyranny in a general context instead of attaching it simply to fortuitous and particular causes such as the specificities of Russian history. This characterization is as disturbing as it is pertinent. For the idea of unlimited progress in the conquest of nature as well as the idea of the popularization of philosophy or science are inseparable from modern democracy. Strauss thus suggests that certain notions proper to modern democracy played a decisive role in setting up modern tyranny, and particularly Communism, in transforming ancient tyranny into modern tyranny. Communism is tyrannical, contrary to democracy and, in another sense, it is its creature. It actualizes and implements in a simplified and brutal form ideas that are proper to the modern democratic world.

You recall Kant's definition of the Enlightenment. He defines it as

> man's emergence from his self-imposed immaturity. Immaturity is the inability to use one's understanding without guidance from another. This immaturity is self-imposed when its cause lies not in lack of understanding, but in lack of resolve and courage to use it without guidance from another. *Sapere aude!* "Have courage to use your own understanding!"—that is the motto of enlightenment.[8]

So goes the simplest and noblest expression of the democratic movement. Kant affirms that the time for living under tutelage is past, the time for living under the guidance of God (or rather of God's representatives), of princes, of the past—of all that imposes an external law, a law *other* than human reason, of all that imposes *heteronomy*. Humanity must now have the courage to be *autonomous*. In this Kantian version of modern liberty, human beings emancipated from each other do not emancipate themselves from the law. They obey the law of reason, the law they give themselves as rational beings.[9] Kantian law, the law of autonomy, is the most rigorous of all laws.

Herein lies the problem: the noble Kantian equilibrium between *autos* and *nomos* is difficult to maintain. Humanity is faced with the temptation to reject every law, to see one's liberty in the rejection of every law, to think of oneself as the sovereign author of the human order. Since at least the seventeenth century, European philosophy and politics have been animated by the idea of a human order *conceived and willed* as an artifact, as a great machine that orders the state of nature.

The sovereign state, thus politics, is this great machine, the agent of this order. At first the idea of human nature as something *definite* and *given* was maintained. During the eighteenth century a great change appeared. The idea of human nature, which was a limit to human sovereignty, gave way and soon collapsed. Human beings were thereafter no longer defined as having a certain nature but lived in "history," of developing in history, of being "historical beings." Human beings have no nature; they evolve, transform, and create themselves over the course of historical time. Taking these two ideas together—the idea of the political order as artifact and supreme instrument and the idea of the human being as a historical being—a fundamental presupposition of totalitarianism emerges. Let us make a clean slate of the past; the creation of the new human being is in our hands.

Lenin and his companions were confident that they held in Marxism the science of history, that is, the science of the creation of man by man. Their extreme violence, their immoderate measures derive directly from this intoxication of omniscience and omnipotence. The Bolshevik Party was not simply a party habituated to secrecy and conspiracy and desirous of seizing all power, it was a group of men who were dead serious in thinking of themselves as the conscious and active head of humanity, with the rest of humanity being at best a passive and ignorant mass that one could deceive and brutalize, at worst a bunch of "harmful insects"—to use Lenin's expression—that one must exterminate.

The Communists thus felt that they were engaged in a great experiment, *the* great work nothing less than the creation of the new humanity. In such an undertaking, the ordinary moral rules do not apply. The party is above all law; it itself is the law. Even the rules of good sense lose their validity; even those of perception. This is, perhaps, why Communism, for a long time, kept its prestige, not only among Communists and "sympathizers" but also among "neutral observers," while unprejudiced and neutral observations of life in Communist regimes revealed the lie of their claims. After the fall of the Wall the West Germans, measuring the economic and technical backwardness of East Germany, asked anxiously how they did not *see* what was before their eyes. There is indeed something very troubling in this. One explanation is that the Communists and their sympathizers managed to impose their conviction on the observers who considered themselves impartial. The Communist reality has no objective, measurable properties. It is the phenomenon that manifests what alone matters to the creative will. Reality is the will that scorns reality. Everything in Communist life was destined to make this will felt and thus to prevent one from seeing what is before one's eyes or from recognizing that which one sees.

This interpretation of the Communist project as the project of the creation of humanity by humans themselves in history allows one to explain or to understand many aspects. Yet, it comes up against a common sense objection that we have already mentioned. These ideas that seem decisive in the genesis of Communism, especially those that set forth humans as sovereign rulers of the human world and as historical beings, are not the preserve of the Communists. It is thus not only with a subjective sincerity but with an objective plausibility that the Communists could declare that they were only taking seriously the democratic ideal itself, that they, the Communists, deep down were the only serious democrats. For a long time, this reasoning disturbed and intimidated many good democrats because they felt that this was an imposture but at the same time a sort of truth.

As I have said, Communist "ideas" are in large part the "ideas" of the democratic movement as it developed during the modern centuries. Nonetheless, the Communist regime and the democratic regime are radically opposed. Where then lies the opposition between Communist and democratic propositions? Democracy, like Communism, clearly states that human beings are sovereign over themselves and create themselves in history. But *how* does it say it? At the same time that it affirms this truth, it affirms that no one can appropriate this truth, no one holds it exclusively. The democratic power, the democratic state is the instrument of the sovereign social will, the instrument of the creation of human beings by themselves. But the locus of power in democracy, as expressed by Claude Lefort, is an *empty place*. Those who occupy it, the governors, our governors, occupy it without occupying it, since they are destined to give way to their successors at the next election. Unlike kings who embody the society and who *are* the society, the democratic governors only represent it and *are not* the society. The king's body is a concrete presence. Representative governments are in some way an abstract presence. That is the very pivot of democracy, its center and meaning, and it is precisely the rift through which the Communist temptation enters. There is a problematic, almost painful contrast between the essence of power—the power of the people—and its appearance. This contrast is also its reality in democracy, that is the necessarily disappointing particularity of those individuals who succeed one another in this place of power. Lefort writes:

> Political power, as circumscribed and localized in society at the same time as being an instituting moment, is exposed to the threat of falling into particularity, of arousing what Machiavelli regarded as more dangerous than hatred, namely, contempt; and similarly those who exercise it or aspire to it are exposed to the threat of appearing as individuals or groups concerned solely to satisfy their desires. With totalitarianism an apparatus is set up which tends to stave off this threat, which tends to weld power and society back together again, to efface all signs of social division, to banish the indetermination that haunts the democratic experience. But this attempt, as I have suggested, itself draws on a democratic source, developing and fully affirming the idea of the People-as-One, the idea of society as such, bearing the knowledge of itself, transparent to itself and homogeneous, the idea of mass opinion, sovereign and normative, the idea of the tutelary state.
>
> Since the advent of democracy, and in opposition to it, the body is thus revitalized.[10]

This body is of course no longer the living and fruitful body of the king. It is an abstract body, a dead body, so to speak. The Communist order, whose center is Lenin's mummy, has as its goal to make visible the unity of power and society, the phantasm of the People-as-One over which rules not a king with his living body, but the image, the photograph, the presence-absence, threatening and anguishing, of the *Egocrat*, as Lefort calls it, borrowing a phrase from Solzhenitsyn. On holidays, on the balcony of the mausoleum, a hand with no body and no face, motioning with a wave.

Why does the Communist temptation, irresistible at certain times and in certain countries, appear nearly inconceivable at other times and in other countries? One could say generally that the temptation is present more or less once the body politic has not succeeded in developing a method of representation. This can be tied to a slower democratic development in a world otherwise dominated by the democratic idea. In fact, Lefort remarks that Communism "has taken root . . . initially, in countries where the democratic transformation was only just beginning."[11] Or else the temptation can be tied to an experience of representation that was originally so intense that the citizens subsequently found it difficult to accept the prosaic particularity of their representatives. If France was one of the rare countries of the non-Communist world where the Communist Party and its ideology constituted a fundamental element of national life, this was due to the revolutionary foundation of modern France, which was representative but suspicious of the contingency of the representatives and fascinated by the idea of the People-as-One.

Be that as it may, the disappearance of Communism in Europe leaves the structure of democracy intact, together with its problematic character. Power is more than ever an empty place, occupied more abstractly by individuals who are interchangeable. It would not be surprising that in spite of our being long accustomed to the ways of representation, other totalitarian temptations and undertakings should arise in the future, whose forms may be more difficult to foresee today as Bolshevism was in 1916.

CHAPTER 15

Is There a Nazi Mystery?

O UR CONCERN is to study a political phenomenon. It does not have to do with what today is called the "obligation to remember," however legitimate and imperative that may be. Nazism offers us a peak example of a phenomenon to which modern political science and even philosophy have not paid much attention, namely the corruption of a regime, in this case the Weimar regime, or of a body politic, in this instance Germany. In an article he wrote near the end of his life, Raymond Aron states the difficulty clearly:

> Suppose that a historian formulates the question: Why, and in what circumstances, did a highly civilized nation surrender itself to a demagogue like Hitler, and follow him to the bitter end, almost to the point of national suicide? Put in this way, the Nazi question will never receive a satisfactory answer; or rather (and this comes to the same thing) it may receive several answers none of which is totally wrong but which do not give satisfaction even taken all together. On the other hand, in response to most of the questions *"why?"* which concern single aspects of the Nazi phenomenon, historiography does provide plausible or demonstrable answers.[1]

Thus, every aspect of the phenomenon of "1933," if considered separately, is intelligible. What does not appear to be intelligible is the whole, the movement that leads from 1933 to 1945, the way the different aspects are knit together to produce a final result that not only no one foresaw, but that no one knew how to approach in retrospect, so much does it seem to be "incomprehensible." The different causes uniting through the worst of each, that is the corruption, is most difficult to understand. It seems that nothing produced any good, and that everything served to bring about evil. For example, military honor, which ought to have led the *Wehrmacht* to refuse obedience to Hitler (and some did, very late, on July 20, 1944), instead contributed chiefly to make the army docile to Hitler, to whom the officers had sworn an oath. For at least two centuries now, we have been spontaneously "progressives"; we think that on the whole, the interplay of causes necessarily in the end produces a globally positive effect. In the case of Nazi Germany, the interplay of causes raced toward the worst catastrophe.

When one wishes to understand the phenomena of the twentieth century, one always needs to return to their founding event, World War I. The first link in the chain of the catastrophe was that in November 1918, Germany, although it was defeated and had signed the armistice, refused to acknowledge its defeat. Of course, no country willingly accepts its defeat; the people grumble, and sometimes revolt against the leaders who they believe are responsible for the defeat. But here something unique intervened in Germany in the aftermath of World War I. Subjectively, Germany considered herself as unconquered, in a sense, victorious. It had good objective reasons to think so: German territory was not invaded, the German army threatened its enemies until the last moment, until it was on the verge of victory almost to the last days. If Germany was forced to sue for armistice, it was because of the massive intervention of American troops. Their decisive role proved that, within the European framework, Germany "should have" won the war.

However, to these objective facts were added elements of an altogether different nature. It was the German *army* that demanded its civilian leaders to negotiate an armistice but, as soon as the armistice was officially concluded, the army chiefs declared that they had been betrayed. They declared that Germany itself had been betrayed and began to propagate the legend of the "stab in the back." Thus, democratic politicians, in particular the Social Democrats, to whom was left the thankless task of governing the large vanquished and despairing country, immediately in prey to anarchy, were immediately discredited in the eyes of an important part of public opinion, particularly the ruling class. They were considered traitors, responsible for the defeat.

Pre-1914 Germany, the Wilhelmine regime, was only half democratic. To establish a truly democratic regime under conditions of defeat was an extremely difficult undertaking. In addition, the Weimar regime was held in disdain and accused of treason by a great part of the social authorities. Its task became nearly impossible. Not only was a vital part of the elites hostile to the regime, it acted in bad faith. It lied to the public and to itself. The man who played the decisive role in this fatal moment was the one who, under the nominal authority of Hindenburg, was the true head of the army, the quartermaster Ludendorff. In 1923, he participated in Hitler's attempted putsch in Munich. Such was the first link in the fatal chain.

Furthermore, the peace treaties ending World War I were not negotiated in conformity with the tradition of European public law. Rather they were imposed on Germany, which had been declared responsible for the war, and for that reason, forced to disarm and made to pay reparations. From the first moment, resentment against the *Diktat* of Versailles affected the German population as a whole. Germany was fundamentally hostile to the European order that emerged from the war. Yet, it was so weakened by the treaties that it would lack the means to the consequences of the *Diktat*. Hitler proved himself in the eyes of the people and the army precisely by his skill in abolishing the consequences of the Treaty of Versailles within three years.

Thus the postwar period saw the worsening of the difficult relations the Germans had with the "West," chiefly the French, the English, and the Americans. The Wilhelmine regime, half democratic, had been vanquished by the old democracies of the West. The new Weimar democracy was the expression of the German defeat. But something more profound than democratic institutions was in play. France and England were more than rivals with Germany, they represented two versions of "civilization": France, the civilization founded on intelligent sociability or "manners," and England, the civilization founded on individual initiative or "commerce." Now, since the beginning of the nineteenth century, even the end of the eighteenth, a growing part of German philosophy rejected the civilization of the West, an "exterior" civilization, that was without interiority or spirituality. In the case of the French, they were "superficial" and "corrupt"; the English and American were "greedy" and "vulgar." To the civilizations of the West, Germany opposed its own way, its *Sonderweg*, characterized by the true culture of the mind and the soul, the *Bildung*.

The opposition between "culture" and "civilization" can take very subtle, "dialectical" forms and so enriched the European debate. But it took less and less subtle forms. Whatever the merits of French civilization, it was the English and American civilization of the individual and of commerce that set the tone for the new world. As Nietzsche had said, modern ideas are "English ideas." The world of the individual and of commerce is a world founded on self-interest and the calculation of this interest. Being inimical to all true generosity, it is a world in which a truly human, that is, a disinterested life, is impossible. At least that was the complaint of the critics of the spiritual effects of commerce and modern economic life. These cities were numerous and in any case vocal and often brilliant in all the countries of Europe. But it was in Germany that the rejection of commercial civilization, the contempt for English civilization, crystallized to the point of forming a spiritual, social, and political phenomenon, a major phenomenon, heavy with fatal consequences.

If commerce and the calculation of self-interest is the enemy of human greatness, how can this greatness be preserved or recovered? Which human activity can be said to be *not* founded on the calculation of private interest? There is only one: war. The only truly disinterested action is to die for one's country.[2] Thus, while the liberal philosophers like Montesquieu or Constant rejoiced in seeing commerce taking the place of war as the principal activity of civilized peoples, the critics of commerce now preached a return to war, particularly in Germany. Thus war had become not an unfortunate characteristic of the state of barbarism that civilization must overcome, it belonged to a truly disinterested human life. German philosophy, from Hegel to Nietzsche and others, showed a particular sympathy for war. In summary, this spiritual attitude held that war was noble; commerce was base and vulgar.

This spiritual disposition that sustained German militarism during the Empire, was radicalized during the World War I. It transformed itself, Leo Strauss says, into nihilism. The "experience of the front" appeared to many young Germans as the decisive human experience, the one that nullified and ridiculed all other experiences of social and civilized life. This disposition found a particularly striking expression in the work and life of a German writer-soldier, who is much appreciated in France and a great friend of France: Ernst Jünger. Leo Strauss refers to a few lines from an essay published between the two wars: "What kind of minds are those that do not even know there can be no deeper and wiser mind than the mind of *any* soldier fallen anywhere at the battles of the Somme or Flanders? That is the standard we need." This was published in 1931, more than ten years after the end of the Great War!

Texts such as this one suggest that Nazism cannot be adequately defined as a "falling back" into barbarism. After World War I a good part of educated German youth, those who read Jünger, had deliberately rejected the principle of civilization in the name of an "authentic" experience of which the experience of the front provided the model and the criterion. These young people would not all become Nazis, far from it. Jünger was never a Nazi. But these youths were dangerously available for any adventure that promised the rejection of civilization and the established order, in short, the rejection of the "system." In this sense, they consented beforehand to barbarism; they chose it. And barbarism that is chosen, willed, is a separate thing, something worse than the natural barbarism that precedes civilization.

At this point the question arises as to why these young Germans did not become Communists. After all, the Communists also manifested strong hostility toward commerce and bourgeois life. If these young people needed adventure, why not become engaged in the Communist adventure, in the construction of the new humanity? In many European countries this perspective incited many to Communism. In Germany also, the Communist movement gained numerous followers. But the resolute enemies of the bourgeois world not only did not become Communists, but on the contrary became the fierce enemies of Communism. In their eyes Communism did not signify the overthrow of capitalism, but its culmination. Communism for them represented the definitive, crushing, inescapable victory of the "most contemptible man," that Nietzsche's Zarathustra spoke of, the "last man," the man of needs and the satisfaction of needs, the altogether "economic" man.

Although they scorned and hated Communism they were also impressed and intimidated by it. They wondered if Communism did not hold the keys to the future, if modern civilization was not going to roll irresistibly in the direction of Communism. Moreover, they often shared with the Communists the idea that humans are "historical" beings, that they "create themselves" in history. The Communists were in the process of seizing history; they had to be stopped at all cost, and since the Communist revolution had to be defeated by an anti-Communist revolution, the man of needs had to be opposed by the man of risk and war. In itself this reaction to Communism was not without some legitimacy, but it was fatally unbalanced. It was blind to the human possibilities that democratic and liberal regimes still hold. It was devoid of any vast and complex idea of the humanity of man. Instead, it wrapped itself in the historical moment for a duel with its mortal enemy and, being drawn into the logic of the duel, it imitated the enemy's worst features that brought them to its extremes.

These remarks, which concern anti-Communist and nihilist youth and not the Nazis properly speaking, help formulate the mimicry between Nazism and Communism. A number of historians contend that the idea of "great purges" was provided to Stalin by the action of Hitler in the "night of the long knives." But I speak of a more essential mimicry, such as the one described by the German historian Ernst Nolte, for whom Nazism was a reply to Communism, an inordinate and criminal one, yet after all, a response.[3] Nolte has been strongly criticized on this point. He has been charged with allowing Hitler extenuating circumstances by claiming that it was Stalin who started things. I do not believe that Nolte had such intentions. But it is true that Nolte presents an untenable thesis, although he draws attention to accurate historical elements. It is frankly absurd to suggest that the Nazis killed because they felt directly threatened by the Bolsheviks and so they themselves would not be killed. It is to take the rationalization of the criminal for the explanation of the crime. This question of mimicry has to be considered in a less summary way.

What is true is that Communism was a daring, ambitious, and extremely violent ideology that appeared to succeed. The anti-Communists reacted to this challenge according to their own quality of soul. Some of them strove to preserve the humanity of man imperiled by Communism; the criminals drew from it techniques of manipulation and violence to accomplish the crimes they themselves had conceived and willed. There probably was a sort of "emulation in crime" between Communism and Nazism, but it did not constitute an attenuating circumstance for Nazism. Those who imitate and outdo the crimes of their enemies, whom they denounce as criminals, are worse than their enemies.

The anti-Communism and the nihilism are intellectual and spiritual phenomena. Those anti-Communists—students, writers, soldiers—were not especially threatened in their immediate personal interests by Communism. But the various economic and social crises of the 1920s and 1930s provoked the proletarianization of a large part of the middle classes in most of the countries of Europe. These populations reacted to their loss of status by voting quite largely for the Fascist or Nazi parties that would protect them from proletarianization. Thus Fascists and Nazis were able to politically exploit the fear of Communism that was widespread throughout society.

Why did these social strata, threatened by proletarianization, react to the pain inflicted by capitalism by turning against Communism? It was because Communism sealed for good a fate that in capitalism one could hope was temporary. Besides, Nazism spoke of itself as anticapitalist no less than anti-Communist. It denounced the *Zinsknechtschaft*, the bondage to the interest rate. It claimed to reestablish hereditary farms, the *Erbhof*, to defend the small tradesmen, artisans, and entrepreneurs against the *Konzern*, etcetera. To vote for the Nazis was to vote against Communism *and against capitalism*. There was something artificial in this.

Was a third way genuinely offered? Nazism did not offer a third way. It would preserve the essentials of capitalism. However, it rejected both Communism and capitalism by casting opprobrium on a segment of the population, the Jews, the public viewed as the "common factor" between Communism and capitalism. It was difficult to articulate in rational terms a third way that was neither Communist nor capitalist. But as soon as Communism and capitalism were both presented as "Jewish enterprises" both equally expropriating and despoiling the German people, it became easy to be at once anti-Communist and anticapitalist. It was enough to be anti-Semitic.

At this point a simple but fatal mechanism was triggered. In these troubled times, many Germans, like many in other European countries, were indeed anticapitalists and anti-Communists. They resolved their intellectual confusion by abandoning themselves to anti-Semitism. The pendulum of their unease and their wrath, oscillating from anticapitalism to anti-Communism, zeroed in on the Jewish "common factor." Many Nazis were caught in this mechanism that they exploited with such extreme cynicism. But before considering Nazi anti-Semitism, let's explore the Nazi "worldview," since they were so keen to possess one.

Underlying the nihilism that led the way to Nazism is the resolute, scornful, and violent rejection of civilization, the rejection of "base" civilization in the name of "noble" nature. But what kind of nature is involved here? It is not nature in the ancient sense, the Aristotelian or Christian sense of the term, the hierarchically ordered whole that culminates in the Idea, in Reason, or in God, and that ultimately culminates in Peace. It is a nature that is synonymous with war. One is reminded of Hobbes's "state of nature," which is the "war of all against all." But with Hobbes, life in the state of nature was "solitary, poor, brutish, nasty and short," in brief, unbearable, and that is why people left the state of nature to construct civilization. The Nazis wanted to regain the state of nature, the state of war against the artifice of civilization. Their ideal is exactly the opposite of Hobbes.

There is yet another important difference. The Hobbesian state of nature includes a decisive experience of equality. The war of all against all makes everyone realize that they are *equally* threatened. According to Hobbes, the weakest has strength enough to kill the strongest. In discovering their equal vulnerability, human beings discover the root of their equality. And it is because they discover they are equal that they are then able to agree in order to build the peaceful and civilized political order.

For the Nazi, however, the state of nature is essentially inegalitarian. Left to itself nature reveals the triumph of the strong. This is a thesis that goes back to Callicles, according to which civilization is a trick of the weak to subjugate the strong. But to this ancient idea is added the recent, scientific, biological idea of the "struggle for life" promoted by Darwin's theory of evolution. To the old Calliclean resentment against civilization that masks and crushes true natural differences is added the new idea according to which the survival of the fittest is the law of life. Hence, by eliminating the weak, life is best served. Whoever kills assists life and works for the good of humanity. This perverse use of Darwinism will play a central role in Nazi self-justification.

To better emphasize the reversal to which Nazi naturalism subjects the notion of nature, I'll add that in the traditional conception, nature, in particular under the form of the "law of nature," implies a limit to human arbitrariness and human will. If there is a "human nature," or "natural law," then human beings cannot do whatever they want to do. For the Nazis, however, nature is the opposite. It is so conceived that the human will can do whatever it wants with nature, once nature is taken to be the nature of the "weak" and the will to be the will of the "strong."

In this model, in which only the fittest survive, the chief protagonist is not the individual, but the "race." On this point also, the Nazis took up a banal idea from modern anthropology. The theory that the various races of humans were in some respects unequal was widespread in the nineteenth and at the beginning of the twentieth century. But Nazism renders the idea of race absolute to the point of destroying the very idea of the human species as a whole.

Nazi anti-Semitism appears to be a particular case of Nazi racism, according to which the Jews represented the lowest rung on the racial ladder, not to be subjected like the Slavs, but to be completely eliminated. At the same time, anti-Semitism is so central, so obsessive in Nazism, that it could not be considered only as a form of racism. Rather, racism should be considered here as a "generalization" of anti-Semitism. In any case anti-Semitism is the center of gravity of Nazism. Certain historians argue that the "final solution," the killing of the Jews, resulted from a chain of circumstances linked to the war rather than the effect of a deliberate plan. I disagree. This "functionalist" thesis is untenable, and its rival, the "intentionalist" thesis, is the only acceptable one. One does not kill six million people in three years—the majority of them women, children, and the elderly having no military potential—as the result of a chain of circumstances.

There remains the central question, the mystery of the murderous hatred of the Jews. Of course, the Nazis did not invent anti-Semitism, but Nazi anti-Semitism cannot be taken simply as a particularly virulent case of a general and diffuse anti-Semitism. Scholars distinguish in general between anti-Semitism and anti-Judaism.[4] "Anti-Judaism" is the term used for the traditional hostility toward the Jews as it manifested itself in the Christian world for reasons that were initially religious. This anti-Judaism presupposed and produced separation: it relegated the Jews to their ghettos. It was transformed into anti-Semitism when, with the French Revolution and its aftermath, the Jews were emancipated and took their place in public life. Anti-Semitism was a reaction to the emancipation and assimilation of the Jews. Why did this reaction take place?

This question is very difficult to answer in a satisfying way. Besides, if one explains anti-Semitism in a truly satisfying way, does that not in some way justify it? This would be but a particular instance, but an eminent one of trying to explain evil.

I have already argued that anti-Semitism supplied a kind of synthesis of two otherwise contradictory political and social passions, anti-Communism and anticapitalism. Previously, the Jews played a visible role in certain developments of the modern world, such as financial process, opinion process, intellectual process, all of which give modern society a network that cannot be seen or grasped and thus is cause for anxiety. Modern society substituted commerce for command, and the withering of command was disturbing: people want to know *who governs*. But when *no one* governs, the desire grows to *identify* those who govern the society that no one governs. Who governs then? The Jews govern, the Jews were the "kings of the age," according to the title of one of the first books expressing this modern anti-Semitism. Of course this answer is false, illusory in the sense that it answers to a social anxiety and can easily become delirious.

Why is the invisible power attributed to the Jews rather than to other groups or segments of the population? In fact, other groups are often incriminated: the Jesuits, the Freemasons, the capitalists. But the phantasm of invisible power always comes back to the Jews because the modern history of the Jews seems to provide the model of the general process. The Jews, in assimilating, disappear as Jews at the moment when the visible power of command tends to disappear. Thus the Jews seem to want to become invisible at the moment when power in general becomes invisible. Therefore this invisible power is the secret power of the Jews. So goes the conclusion reached by anxiety and phantasm.

Another important element is that democratic politics in the nineteenth and twentieth centuries was "territorializing." The traditional aristocratic and religious order crossed or overlooked borders. The new national order has a sharp awareness of territory and border. In spite of their sincere efforts to "nationalize," and become patriotic in each of their European homelands, the Jews still seemed to be "transnational" or "homeless," *heimatlos*.

Moreover, modern nationalism affirms the particularity of the nation as such. But paradoxically in modern democracy, it is difficult to affirm only particularity. Universality has been fully brought out; humanity as the totality of human beings has been made explicit. How could the sole particularity of the nation be a match for the universal? The particular nation must have a universal task. This national task can be universal and become the gift of civilization that each nation can make to the others. By a perverse reversal, anti-Semitism supplies the narrowest nationalism with what it seems to lack absolutely: a universalism—a caricatured, inverted universalism. If Jews are the enemies of the human race, the Nazis, in making the destruction of the Jews their primary task, fulfill the good of humanity and are the good servants of the universal. By declaring the Jews enemies of the human race, Nazi "particularism" accedes to the universal. In this sense, anti-Semitism is the universalism of the Nazis.

The extermination camp is both the first and the last expression of the Nazi project. The Nazi camp enacts the omnipotence and total domination of men over other human beings. The domination seen in the camps differs from all other forms of domination. It is not the domination of the victorious warrior; it is not even the domination of the sadist (even if sadism was found in the camps). It is a matter of duty and a scientific program of reducing certain human beings to what the Nazi doctrine proclaims: that the Jews are not human beings, but animals, indeed vermin. This is the dehumanization of the human being. It is an inconceivable undertaking whose primary impulse escapes human scrutiny, an attempt at "decreating" humanity. Primo Levi has described this inconceivable undertaking of dehumanization with admirable simplicity:

We already find ourselves in the open, in the blue and icy snow of dawn, barefoot and naked, with all our clothing in our hands, with a hundred yards to run to the next hut. There we are finally allowed to get dressed.

When we finish, everyone remains in his own corner and we do not dare lift our eyes to look at one another. There is nowhere to look in a mirror, but our appearance stands in front of us, reflected in a hundred livid faces, in a hundred miserable and sordid puppets. We are transformed into the phantoms glimpsed yesterday evening.

Then for the first time we became aware that our language lacks words to express this offence, the demolition of a man. In a moment, with almost prophetic intuition, the reality was revealed to us: we had reached the bottom. It is not possible to sink lower than this; no human condition is more miserable than this, nor could it conceivably be so. Nothing belongs to us any more; they have taken away our clothes, our shoes, even our hair; if we speak, they will not listen to us, and if they listen, they will not understand. They will even take away our name . . .

Imagine now a man who is deprived of everyone he loves, and at the same time of his house, his habits, his clothes, in short, of everything he possesses: he will be a hollow man, reduced to suffering and needs, forgetful of dignity and restraint, for he who loses all too often easily loses himself. He will be a man whose life or death can be lightly decided with no sense of human affinity, in the most fortunate of cases, on the basis of a pure judgment of utility. It is in this way that one can understand the double sense of the term "extermination camp," and it is now clear what we seek to express with the phrase: "to lie on the bottom."[5]

CHAPTER 16

The Empire of Law

I

AMONG THE ILLUSIONS that tempt our laziness, none is more present today than this one: the law must be and will be increasingly the sole regulator of social life. The emptiness of this illusion must be brought to light.

What is an illusion? An illusion is a representation linked to a desire. But to what desire? After all, if we speak of the law, to desire that human relations be organized according to law, is the very project of civilization and there is nothing illusory about it. We thus speak of "Roman law" or "Germanic law" or "common law" as great achievements of civilization. But something more specific characterizes the contemporary situation. Not only the desire that law should rule, but that it *alone* should rule. In a vigorous formulation, Kant in 1795 wrote in *Perpetual Peace* that "nature irresistibly *wills* that right should finally triumph."[1] Without any doubt *we* will that "right should finally triumph." And many among us are convinced that the movement of history leads *irresistibly* in this direction. This contemporary will and conviction encompasses numerous aspects that we shall attempt to identify, but two motives for our enthusiasm for the law come to mind immediately.

The first is ancient, going back to the origins of the modern democracy. As we have had occasion to see in greater detail, modern humanity declared its coming of age in declaring human rights. Human beings are not born subjects of law, ancestral or divine, more generally the law of "superiors;" they "are born and remain free and equal in rights." The human being is the being that has rights. Proclaiming these rights is different from implementing and guaranteeing them through stable institutions, but it is natural that societies born out of human rights should end up explicitly placing law at the center of their action and consciousness and becoming societies wholly governed by law.

The second motive is of much more recent origin. It is tied to the weakening of the national state regulations and territorial political sovereignties. This very broad movement is called "globalization." We live our lives more and more in the context of this global civil society composed of individuals, businesses, nongovernmental organizations, and humanitarian organizations, a global civil society ruled by institutions that are not political, but by tribunals or quasi-judicial bodies charged with assuring respect for freedom of commerce, the rules of competition, and human rights. In short, it is the judicial branch augmented by rating agencies and arbitration boards. These nongovernmental agencies are not tribunals, but replace them in arbitrating disputes without going to court. They contribute even more than the judicial institutions to the denationalization and depoliticization of the rules of social life.

Thus it is quite natural that having lived for two hundred years under the spiritual authority of human rights and recently under the functional logic of "globalization," we would envisage social life from a legal perspective. In other words, we are organized increasingly according to rules of law administered and guaranteed by judges or quasi-judges. But why did a process that seems so natural take so long to come to completion? It is because, for nearly two centuries, the Europeans sought to establish human rights in the framework of the sovereign national state—the same sovereign national state that the law and civil society are in the process of eroding, leaving it but an empty shell. Thus our fathers claimed to "make real" the rights of man by means of the sovereign state that now appears to be the principal enemy of these rights. In any case, we want to make human rights independent of it. We envisage a world where the law would be guaranteed without the national state.

I shall first consider the history and meaning of this transformation *within* states. How did we come to consider "government by judges" as the best, most civilized way to order common life? Then I shall consider the international order. If the sovereign states weaken into empty shells, the perspective of a truly international order imposes on itself an order that falls outside interstate logic. The logic of independence, of competition, of war, of an international order founded on a true *international law*, not an interstate law, but a truly *cosmopolitan* law, whose subjects are no longer the states, but individuals and groups, that have rights simply because they are human.

It is quite natural that societies born under the sign of human rights should end up placing law at the center of their action as well as their consciousness by aspiring to be societies governed wholly by law. The argument is plausible, but misleading since things did not happen this way historically and politically. Human rights at first imposed themselves against the law of the land, by means of the state.

The enlightenment modern state opposed its rational law to supposedly irrational jurisprudence—that tangled web of "feudal," ecclesiastical, familial laws, of "customary" laws that carried weight because they were passed down from past generations and incorporated precisely their "juris- prudence." There were several laws from diverse sources, and that was cause for confusion and abuse. Law was born in diverse places. Hence- forth, the rule, the law arises from one place only, that place where the state legislates, be it Parliament, King-in-Parliament, Congress, or the National Assembly. The fact that there is only one source of rule guarantees the rule's impartiality and rationality.

The logic of the modern state is most visible in the doctrine of Hobbes. Hobbes argued that people *naturally* live in a state of war, which is the war of all against all. This war is due to the fact that human beings desire the same things and thus are in competition, that they are proud, and thus each man or woman wants to be first, that they have diverse ideas of truth that they want to impose on one another. The consequence of this war is that people live in continual danger. Life in the state of nature is "solitary, poor, brutish, nasty and short."

People risk their life and thereby discover that they want above all else to live and cannot avoid wanting to live. They risk losing the little they have and discover that they want to keep the little they possess and cannot avoid wanting to keep it, to keep and even increase their property. People risk their liberty, and discover that they want to keep it, and cannot avoid wanting to keep it.

The war of all against all leads everyone to reflect on their condition, which turns out to be a common condition. They discover themselves to be *equally* threatened in their life, their property, and their liberty. To live, to keep and even increase their property, to preserve their liberty: these are their rights. Discovering themselves equally threatened in their rights, they discover that they have equal rights. Thus they desire to see these rights guaranteed. How then to guarantee and protect the rights of the members of society? By constructing a *separate* place *above* society, a *neu- tral* place that will be occupied by the *sovereign*, a sovereign who is neces- sarily *absolute*. To say that the right of the sovereign is absolute is to say that it is *without common measure* with the right of any of the members of society, essentially it trumps all other rights. If this were not the case, the members of society would quite simply not be able to leave the state of war. This is the Hobbesian doctrine, but also describes an essential fea- ture of the modern state.

First, the sovereign state is the instrument of the protection of rights. It is sovereign in order to have the force to protect them. Moreover, a sovereign state is necessary to guarantee *equal* rights. Of course, such a state is also dangerous for the rights and liberties of the members of soci- ety since it has so much more power than any social entity. We are today very sensitive to the way in which the state endangers the human rights.

Nevertheless we must not forget the first aspect: without a sovereign state the naturally inegalitarian logic of society wins. That does not of course mean that the sovereign state is the sole guarantor of the equality of rights, but it is the final guarantor because it has a monopoly on public force. That is what happened in the United States in the 1960s. The civil rights for the African American minority would never have been achieved in the South if the *public force* of the federal government had not imposed it. One could say that in the modern regime, the state and citizen's rights are both partners and adversaries. They are adversaries as a consequence of their prior partnership.

Secondly, Hobbes criticizes customary rights, jurisprudence, common law, social powers (what the French revolutionaries called feudal society and the ancien régime), by virtue of a juridical logic. To overcome the conflicts that inevitably arise in society, a neutral place is needed, between the contending parties, a place essentially superior to them and whose decisions are binding; there is need for a supreme arbitrator or judge. Other judges, and more generally other powers, have power only by the permission of the supreme judge. Other judges and powers, ecclesiastical or lay, invoke a truth, be it the legal truth of common law or the religious truth contained in the dogmas professed. These diverse truths cannot constitute the supreme law of society because they are diverse and subject to debate and interpretation. The supreme law of society resides thus in the supreme judge, the sovereign, who alone determines what is law. According to Hobbes's decisive phrase, "*auctoritas, non veritas, facit legem.*"

Thus, the modern state has as its raison d'être the protection of rights; and it develops and proceeds according to an arbitral or judicial logic. In this sense, the contemporary phenomenon of the law being the unique regulator of society is but the natural continuation of the modern state as an arbiter state, but at the cost of a reversal. The sovereign law replaces the sovereign who determines the law. In short, we have gone from the sovereign who is judge to the judge who is sovereign.

But between these two extreme formulas, and also between the periods they define, an altogether different ideal of law and its place in free society held sway for a long time: the ideal of the separation of powers, which is in principle still ours. The separation of powers allows the problem Hobbes left hanging to be resolved: how to avoid the power of the state, constructed to protect society, to be turned into oppression? By "dividing" or "distributing" the power of the state into three powers: the legislative, executive, and judicial powers. It was Montesquieu who gave the most rigorous and ingenious analysis of the mechanism of the separation of powers. We have discussed the interplay between the executive and the legislative. What about the judicial?

People are often confused about Montesquieu's thesis. For him, there is not *the* judicial power; its form and function depend on the political regime. In the monarchic regime, in the France of Montesquieu's time, where the king holds the executive and legislative powers, it was essential that the judicial power be truly a distinct power, lest the regime be despotic. Not only do parliaments, composed of judges who own their offices, judge particulars, but they must also be responsible for "the depository of the fundamental laws" of the state.[2]

In the modern English regime, the function and nature of the judicial are altogether different. Liberty is guaranteed, by the interplay of the other two powers and by the effects this interplay induces. The judicial is thus not the guardian of liberty as it was in a monarchy. And to assist liberty, it must even in some way disappear as a power. This is possible because in a democratic regime the laws are fixed and clear, and the necessity of interpreting the laws is reduced to a minimum.[3] At the same time, judgment is rendered by a jury, "drawn from the body of the people" and who return to society once judgment has been rendered. Thus justice is rendered without the judges playing any decisive role in the process: "In this fashion the power of judging, so terrible among men, being attached neither to a certain state nor to a certain profession, becomes, so to speak, invisible and null. Judges are not continually in view; one fears the magistracy, not the magistrates."[4]

Montesquieu's ideas are crucial to our discussion, but they are rather inexact historically. Judges played a greater role, and the jury a much lesser role, in eighteenth-century England, than Montesquieu says here. Not a trace of the hanging judge in his pages devoted to the English Constitution! But these inaccuracies are deliberate. Montesquieu sketched the ideal model of the representative republican regime. Such a regime does not know what we call the "power of judges." That surprises us because we have learned to establish a kind of equivalence between the liberal regime and the power of judges, to measure the quality of a liberal regime by the quantity of the power of judges. Montesquieu is the most incisive analyst and the most competent theoretician of liberalism, and yet he wants to reduce the power of judges to a minimum or render it "invisible" and "null." Why? Because the "power of judging" is "terrible." The power that seems to us the most inoffensive, in truth the most salutary, is the one that in the eyes of Montesquieu is intrinsically the most fearsome, even if he would acknowledge that it is necessary and therefore salutary.

Montesquieu would be surprised to see the enthusiasm in Europe today for the power of judges, but he would not be surprised that the free country that grants judges the most power, the United States, is also the country where there are by far the most citizens in prison or under judicial control. I note that we do not fear judicial power because in principle it ignores arbitrariness, limiting itself to "applying the law." That may be, but its virtue risks becoming its vice, its lack of arbitrariness becoming mechanical rigidity.

Such mechanical rigidity produces rather perverse cumulative effects, as is seen in the United States, where certain laws are so clear and rigorous, so "fixed" Montesquieu would say, that judges must apply them strictly. Thus the judges are obliged to imprison for an extended time the perpetrators of minor offenses in cases where these are drug offenses, or as in California, to condemn to life imprisonment with no possibility of release third-time offenders even if the third crime is a minor offense. Thus one cannot speak of an excess of judicial power, since these unreasonable laws are enacted by legislatures, and judges only apply these laws. That is true, but that means that the legislature assigns to the judiciary the care of solving certain social problems by exercising a repression that many deem excessive. Thus a consequence manifests itself that Montesquieu did not contemplate. Because the judicial power is "invisible," a "terrible" task is assigned to it.

The advance of the power of judges is rooted in the matrix of neither the sovereign state nor the liberal state. Where then does it come from? It derives, Philippe Raynaud writes, "from the political experience of the liberal regimes, notably from the Anglo-Saxon tradition."[5] He underlines the decisive role of the American Revolution and constitutional experience. What is distinctive about this constitutional experience? Raynaud points to two reasons. One, unlike the French and the English, the Americans were aware very early of the despotic potentialities of representative government, that is, of the legislative power. The American colonists felt that they were victims of the Parliament in London that was supposed to "represent" them without actually including any "representatives." Then, as a consequence of the federal nature of their country, the Americans needed a complex, written Constitution that distributed powers and functions among the different levels of the federal structure, and this Constitution was to give the American body politic its form and soul.

Raynaud writes:

> The evolution that led first from the adoption by the States born of the thirteen colonies of Bills of Rights that limited the power of the legislature, to the Constitution of 1787, and lastly, to the control of the determination of the constitutionality of federal laws by the Supreme Court of the United States (*Marbury vs. Madison* decision of 1803) obeys an indisputable logic.[6]

The power of constitutional judges is not a sovereign power. As the authors of *The Federalist Papers* already pointed out, the power given to a court to declare legislative acts null can only be founded on the superiority of the Constitution, that is to say, on the popular sovereignty as declared in the Constitution.[7] But for the Constitution to have a voice, the judges must interpret it.

What does it mean to "interpret the Constitution"? On this point, there are strong opposing views about the American Constitution, which are much more a part of political debate than in most other countries. According to the conservatives, in order to interpret the Constitution, one must always go back to the original intent of the Founding Fathers. According to the progressives, the rules should be adapted to new needs and new insights. In the latter view, the judge "creates" law. A philosopher of law such as Ronald Dworkin gives his "progressivism" a "rationalist" turn. I quote Raynaud once again: Dworkin "seeks to avoid the charge of 'judicial activism' by making the judge the guarantor of the law's unity, who progressively draws from the different rules a coherent conception of justice and equity, and who, whatever may be his liberty, implicitly acknowledges that for each case there exists a 'good answer.' "[8]

The profound recent changes of the French constitutional system have been influenced by the American system and experience and the American debates about it. To put it simply, if there were no United States Supreme Court, there would, in France, be no constitutional Council or at least the French constitutional Council would not have acquired the powers it has acquired in recent years. These new powers are a departure from the French constitutional tradition, which is from France's two rival constitutional traditions—the republican, revolutionary, "legicentric" tradition that favors the legislative power, and the consular, "revisionist," or Gaullist tradition that wants to strengthen the executive.

Of course, the French constitutional evolution is not only an effect of American influence. First of all, it corresponds to the new political and moral situation of the democracies that increasingly reject the exercise of political power by the legislative and executive branches to the benefit of a moral protest that is as strident as it is vague. By favoring the judicial power, these two demands are satisfied in one fell swoop, one negative and the other positive. On the one hand, the judicial power is a politically "invisible" power, even when its decisions amount to a political revolution; on the other hand, the judicial power appears as a power that ultimately takes only justice and morality into consideration. For in France particularly the Declaration of the Rights of Man has constitutional standing and is taken as the ultimate foundation of all judgments. One could say simply that the judicial power is a power that seems not to be a political power, and appears to be a spiritual power.

We have considered the advances of law or the advances of the "government of judges" within nations. Of course, an "empire of law" is not limited to the internal order but encompasses the international order. This is what President George H. W. Bush meant when he spoke of a "new world order" at the time of the first Gulf War. The invasion of Kuwait by Iraq was to be repelled and punished by the international community. The military coalition led by the United States implemented a sort of "police power," focused no longer on delinquent individuals but on delinquent *states*. The Americans use the expression "rogue states" to designate those states that in their view represent an acute danger for the common peace and security. What interests us here is the "paradigm shift" that these recent developments signal. What are the implications of this paradigm shift for what until then was considered as "international law"?

In short, one assumes that states can be motivated to act, in particular militarily, by a pure respect for law, a respect that is detached from their particular state interest. If military action is an international police action, those who engage in it have no greater particular interest in this action than do the police who arrest a murderer or bank robber within a state. The police arrest a bank robber for violating the law, not for attacking *their* bank and taking *their* savings. In this sense, they are perfectly disinterested. Can one imagine that states will be more susceptible of acting on these principles, thereby abjuring the motive of national interest whose legitimacy was generally acknowledged? In any case, it is this change of scope that is implied in the two large-scale military actions by the United States and their allies, the Gulf War and the bombing of Serbia, followed by the intervention in Kosovo and the turning over of Milosevic to the International Tribunal in The Hague.

Some argue that these recent developments do not signal any important political change, save perhaps an advance in American and Western hypocrisy. In the Gulf War as in Kosovo, the Americans and their allies only put the language of law on an action motivated solely by their national interests. In doing so, they behaved as states have always done. I do not think that this "cynical" assessment is sufficient. Assuming that the Gulf War can be tied easily to the immediate interests of the United States and its allies in the region, this is not the case in Kosovo. The images and ideas we form of the world in which we act, including our interests, directly motivate our action. Besides, we are aware of our interests only within a certain representation of the world that does not derive simply from our interests. One should not underestimate a priori the role of the image of a virtually unified humanity that would make the old interstate logic obsolete.

In the traditional order of things, which held sway for the greater part of human history, law properly holds meaning only *within* political bodies. Since it regulates common life, law holds meaning only in the context of common life, that is, of the res publica of the city. Of course, the notion of jus gentium has circulated in Europe for a long time, being translated into English as the "law of nations." This notion goes back to Roman law. It designates those laws that are not covered by the *jus civile* (civil or political law), as the law within the city. Thus it includes at times several types of law: international laws (as the moderns call them), laws concerning human beings as humans independent of their political affiliation (i.e., the laws regarding foreigners), laws concerning institutions that are common to all people (i.e., the general laws of the family, which prohibited the separation of children from their parents even for desirable or legitimate reasons), and laws regarding living creatures (i.e., laws concerning animals). Once again, the vagueness or plurality of meanings of the notion of res publica stems from the fact that it encompasses all the laws that do not come under the civil law or the law of cities in a haphazard way. Thus this negative definition confirms the primacy and centrality of law within political bodies.

This duality and dissymmetry of law were settled and clarified by the progressive constitution of "European public law" that unfolded from the seventeenth to the nineteenth century, (from the Treaty of Westphalia to the Berlin Conference of 1878). According to the provisions of European public law, law was principally the law within states and thus civil or political law. It was more so than ever since "sovereign" states distinguished rigorously between internal and external law. And in the external order, states were the only legal subjects, while individuals were legal subjects inasmuch as they were nationals of a state.

This "external" law was "international law" set forth by conventions established among states. These conventions codified relations among states, particularly the relation that seems by nature alien to law, namely war. War had to be declared, ambassadors and plenipotentiary envoys had to have their security and liberty guaranteed, civilians had to be spared, prisoners of war well treated, and the use of certain types of weapons prohibited. These conventions concretized the fact that war in civilized Europe was deemed to be a relation of state to state and not a relation of person to person. European public law constituted a great achievement of civilization precisely because it gave some form and effectiveness to this salutary fiction.

At the same time, since the legal subject was states and the states were independent and sovereign, the conventions were only valid as long as the states considered them to be. In other words, as long as the states considered that the convention answered to their interests. International conventions were thus subordinated to national interest even if certain of these conventions normally appeared to conform with the interest of all and carried a particular authority. Thus in spite of conventions and treaties, states in the end continued to live in the state of nature, sovereign and answerable to none. When Hobbes wanted to give an idea of the original condition of humanity, of the state of nature, he evoked the relations that prevailed among states. States remain in the state of nature, whereas individuals leave it precisely by constituting states. Essentially, European public law can be described as follows: there is no law except within sovereign states; without, among sovereign states, the state of nature reigns, a state of nature civilized by fragile but invaluable conventions.

Something needs to be added. An international order of this kind appears to be extremely fragile. After all, the state of nature is ultimately the state of war or the permanent threat of war. Yet, in spite of bloody cycles— the war of the Spanish Succession, the wars of the Revolution and the Empire—Europe, from the seventeenth to the nineteenth century, tended toward peace. One of the causes was the development of commerce, which substituted the spirit of trade for the spirit of conquest. Another factor concerning international relations was the cause of optimism for Europeans. It was the phenomenon of the European balance of power. The eighteenth and nineteenth centuries were realist and scientific times; they were Newtonian. They believed in the equality of action and reaction, that relations among states, like relations among the planets, formed a stable, predictable, regular system. The secret of European civilization was that the different nations of Europe were linked to each other, through alliances and reversals of alliances, through coalitions of variable geometry, in such a way that none among them was in a position to seriously threaten the others, so that the European balance was preserved. In this mechanism, the United Kingdom obviously played a pivotal role. English policy consisted, on the one hand, in assuring its mastery of the seas, and on the other, in preventing, by direct military intervention or by financial assistance to its allies, any continental power from achieving continental hegemony. Thus in the classical European order, law belonged properly to the internal life of states. States were sovereign, motivated principally and legitimately by national interest; while among states reigned a state of nature civilized by conventions; and this state of nature tended toward a peaceful balance because it was ordered, by the balance of power.

This system, which prevailed during the most glorious period of European history, was not without merits. It appeared to represent an appreciable advance in civilization. In retrospect too, considering that the wars of the twentieth century ignored the distinction between combatants and civilians and in which all means were acceptable, it seemed a sort of golden age. Of course, it is not true, as pointed out long ago be the two philosophers most critical of the classic European public law, Rousseau and Kant. Kant considers that the system of the balance of power is "a mere figment of the imagination" similar to "Swift's house, whose architect built it so perfectly in accord with all the laws of equilibrium, that as soon as a sparrow lit on it, it fell in."[9] As for Rousseau, he denounces the classic political arrangement:

> We shall examine whether the establishment of society accomplished too much or too little; whether individuals—who are subject to laws and to men, while societies among themselves maintain the independence of nature—remain exposed to the ills of both conditions without having their advantages; and whether it would be better to have no civil society in the world than to have many. . . . Is it not this partial and imperfect association which produces tyranny and war; and are not tyranny and war the greatest plagues of humanity?[10]

These two philosophers found it impossible to be satisfied with the so-called civilized status quo. Kant obstinately searched for the means to overcome the political and human order that presupposes and supports war, in order to arrive at "perpetual peace." Rousseau, on the other hand, was too deprived of hope, too skeptical toward human artifices to attempt it seriously. Pierre Hassner reviews Kant's procedure.[11]

Kant is not a "bleating pacifist"; he recognizes the civilizing virtues, the formative value of man's aggressive dispositions: "[T]hanks be to nature for the incompatibility, for the distasteful, competitive vanity, for the insatiable desire to possess and also to rule. Without them, all of humanity's excellent natural capacities would have lain eternally dormant. Man wills concord; but nature better knows what is good for the species; she wills discord."[12] At the same time, Kant detests war. Thus Kant writes at one point: "[T]he greatest evil that can oppress civilized peoples derives from *wars*, not, indeed, so much from actual present or past wars, as from the never-ending and constantly increasing *arming* for future war."[13] Yet, he also writes: "Thus, at the stage of culture at which the human race still stands, war is an indispensable means for bringing it to a still higher stage; and only after a perfect culture exists (God knows when), would peace that endures forever benefit us, and thus it is possible only in such a culture."[14]

Kant introduces an ambiguity here by saying that peace will be morally necessary when it will be possible and that peace is possible because it is morally necessary. In effect,

> moral-practical reason within us voices its irresistible veto: *There shall be no war*, whether between you and me in a state of nature or among states. . . . Accordingly, there is no longer any question as to whether perpetual peace is a reality or a fiction. . . . We must, however, act *as though* perpetual peace were a reality, which perhaps it is not, by working for its establishment. . . .

> It can be said that the establishment of a universal and enduring peace is not
> just a part, but rather constitutes the whole, of the ultimate purpose of Law
> within the bounds of pure reason.[15]

But how can this imperative of morally practical reason be implemented? How does one found this perpetual peace? In his 1795 *Project of Perpetual Peace*, Kant formulated his ideas more precisely. The peace treaty, the condition and means of pacification, is composed of three articles:

(1) "The civil constitution of every nation should be republican." Why should it be? Because in such a constitution, "the consent of the citizenry is required in order to determine whether or not there will be war," and they will "consider all its calamities before committing themselves to so risky a game."[16]

(2) "The right of nations shall be based on a federation of free States." Kant is not clear and interpreters disagree. Does Kant envisage a universal republic, a sort of world federal state? It seems rather that he restricts himself to the more practical idea of a loose alliance, or if circumstances are favorable, of a tighter association of (republican) states against war.

(3) The third clause concerns "cosmopolitan right." This clause derives from the fact that "because a (narrower or wider) community widely prevails among the Earth's peoples, a transgression of rights in *one* place in the world is felt *everywhere*." From there, a cosmopolitan right, one that protects every human being qua human being is no longer a figment of the imagination. We would speak today of "humanitarian right" or simply "human rights." One hails in Kant the clear anticipation of a theme that is dear to us, but one is struck by the narrow limits in which Kant constrains this "cosmopolitan right." In practice, he limits this right to the "conditions of universal hospitality," that is, to "the right of an alien not to be treated as an enemy upon his arrival in another's country."[17]

Kant leaves us in uncertainty. One would willingly consider him to be the most idealistic of realist philosophers, or the most realistic of idealist philosophers, but that does not get us very far. Universal peace, or the rule of law, is morally desirable, thus morally necessary. It can be approximated thanks to the progress of civilization, the progress of the republican constitution within states, which includes the progress of communications and commerce among states, and the progress of the "republican resemblance" among states. But this progress, like every advance of civilization, presupposes the activation of the aggressive faculties of human beings—people must "fight for the republic"—which Kant calls their "unsociable sociability." Thus humanity is forever getting closer to this universal peace, but like the curve to its asymptote, without ever really reaching it and with relapses or regressions that are necessarily involved in the activation of man's aggressive faculties. Leo Strauss has summed up the difficulty in an epigram: the continual progress toward perpetual peace is perpetual war.

On the other hand, what are the *motives* of people engaged in this long march toward peace? In most cases, the motives are self-interested: the "material" interests of those who seek in peace chiefly the guarantee of their "pleasures"; the "moral" interests of those who want to "win the battle for peace," "defeat the warmongers for good." In any case, these motives are not "moral" in the rigorous Kantian sense. Rare, very rare among the "combatants" for peace are those who act out of pure respect for the moral law!

If peace is attained, it will be an external peace, that is, an absence of war. If the object of our desire is a true peace, thus internal and moral, one has to imagine that humanity as a whole is capable of making a leap, of accomplishing a moral conversion. But this conversion to the moral law can only be the rare attainment of rare individuals. Kant subjects humanity to the torture of Tantalus. He brings peace by law close to us, thanks to the progress of civilization, and at the moment we are about to grasp it, he takes it from us entirely, for this peace is not peace, but an external tranquility accessible "even for a people comprised of devils (if only they possess understanding)."[18] But can one imagine happy devils, devils at peace with themselves?

This is what we have come to; we are no more advanced than Kant. His hopes are ours, as are his hesitations and perplexities. We too seek peace through law at the end of the asymptotic progress of civilization, of commerce and communications. But we also recognize the necessity of a moral conversion or, in modern terms, of a "humanitarian awakening of conscience." We do not know any better than Kant how to articulate the internal change and external transformations. Between the two there is no natural and intrinsic link. The existence of such a link would be necessary for us to have the right to hope seriously for peace—true peace—through law. And in the end we think, like Kant, that we have the duty to work at this peace through law that we have no right to hope for but for which we hope nonetheless.

What are the difficulties that confront our "Kantian conscience" of war and peace today? Kant made us undergo the torture of Tantalus. But it is, of course, *we* who inflict the torture of Tantalus on ourselves. We think that we are forever coming closer to peace, that peace *ought to* be with us. And if it is not, we think it is the fault of certain political actors who are called the enemies of peace. For example, delinquent states, those rogue states that the American State Department lists every year: North Korea, Iran, etcetera.

After the World Trade Center massacre in New York, no one will contest that certain states or terrorist groups act as if they were moved by hatred of the human race and that it is vital that they be stopped. Yet, we act as if once criminals are brought to justice, peace will prevail. Now this assumption is either tautological or eschatological. Tautological: if in thought we suppress all the factors of trouble, what in effect remains if not peace and tranquility? (We only forget to think of the new trouble that will no doubt arise.) Eschatological: we suppose that the "last times" have arrived and that after a "final struggle" we will enjoy the golden fruits of peace. So we anticipate these "last times," we anticipate this peace to come and we act *as if* it were already here. The consequence is that the wars we conduct are of an unprecedented type. Our governments present them as police operations. We bombarded Serbia massively for seventy-eight days without declaring war against the country. The serious mistake we made is not in waging war against Milosevic, but, in failing to declare war on him.

We have engaged in a moral lie on a grand scale. We have lied to ourselves about what we were doing. Instead of telling the simple and honorable truth that we were waging war for reasons that were inseparably political and moral, we have adopted a simply moral posture. We have placed ourselves at the pinnacle of all the virtues, we were simply waging the pure fight of justice and right, our Albanian allies were waging the good fight of liberty and the right of nations. Of course, the adversary had to appear as a criminal pure and simple. Since the real crimes they had committed were not enough for our good conscience, we imputed to them some crimes they had not committed. All this was no longer very honorable.

The refusal to declare war did not stem principally from our "hypocrisy." All kinds of diverse interests were boiling in the cauldron of our deliberations, but the Western councils were in some way awed by the pure idea of humanity on the one hand and the pure idea of crime against humanity on the other. Our leaders seemed incapable of thinking or saying anything without having recourse to this contrast. If the disproportion of forces had not been so enormous—so enormous that it made our martial postures look comical—we would have paid dearly for such a flawed approach to reality.

The most serious political consequence of this refusal to recognize war is no doubt the extreme difficulty of making peace. In Bosnia, Kosovo, and Macedonia we are in the position of occupiers and protectors, albeit well-intentioned occupiers and protectors. We have only our good intentions to guide us in the midst of populations that have needs and passions. Most often these populations *do not want* to live together. On our part, we *do not want* to recognize this fact, or we assimilate it to the crime of "ethnic cleansing." We want to envisage only a purely moral politics.

Consequently, we are torn between the status quo borders that for mysterious reasons we refuse to touch and the purely moral politics that we pretend to impose on human beings, who nonetheless have the right not to be angels: torn between what is and what ought to be, we do not consider what is possible politically. In the name of humanitarianism, we are inhuman.

I spoke of our "Kantian conscience" of war and peace. In truth we are on this point more Kantian than Kant. We have completely delegitimized war (something Kant had not done even if he came very close, when he stated in the *Doctrine of Right*: "Practical moral reason enunciates in us its irresistible veto: *there must not be any war*"). We accept war only as war against war, against tyranny, against crime, thus in the service of pure justice. That is why we refuse to call it war and to declare it as such. The cause or consequence of this refusal is that we refuse to acknowledge that states, bodies politic have particular interests, susceptible of diverging to the point where at least a *risk* of war can appear. We suppose that the material and moral interests of political communities either are in a natural harmony or can be harmonized by implementing common rules that do not impose any unacceptable sacrifice on anyone. That is a salutary postulate to the extent that it incites everyone to seek grounds for agreement in a given situation rather than disagreement. To think that peace is possible, that it is normal, is a conviction that certainly helps in finding the ways to peace. At the same time, this postulate rules out that situation in which a body politic or state can legitimately judge that its material or moral interests have been wronged or neglected to such a point that the use of force remains its only recourse to defend its liberty and its honor. In postulating that the liberty and honor of a body politic never justify the risk of war, do we not, in the name of morality, deprive political life of an essential part of its morality?

CHAPTER 17

The Empire of Morality

I HAVE UNDERLINED what seems to me the main trait of the present world, which is the tension between the old order, what some would call the "natural" order of politics and the project and hope of a new metapolitical or postpolitical order of unified humanity. Contrary to the predictions or hopes of many, I argued that the political order remains still largely determined and that people's lives are still largely defined by political circumstances and context, by the political regime and form.

There are two principal ways to conceive a metapolitical humanity that has overcome or transcended its political condition. It can be humanity organized according to law or humanity living in accord with morality, which is humanity living in respect for human dignity. In the two preceding chapters, I have dealt with humanity organized according to law, distinguishing between internal law and external (international and "cosmopolitan" law). Regarding internal law, I considered the increased power of judges. On that subject, I used the expression "spiritual power," which originated with Saint-Simon.

What justifies this expression is that the power of judges today rests ultimately not on the laws of the nation, not on its constitution, but on the foundation of the laws and the constitution, that is, "human rights" and the idea of "humanity." Setting aside local laws, accepted usages, and international conventions and treaties, judges more and more claim to speak *immediately* in the name of humanity. For very understandable reasons, this appears to be progress. The complicated formalities that held back and at times prevented the exercise of justice have been brushed aside like so many scraps of paper. Judges exercise an immediate right to inculpate alleged guilty parties, whoever and wherever they may be, as a Spanish judge made clear recently by having the Chilean General Pinochet arrested by British authorities, and as the International Tribunal of The Hague shows every day in conducting the trial of Milosevic, the former president of Yugoslavia.

However natural and legitimate our desire to see criminals punished, this unconditional jurisdiction that judges rely on more and more raises serious difficulties. As an example of the incoherencies of the current political and juridical situation, consider how the United States has demanded that Milosevic appear before a type of tribunal whose legitimacy the United states refuses to recognize as a matter of principle. I will mention three principal difficulties of the present international judicial system.

First, the declarations of human rights are nobler but much vaguer than national laws and constitutions. If one relies chiefly on human rights, there can be no "fixed way of judging." Arbitrariness, against which our constitution is supposed to protect us, will only increase paradoxically by the actions of judges.

Second, a power that discovers that it can act arbitrarily will soon use and abuse this latitude. It tends toward despotism. Perhaps operation "Clean Hands" in Italy gave us a first glimpse of what the despotism of judges will be if the current tendency is confirmed. The Italian judges changed the political map of the country without the Italian people being consulted at all.

Finally, if the principles of justice are immediately human rights, why would their activation be reserved to judges? Hitherto judges meted justice because they held the science of right and the laws. As soon as the mediation of right and the laws is swept aside in favor of the immediate appeal to human rights, the mediation of the judge loses its raison d'être. Every human being is capable of understanding human rights and of applying this knowledge to a case at hand. But that is exactly the definition that the early liberal authors, particularly Locke, gave of the state of nature! The power of judges risks returning us to the state of nature, which is another name for the state of war.

In any case, the new power of judges illustrates our impatience with mediations, in particular political mediations, and our desire to recognize and achieve humanity *immediately.* This desire is natural to our democratic societies dominated by the sentiment of human resemblance, by the self-evident character of the humanity of the other person. I would like now to consider the different versions of this immediate moral recognition of the humanity of the other person that preoccupies us so much today.

One must first distinguish between the different versions of the democratic recognition of those like oneself, the different versions of humanitarianism on the one hand, and the specifically Christian love of neighbor on the other. Although this analysis is complex, a certain number of its elements is clear. Generally, the Christian love of neighbor is essentially different from the democratic sentiment for those like oneself. Of course they can have many comparable or even identical practical effects. Nothing distinguishes materially a meal served in a Goodwill soup kitchen from a meal served by a church aid society. But the inner disposition of those who serve it is in principle different. (I say "in principle," for many Christians are

moved by the democratic sentiment for those like oneself as much as or
more than the Christian love of neighbor.)

What is the difference? It is that the Christian love of neighbor is never
focused uniquely on the neighbor. It does not stop at the neighbor. Or,
more bluntly, neighbors are not loved for their own sake but "for the love
of God." (Nietzsche, though furiously anti-Christian, nonetheless says that
to love the neighbor for the love of God is the most refined moral sentiment
attained by human beings.) The neighbor is loved as a creature, as an
image of God. And the neighbor is loved "in Christ." These various expressions are not equivalent, but they all aim at the same central tenet of the
Christian conscience. Human sentiments, human dispositions and actions
fall under the Christian perspective only if they are first addressed to God.
After all, that is quite logical.

Christian love of neighbor bears a particular name, a name that is technical, charity. Now charity is not only a religious notion. It is a political
notion in the broadest sense of the term "political." If love of neighbor
presupposes love of God, it presupposes love of the true God. Consequently, it is only true, only charity in the full sense of the term in the true
Church, that is to say in a particular community, vast as it may be. Thus
the expression: no salvation outside the Church. Charity then becomes
separatist, with all the intolerance and persecution that this entails and
that have been observed in the history of the Churches. Herein resides the
historical, political, moral, and logical cause of the substitution of "humanity"—for charity as the foremost virtue. Christian universalism is in
principle without limit. Since every human is in the image of God, charity
is addressed to every human being. Yet, this universalism is particularized
in a church that does not embrace all of humanity, at least in a visible
manner. It therefore seems to be an imperfect or incomplete universalism.
The eighteenth century thus offered a charity separate from any church, no
longer charity but "humanity." "Humanity" is that benevolent disposition
toward every person as a human being, regardless of race, nation, class,
opinion, religion. Europeans then had the sentiment that humanity as the
whole of human beings had come of age, at least in its more advanced
representatives. Maximum universalism had been achieved; every human
being was henceforth simply a fellow human being. Over two centuries
later, democratic societies still live with this idea of humanity. There is no
reason for that to change; the change could only be a regression since
once again this idea of humanity represents maximum universalism. Any
extension could only take place in the direction of our "lower brethren,"
the animals. Besides, that movement has already begun.

Everything then works for the best. Cheers to humanity, and let us consider charity as a preparatory stage on the road that has led to this maximum universalism! Yet, things are not so simple because this maximum

is only a maximum in extension. Granted that the virtue of humanity, the sentiment for those like oneself, applies to everyone, but in what does this sentiment consist? What is the virtue of humanity concerned with? In what does the rapport consist that binds every one to those like oneself?

There are two interpretations of this rapport, elaborated at the same time as the general idea of humanity in the eighteenth century to give it meaning and content. One can say that our good will for other human beings is first addressed to the one who suffers, to the body that suffers— from illness, hunger, etcetera—and it is thus called *pity* or *compassion*. In this version, the universal human bond is the bond of pity or compassion. This interpretation of the virtue of humanity influenced the modern sensibility elaborated by Rousseau. One could say that the foundation of contemporary humanitarianism is pity in the Rousseauan sense.

The second interpretation is altogether different, even contrary. The relation is not addressed to the visible and suffering body, but to something invisible, to the soul, to the *dignity* of the person. The interior disposition that recognizes the dignity of the person is *respect*, as explained by Kant. Pity for the suffering body, respect for the (necessarily spiritual) dignity of the person. These are the two great conceptions of contemporary humanism or universalism.

Why does Rousseau have such confidence in pity, why does he count on it so much to bind people together? Pity is a universal affect in two senses. On the one hand, all human beings are potential objects of pity since they have a body liable to suffering. On the other hand, all human beings are potential subjects of pity, since they can easily identify themselves with the physical suffering of others. Physical suffering is immediately grasped or imagined. One sympathizes with a toothache, a nervous colic, and two days without eating or drinking more easily than with a moral humiliation, an intellectual preoccupation, or a spiritual anguish. In short, because physical pity is rooted in the senses, we communicate immediately with the other, without the mediation of complex ideas. Physical compassion offers us the easiest, most direct, and most general sentiment of those like ourselves. At the end of Celine's *Journey to the End of Night*, the narrator, Ferdinand, witnesses the agony of his friend Leon:

> But there was only me, just me, me all alone, beside him, the genuine Ferdinand, who was short of everything that would make a man bigger than his own bare life, short of love for other people's lives. Of that I had none, or so little there was no use showing it. I wasn't as big as death. I was a lot smaller. I had no great opinion of humanity. I think I'd have found it easier to grieve for a dying dog than for Robinson, because a dog isn't tricky, and Robinson, in spite of everything, was tricky in a way. I was tricky myself, we were all tricksters . . .[1]

At the same time, Rousseau articulated a second great argument, which appears to be less noble. Pity can be relied on to bind people because it is a sentiment, an affect, or a disposition that does not demand any moral transformation or transcendence of the self. Pity is not a disinterested sentiment, hence its social value. Human beings for Rousseau are not capable of a disinterested sentiment, only natural sentiment, that is to say, they necessarily seek their interest and pleasure. These naturally interested beings naturally experience pity. Why? Because the visible suffering of another person tells me that I too could experience it, that I am as vulnerable as the other. In short, in seeing the other suffer, I think of myself, I come back to myself, I *identify* with the other who is suffering. Thus, I make the effort to comfort the other. How could I be indifferent to a suffering that I sense could afflict me? But the interested ruses of compassion do not stop there. For, in fact, I do not effectively experience this suffering that I perceive so vividly. I know well that I do not effectively experience it and so I rejoice that I am exempt from it. I experience the pleasure of *not* suffering. In this way, according to Rousseau's analysis, compassion is an altruistic sentiment that has two selfish motives or components: the fear of suffering and the pleasure of not suffering. Therefore, there is nothing idealistic or utopian in pity as the foundation of social morality. Rousseau thinks that if modern society wants to overcome the isolation, separation, and individualism of the members of society that characterize it, then it must cultivate pity and compassion. Once again, there is nothing in pity that is heroic since its wellspring is the selfishness of each person. Rousseau was giving us the blueprint that has effectively prevailed in liberal democratic society, in bourgeois society. It is the society of the Goodwill soup kitchen.

This system has many political, social, and psychic advantages. Drawing altruism from selfishness is morally economical: it demands little of us. It has however at least one inconvenience. The pity on which Rousseau wants to build is aimed at the suffering body; it is thus by itself not a specifically human sentiment. It focuses on the animal and the workings of the animal in us. If our pity addresses the suffering body, it can take as its object the suffering of animals just as well as of human bodies. Besides, animals too are susceptible of experiencing pity and confirm the wholly *natural* character of pity. Unlike charity, pity is independent of any religious or philosophical opinion, it cannot become separatist and that is crucial to Rousseau's thinking.[2] But in the end, if this sentiment is founded on likeness, then this likeness is not properly human. The physical pity that Rousseau preaches certainly preserves humanity, since humanity is partly animal, but it tends to weaken the consciousness and sentiment of what is specifically human. If it is a matter of taking care of living beings that suffer, then animals have just as much right to our compassion as humans do.

The natural tendency of a society founded on physical pity will thus be to grant the same rights to animals as well as to humans—one right, the right not to suffer. This is indeed the tendency one observes in contemporary society. Efforts are made to assure that animals destined as food for people live in the most comfortable conditions possible before being put to death in the most painless way. Yet, the killing of animals continues. Yes, but in our society, the evil is not so much death as physical suffering. Evil tends to merge with physical suffering. Moreover, this is the reason for advocating euthanasia, the humanitarian death of human beings whose sufferings are extreme or who survive in miserable conditions. Thus the animal condition and the human condition come close to the point of almost merging. Animals are no longer made to suffer and human beings are killed so that they will not suffer.

Some believe that this obsession with physical suffering leads to the loss of what is proper to human beings, of the human difference, to the loss of the sentiment of human dignity. It is true that the supporters of euthanasia invoke the "right to die with dignity." Although my concern here is not to arbitrate between the two parties, my remarks intend to prove that "dignity" is at the heart of the contemporary moral problematic.

"Human dignity" is the loftiest moral notion of democratic humanity. Kant formulated it rigorously and completely fashioned and placed it at the center of his moral and social doctrine. It is of Stoic and Christian origin. The Stoics already formulated a distinction between what has price and what has dignity, in the language of Seneca, between *pretium* and *dignitas*. Kant again took up this distinction. Christianity also affirms the idea of a dignity that is proper to human beings, a distinctive nobility with regard to other creatures. The *dignitas* of human beings is that God has given them the power to follow their own counsel, that unlike the animals who follow the impulse of nature, human beings obey freely and thus can disobey the law of nature and the divine law. One could say that the Kantian conception radicalizes and thus transforms the Christian conception that Thomas Aquinas in particular had articulated. If for Thomas Aquinas human dignity consists in freely obeying the natural and divine law, for Kant it consists in obeying the law that human beings give to themselves. One could say that in the Christian view, human beings *have* a dignity (received from God, Who has given them the power to follow their own counsel); for Kant, and the difference is both radical and subtle, to be human *is* a dignity.

To be human is to be a person; to be a person is to be autonomous; to be autonomous is to act freely, that is, to obey the law one has given oneself. One cannot equate human dignity with human liberty. Dignity resides more precisely in the rapport of human beings to the moral law, a law that they themselves created, but for which they experience a very specific sentiment, a purely spiritual sentiment that Kant calls *respect*. It is an affect that human beings discover in themselves and that they can neither fabricate nor erase. The worst criminals maintain respect for the law deep within themselves. Even if the law is contrary to all our necessarily interested inclinations, we sense that we ought to and thus that we could obey the law. We sense within us—this sentiment is respect—the possibility and the necessity of a purely disinterested action accomplished out of pure respect for the law.[3] This is the content, the heart of the Kantian notion of human dignity: to respect the dignity of others is to respect the respect that they cannot fail to have for the moral law within them (even if they be the worst criminals), the respect that they cannot not experience for themselves as a consequence of the presence of the law within them, is to respect their respect for themselves.

This idea is formulated in the most synthetic and clearest way in the "Doctrine of Virtue," the second part of *The Metaphysics of Morals*:

> Humanity itself is a dignity, for man can be used by no one (neither by others nor even by himself) merely as a means, but must always be used at the same time as an end. And precisely therein consists his dignity (personality), whereby he raises himself above all other beings in the world, which are not men and can, accordingly, be used—consequently, above all things. Even as he therefore cannot give himself away for a price (which would conflict with the duty of self-esteem), so can he likewise not act counter to the equally necessary self-esteem of others as men, *i.e.*, he is bound to give practical acknowledgement to the dignity of humanity in every other man. Consequently, there rests upon him a duty regarding the respect which must necessarily be shown to every other man.[4]

This is the essential of the Kantian idea, impressive and influential. Yet, the contemporary moral consciousness finds it difficult to adhere to it completely. It is a case of split consciousness. One the one hand, this idea of dignity has become indispensable to our moral consciousness. While it was absent from the Declaration of the Rights of Man and Citizen of 1789, it is introduced in the opening words of the preamble of the Universal Declaration of Human Rights of 1948: "Whereas recognition of the inherent dignity and of the equal and inalienable rights of all members of the human family is the foundation of freedom, justice and peace in the world." Here dignity comes even before rights. This change of course was due to the recent experience of war and the crimes against humanity committed by the Nazis. The Nazi camps did not just represent the negation of human rights: as true as that was, the expression would have been too weak. The camps were a systematic undertaking to offend and destroy human dignity. After the experience of the camps, human dignity appears as a more profound principle, more precious still than that of human rights.

The difference between rights and dignity is not from the lesser to the greater on the same scale. There is also a qualitative difference. And so there is a very clear tension between the two ideas of dignity and rights. In their original source, human rights are the rights *natural* to human beings, those that are inherent in their elementary nature, in their needs and desires and above all their desire for preservation. Human dignity by contrast is constituted according to Kant by taking a radical or essential distance with respect to the needs and desires of nature. Human dignity consists in the fact that human beings can be moved by a motive that is completely independent of nature and superior to it, by a purely spiritual causality. To put it rather bluntly: human rights concern natural freedoms, including and above all animal and physical nature; human dignity is freedom against physical or in general selfish nature, and it is spiritual liberty.

The contemporary moral conscience and moral reflection wish to reduce this tension. They seek to maintain the idea of dignity while detaching it from any idea of moral law and spiritual causality, to merge the idea of rights and the idea of dignity. In other words, to absorb, without losing it, the idea of dignity within the idea of rights. That presupposes a complete transformation, in truth an abandonment of the Kantian doctrine—an abandonment that is masked by keeping or wildly using its language, the language of "respect for human dignity." To respect the dignity of other human beings is no longer to respect the respect they hold within themselves for the moral law. Today it is more to respect the choice they have made, whatever that choice may be, in asserting their rights. For Kant, respect for human dignity is respect for humanity itself; for contemporary moralism, respect for human dignity is respect for the "contents of life," whatever it may be, of other human beings. The same words are used, but with an altogether different moral perspective.

Contemporary morality leads to what the English-speaking thinkers call a politics of recognition. Each lifestyle demands equal recognition with all other lifestyles. This claim is very understandable, but it comes up against serious moral and political difficulties. The Kantian formulation appears severe, rigorist, unrealizable; the current formulation appears generous, liberal, realizable. I believe that the contrary is true. The Kantian formulation has the disadvantage of being formal; but that is also its advantage. My respect is addressed to the humanity of the other human beings; as human beings, they are essentially respectable. Now, what they do with their life, the "contents of their life," is another thing; I can approve, disapprove, be indifferent, or be perplexed, in short, here the full scale of feelings and judgments that life arouses in us is naturally deployed. The contemporary formulation has the advantage of being concrete; that is also its disadvantage. Respect is demanded for all life contents, all life choices, or all lifestyles. Yet this formulation really has no meaning. Or its only meaning is that all life contents, all life choices, all lifestyles must be approved, appreciated, valued, applauded. But that is simply impossible.

Respect is addressed to the person, and we can and must respect all persons. But all the life contents, all the political, moral, religious choices people make cannot and must not be approved, appreciated, valued, and applauded. If all life choices must be approved by everyone, life would become truly boring and even sinister, for that would mean that our own personal choices are without importance or meaning. The choice I make can have no value for me unless you react to that choice, with approval or disapproval, even indignation or comprehension. In short, unless the choice I make entails the risk, however minimal, that is inseparable from liberty.

This demand for respect is often advanced today in favor of sexual orientation. But I believe that the problem concerns all life contents. I will take an example that is felt less today but that for a very long time and again recently was the object of much more passionate and widespread discussion than the question of sexual orientation. That is religious choice. People long considered that that was the fundamental choice for every person. Does God exist? If God exists, what is his nature? What does God ask of us, what is his law? How does God reveal himself to us? Since people take to heart these questions that are indeed fundamental, it is difficult to bear with disagreements. Orthodox believers cannot help but think that heretics are moved by pride; heretics that the orthodox prefer power to truth. Believers think that atheists refuse to believe because deep within they reject all law; atheists think that the believers are incapable of autonomy or of courageously accepting the end of their being, and so on.

In short, the positive choices that we make are inseparable from our negative choices. It is inevitable and therefore legitimate that atheists consider believers as affected by a certain moral weakness—they "need to believe," they "need consolation." Reciprocally, it is inevitable and therefore legitimate that believers consider atheists as willfully blind people who proudly refuse to recognize their true condition. Believers can and must respect the humanity, the person of atheists; but one could not ask them to "respect their atheism," an expression that could have no meaning for them. Atheists can and must respect the humanity, the person of believers; but one could not ask them to "respect their belief," an expression that could have no meaning for them.

Some might object that the parallel does not hold because religious convictions are freely chosen whereas sexual orientation has to do with individual nature and not liberty. Implicit in this objection is the reproach that society or the state is wrong not to recognize or "respect" an essential element in a person's life over which this person has no power. It is in some way to condemn that person for what he or she *is*. Whence the assimilation at times of what is called "homophobia" with racism.

I admit that religious conviction and sexual orientation are not the same thing, that there is without doubt more of liberty in the first and more of "nature" in the second. But this contrast should not be exaggerated. What does it mean to say that a religious or irreligious conviction is freely chosen? Does it mean that, in the best of cases, a person has seriously studied the state of the question, examined the opposing arguments impartially, and made a choice without the clouding of the passions? So be it, and certainly this is not how one "chooses" one's sexual orientation! At the same time it was a traditional argument against religious constraint, against state religion that a person had no power over the conclusions of his or her mind: you want me to believe, but even were I to make the most sincere effort, I cannot force myself to believe. I am an unbeliever, a fact that you ought to accept just as I do. Likewise, however, sexual orientation may be determined by individual nature, it is not an objective fact devoid of subjective meaning, it is a rapport with oneself and with others in which liberty is obviously implied. All that matters deeply to human beings is a tangled mix of nature and liberty that engages the whole person.

It is because these choices or orientations engage the whole person that there is something unbearable in the neutrality of the state. What does it mean to say that the state recognizes my dignity if it does not recognize what is most important for me? How does it recognize my humanity if it does not recognize the content of my humanity? We are here at the heart of a great difficulty of our societies.

For a long time, ardent believers denounced this state of affairs: the state calls itself neutral and liberal, in reality it is atheistic; the school calls itself secular, in reality it is "without God." To consign religious life to the private realm is to declare implicitly that religion is without value since what truly matters to a society is recognized in the public sphere. Many of our fellow citizens must observe that things that they take deeply to heart are regarded with indifference by the public sphere, an indifference that seems to them hostile. Our political regime rests on *separations*. And we cannot help desiring, and thus seeking the *unity* of our life. We have to live with this tension. We could eliminate it only at the price of the destruction or corruption of our political regime.

It is possible, in our regime, to satisfy most of the demands of homosexuals and their supporters. Only one is impossible to satisfy. It is impossible for the body politic to "recognize" their "lifestyle" since no "lifestyle" is "recognized" by our regime. That is why it is a liberal regime. But doesn't it "recognize" "heterosexual marriage"? Yes, and for a good reason. Such a marriage produces children, that is to say citizens, and that has to do with *public* interest.

Some argue that many heterosexual marriages are infertile, for reasons of nature or for reasons of choice, and that, moreover, the legalization of adoption by homosexual couples, not to speak of fertilizations by donors, would deprive the "demographic" argument of any validity. But those who propose such solutions contradict themselves. One wants to deprive the "natural division" between the sexes of any validity, any pertinence. But to obtain what result at the end of this great labor? The result is a family, with parents and children, that is to say a human association that *imitates* the family based on the natural division between the sexes—in this nature that one wants to banish. "Homosexual marriage" *imitates* heterosexual marriage, and no invocation of the "equality of rights" will deliver it from this internal contradiction. Those who call for its legalization are thus slaves to the sexual division, slaves of nature, at the very moment they believe they are triumphing over it.

There is much intellectual confusion in a certain homosexual militancy. The expression "gay pride," for example, is a particularly poor choice. How can one speak of "pride" when one is begging for the blessing of approval and the cover of consensus? Not so long ago there was a part of adventure and a truth in homosexuality. Homosexuals now discovered perhaps painfully the range and irregularities of Eros and the limits of its more ordinary expression. They were more apt than others to elude the lies of convention. That was paid for with a certain discretion, but is that not the will of Eros itself that, like truth, likes to conceal itself? All of that is lost in the contemporary staging that only knows how to ape the blandest heterosexual convention: all spouses, all parents!

Nearly all homosexual demands can and must be satisfied. Renting or buying housing together, the possibility of inheriting from the partner, all these elementary rights of bourgeois life the body politic should guarantee to homosexuals. It is respectful and good that older partners can make the younger their heirs without being required as in the past to have recourse to the humiliating convention of false "adoption." At the same time, we are all held, homosexuals or not, to a certain "obligation of discretion." Precisely because our regime is a regime of liberty and so that it can remain so, we do not have the right to demand of our fellow citizens that they approve our "lifestyles" or "life contents." That would be tyranny. That the dignity of each should be respected, that is the least that one can ask for, but it is also the most that one has the right to ask.

CHAPTER 18

The Human Political Condition and the Unity of the Human Race

A CONCLUSION at the end of a book ought to solve the problems that the book has raised. A conclusion of this kind is beyond our reach here. If the problems that we have considered were solvable, as are most mathematical problems, human history has reached its end. Certain authors have indeed thought that the end of history was near because modern humanity was in the process of solving the human problem.

The most profound of these authors, who was the most aware of the breadth and difficulty of the problem, was Hegel. He did not think that the human problem was reducible to technical problems. For Hegel, the human problem is the problem of *mutual recognition*. All human beings without exception desire to be recognized in their humanity, in their liberty by others. Human history is a long struggle for mutual recognition. At the beginning of history, in the Asiatic empires, only the emperor is free. In ancient Greece, only the few who are citizens are free. In modern Europe, from the French Revolution onward, all are free: the humanity of each is recognized by all, since the equal rights of all are declared, recognized, and guaranteed in principle. In that sense, history has come to an end; and Hegel has been proved right. A certain human result has been definitively attained.

Difficulties, of which Hegel was perfectly aware, remain however. He probably considered them as inevitable inconveniences that must be acceptable by rational citizens. These difficulties are related to the modalities and limits of recognition. To whom or to what is the recognition of others addressed? What do the others "recognize" when they recognize me in my "humanity"? Recognition can be addressed to the particularity of an individual, to what makes him or her unique. Or it can be addressed to his or her humanity in general, to the humanity that is an individual. There is a considerable ambiguity here, an ambiguity that is at the origin of lively social and moral debates. Hegel envisaged a recognition that envelops both particularity and generality, transcending one and the other. The modern state represents the institutionalization of mutual recognition that transcends the opposition of the particular and the general. Such a solution is truly concrete: all are recognized not only in their generality as citizens but also for their particular contribution to economic and social life, to the "system of needs." The general rights of their humanity are recognized at the same time that their particular talents are rewarded.

Not only Hegel, but the entire nineteenth century, Europe at least until the war of 1914, believed that the nation-state was the superior form of collective organization, which reconciled particularity and universality. The progressivism of the nineteenth and early twentieth centuries worked toward a humanity composed of independent and democratic nations, linked perhaps by increasing collaboration. This perspective was abandoned, because the credibility of the nation-state in Europe was irremediably damaged by the wars of the twentieth century. More precisely, what the great wars manifested was that the nation-state was not only the principal means or eminent instrument of mutual recognition but was also its complete contrary. It prevented mutual recognition from attaining its end and even produced the opposite of mutual recognition: war. Accordingly, the modern nation-state was also affected and in the end ruined by what I want to call "the phenomenon of the organ-obstacle or instrument-obstacle," that had affected and ruined earlier political forms.

What is the phenomenon of the organ-obstacle or instrument-obstacle? It is something very simple that can be observed in all domains of life. What allows us to reach an objective is also what prevents us from pursuing further the attainment of this same objective and even directs us in an opposite direction. It is in the political order that this phenomenon is most salient and determining. Examples abound: the law, intended to protect the weak against the strong, almost inevitably ends up giving the advantage to the strong over the weak;[1] the sovereign state intended to guarantee peace is a factor of war, etcetera. It seems to me that what the sociologists today call "perverse effect" falls under this phenomenon. For example, the institutions and measures of the welfare state, intending to eliminate misery and prevent exclusion, in the eyes of some contribute, at least in certain circumstances, to perpetuating misery and fostering exclusion. It is at the political level that this phenomenon comes to light most sharply and dramatically. What is perhaps most profound in political life and history, is the way in which a political form appears first as the instrument for resolving a problem and then becomes an obstacle to this solution.

For example, the rise of the Greek city was coeval with the discovery by human beings of their political condition—that they were capable of governing themselves. Human beings fulfilled their nature by governing themselves within and through the city. They fulfilled their universal nature—common to *all*—in a particular city, consisting of a *small number* of people, a city whose particularity was insurmountable, and ended by frustrating the project of self-government. The particularity is limited in that the city is just a city among other cities, with which it is always potentially at war, and also limited in that only a small number of people are citizens. I shall not repeat the history of political forms, but simply recall that from a certain time onward the nation-state underwent the fate of the Greek city. It appeared just as *particular*, just as incapable of solving the problem of fulfilling human liberty.

Thus, reasoning by analogy, it is tempting to say that a new political form, one more universal than the nation-state, will probably appear full of promise, then sooner or later it will be as incapable of solving the problems of mutual recognition as the city or the nation-state. It is tempting to say that the Europe under construction is this new political form, which is to the nation-state what the latter was to the city. I have at length explained why I do not think that "Europe," such as it has been elaborated for the past half-century, offers such a perspective: precisely as a political form, it remains undetermined. The unresolved ambiguity of "Europe" lies in that it designates two rigorously contradictory things: either a new nation, a great nation, capable of being one of the major protagonists of the new century along with the United States, China, etcetera; or else the direct opposite, not a new body politic, but the institutionalization of the end of politics, the reduction of common life to the rights and rules of civil society and civilization. It seems to me that all that is going on pushes us in the direction of the second alternative.

"Europe" is a political promise because it promises an exit from politics. Thus we shall escape the limits and disappointment inseparable from every political form. All the defining elements of the new situation are going in the same direction. The world is disposed to emerge from the age of the political, to organize itself without the mediation of politics. We acquiesce to this movement because it seems to promise the final achievement of mutual recognition. What no political form had permitted to achieve completely, the exit from politics will allow us to accomplish. A meta- or postpolitical world, an immediately human world is shaping up.

The adverb *immediately* needs to be underlined. Modern humanity is impatient with regard to all mediations. In earlier, predemocratic centuries, mutual recognition was conditioned, and therefore, limited by a multitude of forms. Politeness and ceremonies played an eminent political role. There were different forms of address and behavior toward men and women, soldiers and civilians, churchmen and laymen, young and old, superiors and inferiors. Democracy has progressively eroded these forms of mediations, which, in maintaining a compartmentalized and hierarchical order, made it impossible to recognize humanity as such, humanity without social, sexual, professional, and other particularization. Democracy seeks in all domains this common human expression that signifies that one belongs to the same humanity as others. One's bearing, language, and dress must manifest this inclusion. Previously, what mattered was to distinguish oneself by one's dress, language, and bearing, to show precisely that one was "distinguished" and well-bred, one had manners, or one knew how to behave. Today the social imperative has changed; it has reversed itself. It is not that human beings in our societies experience less the desire to distinguish themselves; this desire seems to be inherent in our moral nature. But one distinguishes oneself today by showing one's aptitude to use the language, dress, airs, that manifest an immediate, common, natural, informal humanity. One distinguishes oneself today by being *cool*.

What is *cool*? *Cool* is not the contrary of distinguished; the opposite of distinguished is common, vulgar, even sloppy. Sloppiness manifests only the absence or rejection of the accepted forms of dress or demeanor. *Cool* manifests the immediate presence of humanity beyond forms. The shirt not tucked into the pants is sloppy. The shirt without a tie, with open collar, symbolizes very well the freedom of nature. The shirt without a tie is *cool*. These details, seemingly superficial, are indeed very revealing. Until recently, politicians, even in a democratic regime, had to express through their language, their dress, their general demeanor, the dignity of their position that ultimately represented the dignity and grandeur of the state and the nation. Today, they need to express two things: first, that they are *cool*, that is to say, that common humanity is present in them immediately, without any form that masks or distinguishes them; second, that they are humane, compassionate, caring, capable of responding to the pain of others immediately, independently of any political consideration, rather than being merely concerned with the interests and grandeur of the state. Politicians today are not easily electable if they do not display these two qualities.

What I wanted to note is the force of the demand for immediacy. It is a matter of everyone, including the politicians who represent us, showing their own humanity and of reacting immediately with sympathy to another person's humanity. This phenomenon is not limited to social and political life. The desire, the demand for immediacy, tends to dominate all aspects of modern democratic life.

It would be interesting to study modern art from this angle. It seems to me that the evolution of modern art tends toward the elimination of forms and mediations. Take painting, whose fate has determined the fate of modern art in general. The equalization of genres, the abandonment of perspective, the rejection of the conventions of representation, all point to an experience that aims to be pure, simple, and absolute, the experience that human beings have of themselves as creators. This is an experience detached from the political and social, religious, and intellectual life, an experience that aims to be both elementary and total, an experience that human beings have of their humanity. That is why modern art is essentially nonfigurative. Paradoxically, art abandoned figuration in order to be more purely human. Figurative art, the art of imitation and likeness, comes into contact and resonates with other political, social, and moral experiences, communicates and merges with them to some extent, and for that reason cannot provoke a "pure" experience, or a purely and simply human experience. One understands how nonfigurative art appears to lead to "non-art" or to expressions that fall under "imposture." Its logic is to suppress all that manifests a refined work of elaboration—the signs of such work are a sort of "figuration"—to move toward "brute" art, that is, toward arbitrary proclamation and immediate presentation as a work of art of something that is not elaborated.

One could say that in all domains of life, contemporary people seek an immediate experience of themselves and of humanity. *Cool*, compassionate, artist, or rather "creator," the same desire, or the same project is at work. (I could have spoken also of the refusal of mediations and of the sentimental life: our contemporary idiom replaces the long and slow hermeneutic of love with the abridged version of "sex.")

But the great obstacle to this immediate experience is the political order, because it is the great mediation, or the mediation of mediations.

What do I mean by these expressions? Something simple, but which is often forgotten or interpreted in a reductive or negative way. The rapport of the political to the other aspects of life is viewed as an external and essentially oppressive rapport. Politics intervenes in a thousand ways in the private life of citizens, including the work of artists. In the worst of cases, it imposes, dictates, or forbids or represses certain activities, certain opinions; in the best of cases, it authorizes them, leaves them free, "encourages" them and even "subsidizes" them. But whether it is prohibition or authorization, it is always described as an external rapport. In reality, this phenomenon presents only the visible or external face of political and social history.

Indeed, politics holds together the diverse aspects of human life, individual as well as social. To be sure, a political regime is always partial, and always repressive in some measure, but it is a certain way of holding together the diverse aspects of human life. Politics allows the diverse experiences to communicate with one another, obliges them to communicate according to the form and the regime. That is why politics is the great mediation or the mediation of mediations. It prevents any experience from claiming absolute validity; it prevents any experience from saturating the social arena and the individual consciousness; it requires any experience to coexist and to communicate with the other experiences. In this way, politics is the guardian of the wealth and complexity of human life.

The democratic human being we have described is particularly hostile to the political order to the extent that it hinders the immediacy of experiences. In fact, the democratic political order itself contains something antipolitical, since it claims to reduce the place of politics as much as possible. Politics is the instrument of the individuals who "assert their independence as they please," as Montesquieu says of the English. The democratic order seeks to preserve the authenticity of every experience, authorizing and protecting every experience and every liberty equally. Thus the democratic order encourages every experience to be ever more authentic, ever more immediate and absolute. But the democratic order cannot avoid frustrating each experience, for each one would want to be the only authentic experience and the democratic order must protect all other experiences equally. The democratic political order remains always the great mediation, but it exercises this mediation in a paradoxical way, through separations. Our regime is organized on separations: the separation between state and society, separation of powers, separation among values, and others. We further ask our regime to protect the authenticity, the purity of each one of our experiences, that is, its separation from all the other experiences. The paradoxical nature of the democratic order is that it appears to be the heaviest while it is constructed to be the lightest.

The predemocratic political orders are always explicitly constraining: it is a matter of obeying the law. Every human experience must take the others into account. It would indeed want to be unique, the immediate and absolute one, but this is not possible. Each experience is obliged to account for other experiences and participate in a common effort regulated by law. In the democratic political order, every experience is authorized to be what it is, and protected in its specificity and its authenticity. It is encouraged to see itself as unique, immediate, and absolute. It is thus encouraged to rebel against the democratic order itself.

Two possibilities can therefore be encountered. First, one could rebel against the democratic component of our political order, and this move leads to a totalitarian project that would put an end to the separations. In this case, the political itself becomes the object and the element of the desired experience, the immediate and absolute experience. The overpoliticizing of the totalitarian movements and the accommodating attitude of many artists toward these movements originates here. Or else, one could rebel against the political aspect of the democratic order. This move consists in rejecting the world of mediations. The twentieth century has seen various totalitarian temptations. We are currently experiencing an antipolitical or humanitarian temptation, a much softer temptation to be sure, and so more tempting, but that may soon appear to be hardly more bearable than totalitarian overpoliticizing.

Of course, the desire of leaving the political behind is not engendered solely by the political and psychological mechanism I have just described. It is also motivated by developments that render such a transformation of common life plausible, reasonable, and desirable. We have encountered three great developments that go in this direction:

1. The emancipation of *commerce.* Commerce binds individuals, not necessarily fellow-citizens, each of whom calculate their own interest freely. Mutual dependence is mediated entirely by private interest. One could say that in the commercial relation I depend on the other but I think only of myself. In commerce, the order arises spontaneously from the interaction of individual liberties in quest of their own interest. It is an order among equals ("Commerce is the profession of equal people," Montesquieu writes) that progressively replaces the order of command by rendering it useless.

2. The emancipation of *right.* The independent, free, equal human being is defined as the being that has rights. These rights are not uniquely individual or private rights; they are also political or civil rights. But all these rights, attributes of the being that has rights, are rooted exclusively in the individual. They are attributes of every human being as human. Tendentiously, or ideally, they are declared and guaranteed by judges— judges who are independent of the political order. Nonetheless, since this power of judges is founded on human rights, which every human being can grasp, every human being becomes in some way the judge and the defender of human rights. This brings us to the third development.

3. The emancipation of *morality.* Morality no doubt has never been simply social, never simply the expression of social hierarchies and conventions. In the predemocratic order, however, it was specified according to the diverse subjects and addressees of action or conduct: according to their being men or women, socially inferior or superior, and other distinctions. At some point, morality became detached from the social framework and became the pure human rapport of one human being to another. This is the moment when, in Kant's expression, being human became the supreme dignity.

Commerce, right, morality: these are the three systems, the three empires that promise the exit from the political. Each in its own form: commerce, according to the realism, the prosaic character of interests rightly understood; right, according to the intellectual coherence of a network of rights rigorously deduced from individual autonomy; and finally morality, according to the sublime aim of pure human dignity to which one is joined by the purely spiritual sentiment of respect.

If one considers the three systems together—commerce, right, and morality—it seems that the promise of a new world asserts itself irresistibly, a world that is realistic and idealist, with something to satisfy the body, the mind, and the soul, a new and complete world, but one without politics.

Not that politics must necessarily disappear without a trace, but it will simply be the instrument of these three great nonpolitical realities: the instrument of commerce, the instrument of right, the instrument of morality. This is where we have arrived.

Once again, it is understandable that such a perspective should be alluring. Nonetheless I do not believe that it is reasonable. Why? One cannot be content to say that it is utopian, that it is impossible to govern people or regulate their relations simply through commerce, right, and morality, since command and force will always be necessary in certain circumstances. For the utopia in question does not exclude the use of force. Force will be simply employed exclusively in the service of morality, or right, or possibly the liberty of commerce. The internal weakness of the new humanitarian empire is more subtle and profound than critics who are merely realistic suggest.

It is a question of a *moral* weakness. In humanitarian action, *one does not know what one is doing*. But how is this so, since nothing is clearer, more defined, and obvious than the purpose of humanitarian action: to save lives, to end violence? Sure, let us look at things more closely.

In the first place, the humanitarian principle is silent on the agent performing the action. If one takes only humanitarian emergency into consideration, then anyone is in principle authorized to "intervene." For example, the case of Kosovo, an Islamic alliance instead of NATO would have been justified in intervening, to protect the Muslims of Kosovo. Or Turkey alone, since it governed these regions for centuries. Or why not neighboring Italy? Or any country or group of people moved by the fate of the Kosovars. In short, in the name of humanitarian emergency, anyone is authorized to do anything whatsoever.

More precisely, the language of the "duty of interference" contributes to reestablishing what early modern political philosophy called the state of nature. In the state of nature everyone is authorized to judge and to punish violations of the law of nature, and that leads to the war of all against all. The humanitarian demand is a real demand, but one should not ignore that, left to its logic alone, it means the war of all against all.

Moreover, humanitarian warfare, or rather military action for a humanitarian purpose, necessarily takes on some specific characteristics that make it a loose instrument for ordering human affairs. In a "normal" war, the war's aims, determined by the political heads, direct all the constituents of the action. If the actors are normally civilized, they will strive to limit not only their own losses, but also the civilian losses of the enemy. Of course, this "humanitarian" consideration is subordinated to the achievement of the war aims. The problem with military action for a humanitarian end is that it is not unified or directed by a political end. Our troops in

Bosnia and Kosovo and will remain there for a long time, but *to do what* no one really knows. In humanitarian actions, since the political end is absent, the different elements of the action are independent of one another and each one claims primacy: bringing down the enemy or the criminal, avoiding civilian losses, or reducing the losses of the humanitarian army as much as possible.

In practice, it is the third demand that wins. The normally subordinate consideration becomes the principal one. One finds oneself then in the strange situation where soldiers have as their principal objective not the achievement of their war aims, but the reduction of their losses. So, as was seen in the NATO bombings over Serbia and Kosovo, the military, to reduce their losses, took the risk of multiplying civilian losses, which puts them in contradiction with their humanitarian objective.

This situation is not due to a lack of courage in today's armies, nor even to the entrenched habits of the American army, but to the humanitarian logic itself, more precisely and profoundly to the logic of compassion. Compassion reduced to itself has two effects. The first is the desire to come to the aid of the suffering, and even to risk "dying for Pristina"; but the second is altogether different, and in the end contrary. By turning the attention toward the suffering body, compassion quickens in each of us the desire not to suffer and not to die. As Rousseau saw so well, compassion reduced to itself is inseparable from the happiness of not suffering oneself. The sentiment of the other in which compassion consists exacerbates the sentiment of the self. Reduced to itself, compassion only leads to timid and irresolute action. As a weak and equivocal motive, compassion alone would not motivate a lasting and coherent action. It will not be possible to establish any new satisfactory order on simply humanitarian foundations.

Through this detour we return to the meaning of the political order. It seems less pure, less noble, and less human than the humanitarian order. It is not the universal human order, it is not addressed immediately to human beings as human beings. But precisely because of its nature, it weaves together efficiently the sentiment of the self and the sentiment of the other. Why? Because, in the political order, the self and the other have something *in common*: precisely the political order, the body politic, the republic that is a *common thing*. In the political order, as a consequence of this commonality, there is a sort of active confusion of the self and the other. It is then possible for individuals to forget themselves and to be willing to sacrifice themselves in a sacrifice that is both selfish and generous, the patriotic sacrifice. It is once again Rousseau who, attentive to the virtues and the limits of general human compassion, underlined that patriotism is the source of the greatest virtues and that no other has been found. So that the human sentiment might have force, a lasting force, he tells us, it needs to be concentrated in a particular city. If you extend it to the whole of humanity, it is surely more just and moral, but it is much weaker, too weak to sustain a tolerably just and happy human association.

The promise of moral progress contained in contemporary humanitarian sensibility will remain sterile if we do not know how to delineate the political framework in which it will be able to produce real and lasting effects. There will only be a new order if we resolutely accept the constraints of the old order, that is, the constraints of our political condition. And those constraints in turn hold a promise, the promise of fulfilling the humanity of human beings without illusion, but in the truth of their political nature.

INTRODUCTION

1. Paul Claudel, *Poetic Art*, trans. Renee Spodheim (New York, 1948), 4.
2. Niccolò Machiavelli, *The Prince*, trans. Harvey C. Mansfield, 2nd ed. (Chicago, 1998), 61.
3. *From Max Weber: Essays in Sociology*, trans. H. H. Gerth and C. Wright Mills (New York, 1958), 139.
4. Ibid., 146.
5. Ibid., 155.

CHAPTER 1: THE ORGANIZATION OF SEPARATIONS

1. Adam Ferguson *Essay on the History of Civil Society*, ed. Fania Oz-Salzberger (Cambridge, 1995), 173.
2. Ibid., 175.
3. See Walter Bagehot, "The Cabinet" in *The English Constitution* (Cambridge, 2001), chap. 1.
4. I have found the best political analysis of this affair in the on-the-spot articles by Clifford Orwin. See in particular "Mr. Clinton, the personal, and the political," and "Republicans have only themselves to blame," *National Post* (Canada), December 9, 1998 and February 20, 1999.
5. The comparison that is sometimes made between France and the United States system is groundless. In the United States, a Democratic president often has to govern with a Republican Congress, or vice versa, but this partisan separation parallels the constitutional separation between the executive and the legislative.

CHAPTER 2: THE THEOLOGICO-POLITICAL VECTOR

1. Marcel Gauchet, *La Religion dans la démocratie: Parcours de la laïcité* (Paris, 1998), 11.
2. Ibid., 95.
3. Ibid., 63.
4. Numa Denis Fustel de Coulanges, *The Ancient City*, trans. Willard Small (Gloucester, Mass., 1979), 154–155.
5. Jean-Jacques Rousseau, *On the Social Contract*, ed. Roger D. Masters and trans. Judith R. Masters (New York, 1978), bk. 4, chap. 8.

CHAPTER 3: THE MOVEMENT OF EQUALITY

1. Jean-Marc Ferry, *L'allocation universelle* (Paris, 1995).
2. Ibid., 7.
3. Ibid., 60, 61, and 85–86.
4. Alexis de Tocqueville, *Democracy in America*, trans. Harvey C. Mansfield and Delba Winthrop (Chicago, 2000), 6.
5. Ibid., 4–5.
6. Ibid., 537–538.
7. Ibid., 549–550.
8. Ibid., 531.
9. Ibid., 532.

CHAPTER 4: THE QUESTION OF POLITICAL FORMS

1. See Raoul Girardet, *Nationalismes et nations* (Bruxelles, 1996); Ernest Gellner, *Nations and Nationalism* (Ithaca, New York, 1983); Liah Greenfield, *Nationalisms: Five Roads to Modernity* (Cambridge, Massachusetts, 1992); and Dominique Schappner, *Community of Citizens: On the Modern Idea of Nationality*, trans. Severine Rosee (New Brunswick, N.J., 1998).
2. Jean Baechler, *Démocraties* (Paris, 1985), 338.
3. Aristotle, *Politics*, 1326b.
4. Plato, *Republic*, 422e.
5. Montesquieu, *The Spirit of the Laws*, trans. Anne M. Cohler, Basia Carolyn Miller, and Harold Samuel Stone (Cambridge, 1989), bk. 11, chap. 6.
6. Rousseau, *Social Contract*, bk. 3, chap. 15.
7. See especially *Federalist Papers*, 10 and 51.
8. Dante Alighieri, *Monarchy*, trans. and ed. Prue Shaw (Cambridge, 1996), bk. 1, chap. 3.
9. Rousseau, *Social Contract*, Geneva Manuscript, bk. 2, chap. 4.

CHAPTER 5: THE NATION AND THE WORK OF DEMOCRACY

1. Jean Baechler, "Dépérissement de la nation?," *Contrepoints et commentaires* (Paris, 1996).
2. See Karl Polanyi, *The Great Transformation* (Boston, 1944).
3. Baechler, *Contrepoints*, 487.
4. Ibid., 486–487.
5. Baechler, *Démocraties*, 489.
6. See Ladan Boroumand, *La Guerre des principes: les assemblées révolutionnaires face aux droits de l'homme et à la souveraineté de la nation* (Paris, 1999).
7. Gellner, *Nations and Nationalism*, 1.
8. Ibid., 24.

9. Ibid., 34.

10. Ibid., 131.

11. Ibid., 134.

12. English translation in *Becoming National: A Reader*, ed. Geoff Eley and Ronald Grigor Suny (New York and Oxford, 1996), 41–55.

CHAPTER 6: EUROPE AND THE FUTURE OF THE NATION

1. See Paul Thibaud, *Discussion sur l'Europe* (with Jean-Marc Ferry) (Paris, 1992), 19.

2. "By making the social and fiscal systems that are the nations compete as well as by extending transnational regulation, a similar result is attained: an increase in opportunities for the individual and a restraining of the powers of the citizen." Ibid., 40.

3. Baechler, "L'Europe peut-elle encore faire l'histoire?," *Contrepoints*, 494.

4. On the "philosophical situation" of Europe, see the penetrating article of Philippe Raynaud, "De l'humanité européenne à l'Europe politique," *Les Études philosophiques* (juillet–septembre, 1999), 375–381.

5. Baechler, "L'Europe comme réalité et comme projet," *Contrepoints*, 473.

6. Ibid., 473–474.

7. Aristotle, *Nicomachean Ethics*, 1126b11–12.

8. See Thibaud, *Discussion*, 28.

CHAPTER 7: THE WARS OF THE TWENTIETH CENTURY

1. Auguste Comte, *Cours de philosophie positive*, 5 vols. (Paris, 1892–1894), IV, 239.

2. Ibid., IV, 375.

3. Benjamin Constant, *Political Writings*, trans. and ed. Biancamaria Fonatana (Cambrige, 1988), 53.

4. Jean-Jacques Rousseau, "Considerations on the Government of Poland," in *Political Writings*, trans. Frederick Watkins (Madison, Wisconsin, 1986), 184.

5. See Rousseau, *Social Contract*, bk. I, chap. 6, note.

6. Rousseau, "Government of Poland," in *Political Writings*, 184.

7. Johann Gottlieb Fichte, *Addresses to the German Nation*, ed. George Armstrong Kelly (New York, 1968), 2.

8. French original in *Qu'est-ce qu'une nation? et autres écrits politiques* (Paris, 1996).

9. Raymond Aron, *The Dawn of Universal History: Selected Essays From A Witness To the Twentieth Century*, trans. Barbara Bray (New York, 2002).

10. Ibid., 4–5.

11. Ibid., 12.

12. Ibid., 59.

13. Ibid., 77.

14. Ibid., 82–83.

15. Charles de Gaulle, *The Enemy's House Divided*, trans. Robert Eden (Chapel Hill, 2002), 2.

16. Aron, *The Dawn of Universal History*, 84.

17. Ibid., 85.

18. Ibid., 90.

19. Constant, *Political Writings*, 176.

20. Note: these lines were written in 2000.

CHAPTER 8: THE FORCES OF TRADE

1. Montesquieu, *Spirit of the Laws*, bk. 21, chap. 20. Montesquieu understood by coup d'État an unusual and violent measure of even a legitimate government. The revocation of the Edict of Nantes had been such a coup d'État.

2. Ibid., bk. 5, chap. 8.

3. Ibid., bk. 20, chap. 23.

4. Ibid., bk. 21, chap. 20.

5. Carl Schmitt, *The Concept of the Political*, trans. George Schwab (New Brunswick, N.J., 1976), 70–71.

6. Ibid., 71–72.

7. Ibid., 77–78.

8. Ibid., 78.

9. Montesquieu, *Spirit of the Laws*, bk. 20, chap. 7.

10. Ibid., bk. 20, chap. 1.

11. Rousseau, *Narcisse*, preface. *Oeuvres complètes* (Paris, 1961), vol. 2, 964, note 2.

CHAPTER 9: DECLARING THE RIGHTS OF MAN

1. Immanuel Kant, "What is Enlightenment?," in *Perpetual Peace and Other Essays*, trans. Ted Humphrey (Indianapolis, 1983), 41.

2. French original in Charles Maurras, *Mes idées politiques* (Paris, 1937), 17–19.

3. Karl Marx, "On the Jewish Question," in *The Marx-Engels Reader*, ed. Robert C. Tucker (New York, 1972), 40–41.

4. Claude Lefort, *L'invention démocratique* (Paris, 1981), 56.

5. Ibid., 57.

6. Ibid., 58–59.

7. Ibid., 65–66.

8. Ibid., 67.

9. Ibid., 76.

CHAPTER 10: BECOMING AN INDIVIDUAL

1. Tocqueville *Democracy in America*, 482–483.

2. Ibid., 483.

3. French original *altérité*. This abstract word, so popular today, designates in a suggestive way this dimension of life that evades us or that we flee from in democratic societies.

4. Tocqueville, *Democracy in America*, 489.

5. Ibid., 486–487.

6. Ibid., 487.

7. Quoted by Raoul Girardet, *Nationalismes et nation*, 139–140.

8. Gauchet, *La Religion dans la démocratie*, 106–107.

9. Rousseau, *Social Contract*, bk. II, chap. 7.

CHAPTER 11: THE RELIGION OF HUMANITY

1. Jose Ortega y Gasset, *La Révolte des masses* (Paris, 1937), preface.

2. Victor Hugo, *La Légende des siècles* (Paris, 1964), 774–775.

3. Ibid., 790–791. This set of poems is dated "June 1858 to April 3, 1859."

4. Raymond Aron, *Main Currents in Sociological Thought*, trans. Richard Howard and Helen Weaver (New York, 1965), I, 59.

5. Friedrich Nietzsche, *Daybreak*, Nos. 542 and 132, trans. R. J. Hollingdale (Cambridge, 1982), 215 and 82.

6. Friedrich Nietzsche, *Thus Spoke Zarathustra*, trans. Walter Kaufmann (New York, 1954), 17.

7. See the fine commentary by Martin Heidegger in *What is Called Thinking?*, trans. J. Glenn Gray (New York, 1976).

8. Comte, *Cours de philosophie positive*, IV, 147.

9. "The cult of truly superior men forms an essential part of the cult of Humanity. Even during his objective life, each one of them constitutes a certain personification of the Great Being. Nevertheless this representation requires that ideally one dismiss the grave imperfections that often alter the best natures." Ibid., II, 63.

CHAPTER 12: THE BODY AND THE POLITICAL ORDER

1. On all that, see Book I of Aristotle's *Politics*.

2. Hannah Arendt, *The Human Condition* (Chicago, 1958), 30–31.

3. Ibid., 32.

4. Claude Lefort, *The Political Forms of Modern Society*, trans. John B. Thompson (Cambridge, Mass., 1986), 303.

5. Rousseau, *Social Contract*, bk. III, chap. 15.

6. Lefort, *The Political Forms*, 303–304.

CHAPTER 13: SEXUAL DIVISION AND DEMOCRACY

1. Rousseau, *Social Contract*, bk. II, chap. 7.

2. See Claude Habib, *Le Consentement amoureux* (Paris, 1998), 127–128.

3. See also on this point Rousseau's *Letter to d'Alembert*:

"Popular prejudices!" exclaimed some. "Petty errors of childhood. Deceit of the laws and of education! Chasteness is nothing. It is only an invention of the social laws to protect the rights of fathers and husbands and to preserve some order in families. Why should we blush at the needs which nature has given us? Why should we find a motive for shame in an act so indifferent in itself and so beneficial in its effects as the one which leads to the perpetuation of the species? Since the desires are equal on both sides, why should their manifestations be different? Why should one of the sexes deny itself more than the other in the penchants which are common to them both? Why should man have different laws on this point than the animals?"

"Your whys, says the God, would never end."

"But it is not to man but to his Author that they should be addressed. Is it not absurd that I should have to say why I am ashamed of a natural sentiment, if this shame is no less natural to me than the sentiment itself? I might as well ask myself why I have the sentiment. Is it for me to justify what nature has done? From this line of reasoning, those who do not see why man exists ought to deny that he exists."

Politics and the Arts, trans. Allan Bloom (Ithaca, N.Y., 1968), 83.

4. On this point too see Habib, *Consentement*, 97–101.

5. See Allan Bloom, *Love and Friendship* (New York, 1993), 39–156.

CHAPTER 14: THE QUESTION OF COMMUNISM

1. See François Furet, *The Passing of an Illusion: The Idea of Communism in the Twentieth Century*, trans. Deborah Furet (Chicago, 2000).

2. I have in mind in particular the famine Stalin inflicted on the Ukraine in the early 1930s. On this subject, which is both well documented and strangely ignored, see in particular Robert Conquest, *Harvest of Sorrow: Soviet Collectivization and the Terror-Famine* (London, 1986); Vassili Grossman, *Tout passe* (Paris, 1984); and Vassil Barka, *Le Prince jaune* (Paris, 1981).

3. See Hannah Arendt, *The Origins of Totalitarianism* (New York, 1951). On the validity of the notion of totalitarianism as a "common genre," see the recent observations of Pierre Hassner in "Commuinisme et nazisme," *Commentaire* 92 (winter 2000–2001), 898–902.

4. Giovanni Gentile, quoted by Renzo De Felice, *Le Fascisme: un totalitarisme à l'italienne?* (Paris, 1998).

5. Originally published in 1976 in *Contrepoint* (20), the text was subsequently reprinted in *Présent soviétique et passé russe* (Paris, 1980).

6. Ibid., 146–147.

7. Leo Strauss, *On Tyranny* (Ithaca, N.Y., 1963), 190.

8. Kant, *Perpetual Peace and Other Essays*, 41.

9. See already Rousseau, *Social Contract*, bk. I, chap. 8: "obedience to the law one has prescribed for oneself is freedom."

10. Lefort, *The Political Forms of Modern Society*, 305.
11. Ibid., 301–302.

CHAPTER 15: IS THERE A NAZI MYSTERY?

1. Raymond Aron, "Is there a Nazi Mystery?," in *Encounter* (June 1980), 32.
2. See Leo Strauss, "German Nihilism," in *Interpretation: A Journal of Political Philosophy* (Spring 1999), 353–378. This lecture delivered in 1941, which was not intended for publication, is the most profound analysis I know of the spiritual context of Nazism. I take great inspiration from it here.
3. Ernst Nolte, *Der europäische Bürgerkrieg, 1917–1945. Nationalsozialismus und Bolshewismus* (Berlin, 1987). See the debate with François Furet in François Furet and Ernst Nolte, *Fascisme et communisme* (Paris, 1998).
4. See Leon Poliakov, *Le Mythe aryen* (Paris, 1971).
5. Primo Levi, *Survival in Auschwitz*, trans. Stuart Woolf (New York, 1996), 26–27.

CHAPTER 16: THE EMPIRE OF LAW

1. Kant, *Perpetual Peace and Other Essays*, 124.
2. Montesquieu, *Spirit of the Laws*, bk. 2, chap. 4.
3. Ibid., bk. 6, chap. 3.
4. Ibid., bk. 11, chap. 6.
5. Philippe Raynaud, "Juge," in *Dictionnaire de philosophie politique*, eds. Philippe Raynaud and Stéphane Rials (Paris, 1996), 313. See also the same author's very judicious discussion in "Un nouvel âge du droit?," *Archives de philosophie* 64 (2001).
6. Raynaud, "Juge," in *Dictionnaire*, 314.
7. See especially *Federalist* No. 78.
8. Raynaud, "Juge," in *Dictionnaire*, 314.
9. Kant, "On the Proverb: That May be True in Theory, But Is of No Practical Use," in *Perpetual Peace and Other Essays*, 89.
10. Jean-Jacques Rousseau, *Émile*, trans. Allan Bloom (New York, 1979), 466.
11. See Pierre Hassner, "Guerre et paix," in *Dictionnaire*, 257–266; and "Kant," in *History of Political Philosophy*, ed. Leo Strauss and Joseph Cropsey (Chicago, 1987), 554–593.
12. Kant, "Idea for a Universal History with a Cosmopolitan Intent," Fourth Thesis, in *Perpetual Peace and Other Essays*, 32.
13. Kant, "Speculative Beginning of Human History," in ibid., 58.
14. Ibid., 58.
15. Kant, "Metaphysical Elements of Justice" (*The Metaphysics of Morals*, Part I), trans. John Ladd (Indianapolis, 1965), 128.
16. Kant, *Perpetual Peace*, 112–113.

17. Ibid., 119 and 118.
18. Ibid., 124.

CHAPTER 17: THE EMPIRE OF MORALITY

1. Louis-Ferdinand Céline, *Journey to the End of the Night*, trans. Ralph Manheim (New York, 1983), 428.
2. See Rousseau, "Discourse on the Origins and Foundations of Inequality among Men," in *The First and Second Discourses*, trans. Roger D. and Judith R. Masters (New York, 1964), 131–137.
3. See Kant, "The Incentives of Pure Practical Reason" in *Critique of Practical Reason*, Part I, chap. 3.
4. Kant, "The Metaphysical Principles of Virtue" (Part II of The *Metaphysics of Morals*), trans. James Ellington (Indianapolis, 1964), 127–128.

CHAPTER 18: THE HUMAN POLITICAL CONDITION AND THE UNITY OF THE HUMAN RACE

1. "The universal spirit of the laws of every country is always to favor the strong against the weak and those who have against those who have not. This difficulty is inevitable, and it is without exception." Rousseau, *Émile*, 236 note.

Index